T0318325

Willing, Wanting, Waiting

Richard Holton provides a unified account of the will, pulling together a diverse range of phenomena that have typically been treated separately: intention, resolution, choice, weakness and strength of will, temptation, addiction, and freedom of the will. Drawing on recent psychological research, he argues that rather than being the pinnacle of rationality, these components work to compensate for our inability to make or maintain sound judgments. Choice is the capacity to form intentions even in the absence of judgment of which action is best. Weakness of will is the failure to maintain resolutions in the face of temptation—where temptation typically involves a shift in judgment as to what is best, or, in cases of addiction, a disconnection between what is judged best and what is desired. Strength of will is the corresponding ability to maintain a resolution in the face of temptation, an ability that requires the employment of a particular faculty or skill. Finally, the experience of freedom of the will is traced to the experiences of forming intentions, and of maintaining resolutions, both of which require effortful activity from the agent.

Richard Holton is Professor of Philosophy at the Massachusetts Institute of Technology.

Willing, Wanting, Waiting

Richard Holton

CLARENDON PRESS · OXFORD

OXFORD

UNIVERSITY PRESS

Great Clarendon Street, Oxford OX2 6DP

Oxford University Press is a department of the University of Oxford.
It furthers the University's objective of excellence in research, scholarship,
and education by publishing worldwide in

Oxford New York

Auckland Cape Town Dar es Salaam Hong Kong Karachi
Kuala Lumpur Madrid Melbourne Mexico City Nairobi
New Delhi Shanghai Taipei Toronto

With offices in

Argentina Austria Brazil Chile Czech Republic France Greece
Guatemala Hungary Italy Japan Poland Portugal Singapore
South Korea Switzerland Thailand Turkey Ukraine Vietnam

Oxford is a registered trademark of Oxford University Press
in the UK and in certain other countries

Published in the United States
by Oxford University Press Inc., New York

British Library Cataloguing in Publication Data
Data available

Library of Congress Cataloging in Publication Data
Holton, Richard, 1962–
Willing, wanting, waiting / Richard Holton.
p. cm.
Includes bibliographical references (p.) and index.
ISBN 978-0-19-921457-0
1. Will. I. Title.
BJ1461.H563 2009

Typeset by Laserwords Private Limited, Chennai, India
Printed in Great Britain
on acid-free paper by
Biddles Ltd., King's Lynn, Norfolk

ISBN 978–0–19–921457–0 (Hbk.)
ISBN 978–0–19–969228–6 (Pbk.)

10 9 8 7 6 5 4 3 2 1

Contents

Acknowledgements

Work on the material in this book was started at the Research School of Social Sciences at the Australian National University; continued at the University of Sheffield, the University of Edinburgh and MIT; and concluded whilst visiting the University of Oxford. I thank all of those institutions for their support. I thank the AHRB for giving me leave to work on it whilst at Edinburgh. I thank the members of my department at MIT for allowing a semester's leave in Oxford; the Master and Fellows of Balliol College, where I was a MIT visitor; and the Master and Fellows of University College, where I was an H.L.A. Hart Fellow. Most of the concluding work was done in the idyllic surroundings of Cedar Lodge, Iris Murdoch's former house in Steeple Aston. I thank the Balliol–MIT exchange for making that possible; and Jan Maulden and David Kewley for making it so pleasant.

Although they have all been rewritten for this book, most of the chapters started life as independent papers, and have appeared elsewhere as articles. As a result they have benefited from the comments of colleagues in a huge number of conferences and departmental seminars, and from the scrutiny of numerous referees and editors. I am enormously grateful for this. It strikes me as one of the great things about the philosophical profession that people remain genuinely—critically, but constructively—interested in each other's work.

Conscious that I have left many out, I thank the following for their comments and advice: Roy Baumeister, Kent Berridge, Nick Chater, Elizabeth Fricker, Olav Gjelsvik, Alison Gopnik, Samuel Guttenplan, Caspar Hare, Sally Haslanger, Jennifer Hornsby, Lloyd Humberstone, Frank Jackson, Agnieszka Jaworska, Leonard Katz, Jeanette Kennett, Joshua Knobe, Nico Kolodny, Neil Levy, David Lewis, Alison McIntyre, Alfred Mele, Shaun Nichols, David Owens, Philip Pettit, Agustin Rayo, Amelie Rorty, Kieran Setiya, Nick Shea, Walter Sinnott-Armstrong, Sarah Stroud, Adam Swift, Christine Tappollet, Judy Thomson, David Velleman, Brian Weatherson, Timothy Williamson, Ken Winkler and Stephen Yablo.

I thank Michael Smith, who first taught me some moral psychology at Princeton, and who has continued as a fund of encouragement, criticism, and good sense, ever since; and Michael Bratman, whose work provides the framework for much of this book, and whose continued probing has helped me to understand the issues where our views have diverged.

Three anonymous readers for Oxford University Press gave me excellent comments; I apologize where I have failed to do them justice. I am grateful too for the comments of the participants in the seminars that I gave on this material at MIT—especially Rachael Briggs, Tom Dougherty, Ginger Hoffman, Adam Hosein, Susanna Rinard, Katia Vavova and Kenny Walden.

I thank my parents for their support and encouragement over the years. I thank my daughters, Eleanor and Natalie, for being such wonderful sources of examples and delight, and offer them my apologies for persisting with a jacket illustration that they detest. Lastly I thank my wife, Rae Langton, who has read every word of this book, and suggested I change quite a few of them. Without her it might be a lot worse; I suspect that it would not be at all.

Cedar Lodge, Steeple Aston, June 2008

Origins of the Chapters

Chapter 2 is based on 'Partial Belief, Partial Intention', *Mind* 117 (2008): 27–58; Chapter 3 is based on 'The Act of Choice', *The Philosophers' Imprint* 6/3 (2006): 1–15; Chapter 4 is based on 'Intention and Weakness of Will', *Journal of Philosophy* 96 (1999): 241–62; Chapter 6 is based on 'How is Strength of Will Possible?', in Sarah Stroud and Christine Tappolet (eds), *Weakness of Will and Practical Irrationality* (Oxford: Clarendon Press, 2003), pp. 39–67; Chapter 7 is based on 'Rational Resolve', *Philosophical Review* 113 (2004): 507–35; Chapter 8 is based on 'Determinism, Self-Efficacy, and the Phenomenology of Free Will' forthcoming in *Inquiry*.

Introduction

When I finished my doctoral dissertation I resolved that I would
never write anything as long as a book again. I feared that the attempt
to maintain consistency over a number of chapters was as likely to
result in the elimination of truths as in the elimination of falsehoods;
and that the final product would say as much about my idiosyncratic
preoccupations as about the subject matter of the work. Better by far
to stick with articles.

So there is a certain irony that I break my resolution with a book
that is largely about resolutions. If there is a defence, it is that the
more I thought about the different topics that are the concern of
this book, the more I became convinced that they are related. In
particular, it seems to me that two topics that are treated separately
in most philosophical accounts—on the one hand, that of strength
and weakness of the will, and, on the other, that of freedom of the
will—benefit from a unified treatment. That is what I try to give here.

This is not to say that I aim to account for all talk of the will.
Nietzsche complained that the idea of the will (and he was just talking
about free will) pulls together too much; that 'it is a unit only as a
word'.[1] This is surely to go too far, but in spirit I am inclined to agree.
The notion has a long and varied history, dating, if not to the classical
period, at least to the medieval.[2] It has answered to concerns that
have been variously religious, moral, metaphysical, and psychological.
I doubt that any single conception can be picked out of this history;
and there is much that we would do well to discard.

Nevertheless there is a picture that underlies many of the cases
in which we talk most idiomatically of the will: talk of free will, of
weakness of will, of strength of will and of willpower.[3] It is a picture of

---

[1] Nietzsche, 1886, §19.

[2] For a history of the notion, and a discussion of whether it can be found in Plato and
Aristotle, see the essays collected in Pink and Stone, 2004.

[3] We also use talk of the will quite idiomatically in other ways which may or may not be
related to those discussed here. 'I'm willing to tell you. I'm wanting to tell you. I'm waiting

ourselves as beings who can choose certain courses of action, maintain the choices over time and in the face of contrary desires, and then act upon them. My focus is on what happens in this process: on the willing, and the wanting and the waiting, and on how these interact. It is a picture that is present in much of our everyday thought; but it is also borne out, I think, by results in empirical psychology. My hope is to give it a philosophically adequate treatment.

The central idea is that of an executive capacity. It is a capacity needed by cognitively limited creatures like us, acting in a complex world that is full of uncertainties and temptations. Often we have to act in the absence of a judgement of what is best. That is why we need a capacity to make choices that is independent of our judgements. Even if we can make judgements about what is best, they are often corrupted by ensuing temptation. Temptation does not just change what we want; it also changes our judgements. So again we need a capacity to stick by our intentions that is independent of judgement. The capacities that provide such abilities form the core of our talk of strength and weakness of the will, and of will power. Furthermore our experience of such capacities forms much of the basis of our conception of freedom of the will. It is in making choices, and then in sticking with the intentions that result, that we get an idea of ourselves as free agents: an idea, I will argue, that avoids both the implausible metaphysics of libertarianism, and also the overly mechanical conception that is provided by much traditional compatibilism.

In outline the book runs as follows:

Chapter 1 introduces intentions as states with characteristic features that distinguish them from beliefs and desires, and summarizes the psychological work that supports this characterization. The notion of intention is distinguished from that of intentional action, and various

---

to tell you,' says Mr Doolittle in the lines that provide the inspiration for my title (Shaw, 1914, Act Two). His willing is something like a preparedness to act. Perhaps it can be seen as a conditional intention, but that would need some argument. Similarly we talk of good will and bad will, and of acting wilfully. I suspect that some of these uses are related to those discussed here, but I will not try to develop any account of them.

accounts that attempt to reduce intentions to beliefs and desires are rejected.

Chapter 2 examines the relation between intentions and beliefs, arguing that an intention to do something does not require the belief that one will be successful. Along the way a notion of partial intention is developed, standing to intention much as partial belief stands to all-out belief; and various consistency requirements on intention are investigated.

Chapter 3 turns to how we form intentions, arguing that there is a process of choosing that is not determined by an agent's prior beliefs, desires and intentions. It is argued that this is needed because of the prevalence of situations in which we are unable to form an opinion on which outcome would be best. The process need not be random however: it will often pick up on genuine considerations of which the agent is unaware.

Chapter 4 examines weakness of will, arguing that it should be understood as the over-ready abandonment of a resolution. It thus differs from akrasia, understood as action against one's best judgement.

Chapter 5 discusses temptation, and the standard philosophical distinction between its normal form and the form it takes in cases of addiction and other compulsions. It is argued that this distinction is badly drawn, and should be recast, drawing on the empirical literature. Normal temptation should be characterized in terms of judgement shift: the temptation shifts the agent's judgement. Addictive temptation should be understood in terms of a disconnection between an agent's desires and what they like or judge best. Similarities and differences between the two are then brought out.

Chapter 6 examines strength of will, arguing, again partly on empirical grounds, that it should be explained in terms of a separate faculty or skill of willpower.

Chapter 7 examines whether the employment of willpower, typically acting, as it does, against the current judgement of what is best, can be rational. On the basis of a distinction between when it is rational to reconsider, and when it is rational to revise given that one has reconsidered, it is argued that it can be.

Chapter 8 turns to the experience of free will, and argues that it stems, at least partly, from the experience of choosing an action, and of maintaining the intentions that result. These considerations are used to explain how a belief in determinism can be demotivating.

*

It can help to characterize a position to provide some foils. So, in addition to giving a summary of what I am doing, let me briefly outline some of the things that I am *not* doing, and some of the positions to which I am opposed. As already mentioned, I do not claim that I have captured everything that goes under the name of the will. I do not try to make anything of the idea that there is an experience of willing that accompanies every action.[4] Though I am somewhat sceptical that there is such an experience, I will not say much about it. My focus here is on intentions, not on intentional action more generally.

Since I downplay the role of judgement, my approach also contrasts with those who understand the will as primarily concerned with the implementation of judgement.[5] There is something attractive in the ideal of the perfectly rational creature, unconstrained by cognitive limitations, whose reasoning is transparent to it, and who acts on the basis of that reason. Such a creature would have little need of the aspect of the will that I explore. But it is not one of us. We need the kinds of capacity that I have sketched.

More radically, of course, I part company with those who want to reject the idea of the will altogether. Talk of the will was unpopular in most twentieth-century analytic philosophy.[6] This was only partly because it brought with it an unpleasant whiff of mysticism or of Victorian moralism. More importantly, it was because it was felt to have no useful role to play. The aim, as in so much analytic philosophy, was reduction. Not perhaps to behaviour: behaviourism's day was short and long ago. Rather the received aim was reduction to beliefs and desires.

---

[4] For such an approach, see especially O'Shaughnessy, 1980.
[5] Such approaches date at least to Aquinas. For discussion, see Stump, 2003, Ch. 9.
[6] To get a sense of just how unpopular, see Ryle, 1949, Ch. 3.

To any outside observer this aim for reduction is surprising. What could motivate it? One explanation is a legacy of Russell's programme to secure legitimate foundations in a small set of primitives. Another, which figures much larger, is a certain view of science. Science, it is held, works by reduction. If philosophy is to aspire to the status of science, or even to find a place within the scientific enterprise, it had better be reductivist too.

This may be a reasonable view of physics. It is not, however, a reasonable view of psychology, the science into which a philosophy of action should surely tie. Psychology has not tended to reduce our commonplace psychological concepts to others. On the contrary, it has typically made *more* distinctions. Look for instance at the concept of memory, which has turned out to cover several distinct processes. There is no attempt at the horizontal reduction of one psychological kind to another that has been the goal of so much philosophy.

We are evolved creatures; we should not expect our basic mechanisms to be uniformly simple and elegant. Rather than looking to reduce, philosophers would do better to explore the distinctions that our commonplace psychological thinking, and our commonplace psychological experience, suggest. Such explorations must be done with an eye to what empirical work tells us, for much of what we ordinarily think and feel may simply be wrong. It is, though, a good beginning, especially if we have our eyes on connections back to moral and political concerns. To echo Austin: it is not the last word, but it may be usefully employed as the first.[7]

In the last fifty years or so there has been a huge amount of empirical work in psychology and, more recently, in neuroscience, that is relevant to the will. Much remains controversial, but much is now stable; enough, certainly, that we should use it to inform our philosophy. It transpires, I think, that our commonplace ideas about the will have a lot going for them: not always in how we apply them—we constantly misattribute states and motives to ourselves and to others—and not always in their details; but in the broad outlines of the framework that they provide.

---

[7] Austin, 1956, p. 133.

1

Intention

Suppose that you have been wondering what colour to paint your front door. You have narrowed the options to two: dark red, or dark blue. Both would be nice; both are available. But time is pressing, and you need to decide. So you make your choice. Blue it is.

As a result of your choice you have acquired a new mental state. You still think that both colours would be nice; you still think that both are available. In addition, though, you are now in a state that does not look like either a belief or a desire. You have an *intention* to paint the door blue.

We ascribe intentions freely, both to ourselves and to others.[1] Yet for most of the twentieth century neither philosophy nor psychology made much reference to them. Admittedly theorists were happy to speak of actions being performed intentionally; but this was standardly understood just to mean that they flowed from the agent's beliefs and desires. Little attention was given to the idea that intentions might be self-standing mental states.

Things have changed. In philosophy in the last twenty years, a great deal of work has been done exploring the nature of intentions; and work in psychology has provided good evidence that the philosophical account is basically right. My aim here is to give a sketch of the core philosophical work, show how the empirical work bears on it, and then extend the core account to include a particular kind of intention that I call *resolutions*. I conclude this chapter by returning to the issue of whether intentions should be understood as self-standing states, or whether they can be reduced to beliefs and desires.

[1] For an exploration of how this works, see Malle and Knobe, 2001.

The Features of Intention

Let us start with Michael Bratman's influential account. It has three parts.[2] Bratman identifies the characteristics that a state needs to have if we are to count it as an intention; he explains the useful role that states with these characteristics would have in our lives; and he gives reasons for thinking that beliefs and desires on their own could not fulfil this role. Taken together these provide the basis for the case that we should acknowledge the existence of intentions. For if we seem to have them, and if having them would play a useful role, and if indeed they do seem to play this useful role, then the burden of proof rests in their favour. We will need compelling arguments before giving them up.

Let us postpone for now the third element of Bratman's argument—the contention that beliefs and desires cannot play the role allotted to intentions—and focus instead on the other two elements: the account of the distinguishing marks of intentions, and of the useful role that intentions can play. I start with the distinguishing marks; in particular, with the distinguishing marks of *future-directed* intentions, that is, intentions to do something at some future time.

A future-directed intention to perform a certain action typically has the following characteristics. The agent forms the intention at one time either by making an explicit conscious decision to perform the action or by some less deliberate, more automatic, process. Then, unless it is revised, the intention will lead the agent to perform the action *directly*; it is, as Bratman says, *controlling*. Moreover, it is relatively immune to reconsideration and hence to revision. Once formed, intentions have a tendency to persist. They have what Bratman calls *stability*. Stability is not, of course, absolute. Sometimes we revise our intentions, and it is quite rational that we do so. ('When the facts change,' Keynes reputedly said when accused of inconsistency, 'I change my mind. What do you do, sir?') Stability can best be understood as a shift in the threshold of relevance of information: some information

---

[2] The main statement is in Bratman, 1987.

that would have been relevant in forming an intention will not be sufficient to provoke rational reconsideration once an intention has been formed.

What need do we have of states that are stable and controlling in this way? Part of the answer stems from the observation that we are epistemically limited creatures. Information is scarce, and costly to obtain. Reasoning on the information that we have takes time and effort. It is rational then to allocate our scarce resources by limiting the amount of time we spend looking for information and reasoning on it. We should do a certain amount of searching and reasoning, and then stop and make a decision on the basis of that. Now if we were to act immediately on making the decision, then this would not in itself give rise to a need for intentions. But suppose our decision is a decision to act tomorrow. Then we need some way of storing our decision so that we act on it tomorrow without reconsidering it (for to reconsider it would violate the requirement that we not reason about it further). We need an intention.

This in turn raises another question: why should we want to make a decision now about how we will act tomorrow? It could be that now is a more propitious moment to reason. Tomorrow there will be some factor that will stop us from reasoning well: we will be short of time, or distracted, or under the spell of some temptation. But a more common reason for doing our reasoning ahead of time is that all sorts of other actions will be dependent upon what we decide to do; and we will need to perform some of these actions in the meanwhile. Thus suppose I will not paint my front door till tomorrow. There might still be many reasons for deciding today what colour to paint it. It could be that tomorrow I will start at the crack of dawn when there will be too little light to see the colour charts properly; that will give me a reason of the first kind for doing my deliberation today. More likely, tomorrow the paint shop will be shut, so I should buy the paint today; and since I want only to buy the colour that I will use, I will need to have decided today what colour that will be. I need to form my intention ahead of time. Thus intentions are necessary in the intra-personal case for agents to coordinate their activities. They are also important in the inter-personal case. Suppose some friends are coming to visit me next week, and the easiest way for them to recognize my house is from the colour of the front door. I shall be speaking with them today, but not again before they visit. Then once again I have a reason for forming today an intention about which colour I shall paint my door tomorrow, so that I can tell them what to look for.

It will be important to my argument to realize that there can be good reason for forming intentions even in cases where rational deliberation does not provide sufficient grounds for my decision. One such case involves so-called Buridan examples, examples in which I am indifferent between options.[3] If I am really indifferent between red and blue for my door, it is nonetheless important that I decide on one of them, and form the corresponding intention. Otherwise I won't know what paint to buy, or what to tell my visitors. A more interesting case concerns options that the agent finds incommensurable.[4] Suppose (taking an example at random) that I do not know how to compare the demands of leaving home to fight fascism with the demands of staying to look after my mother.[5] Here the problem is not that each outcome fares equally well on the same scale; I do not know how to place them on the same scale. Nevertheless I need to decide on one course, and to form the corresponding intention; both intra- and inter-personal coordination require this. I need to know whether to start winding up my affairs and packing my bag; and I need to know what to tell my mother so that she too can make her plans accordingly.[6]

---

[3] Named after the example of Buridan's ass, who starves, midway between two piles of hay and unable to choose either. Although the example is standardly attributed to Jean Buridan, the attribution is not substantiated. See the discussion in Ullman-Margalit and Morgenbesser, 1977.

[4] I don't say that they need *be* incommensurable, only that the agent finds them so. I return to this in Chapter 3.

[5] Sartre, 1945.

[6] Bratman points out that cases like these show the utility of intentions even in cases where information is not limited. For we have reason to think that Buridan cases at least will arise even for agents who know everything. He also argues, I think convincingly, that they provide grounds for thinking that we cannot reduce talk of intentions to talk of beliefs and desires. For, by hypothesis, I do not desire that I take one course rather than the other; and my intention to take one course cannot be seen as a belief that I will take it. See Bratman, 1985, at pp. 22–3, and Bratman 1987, pp. 11, 22ff.

Psychological Evidence

The account I have sketched shows us why it is that having intentions would be beneficial. But that does not by itself show us that we have them. After all, wings may well be beneficial, but we certainly lack them. Admittedly, we don't come with a prior commitment to the view that we have wings, whereas we are committed to intentions. Still, it would be good to know if there is solid psychological evidence that we have intentions along something like these lines.

There is. Indeed, there are two distinct bodies of evidence supporting his account, both stemming from the work of Peter Gollwitzer. The first provides evidence of something like the stability brought on by forming intentions. The second provides evidence of their controlling nature. And while both basically support the account of intention that we antecedently hold, both require refining that account in an interesting way.

Stability

To get an understanding of the first body of evidence it will be helpful to step back to consider a famous article published by Alloy and Abramson.[7] Their aim was to understand how much control subjects think that they have over the world. They set up a simple apparatus consisting of a button and a light, and asked subjects to estimate the degree of control that the button gave them over the illumination of the light. The start of each trial would be marked by a secondary light coming on, at which point the subjects would either press the button or not; this was followed by the main light either coming on or not. Subjects were asked to judge how responsive the main light was to the pushing of the button. Alloy and Abramson found that normal subjects were pretty good at realizing that they had no control when the light only came on rarely, i.e., when it came on in 25 per cent of trials. But once the light started coming on frequently (in 75 per cent of trials) they hugely overestimated how much control they had.

[7] Alloy and Abramson, 1979.

Much of the interest of Alloy and Abramson's article came from their finding that depressed subjects were not vulnerable to this illusion: unlike normal subjects, they did not overestimate their degree of control. And this gave rise to a large literature suggesting that over-confidence in one's ability to control the world, together with over-confidence in one's abilities more generally, could be beneficial: people who are over-confident are more likely to persist, and ultimately to succeed, when more realistic people would give up.[8]

This raises an interesting question. For whilst over-confidence can bring certain benefits in enabling agents to persist in the face of adversity, it can obviously also be a liability if it makes agents choose projects that they are unable to complete. It is here that Gollwitzer's work comes in. He found that in non-depressed agents, over-confidence comes and goes depending on their attitude. If the agent is in what he called a *deliberative mindset*, i.e. a mindset that is focused on deciding what to do, they are much less prone to illusions of control. In contrast, if they are in an *implemental mindset*, i.e. a mindset that is focused on implementing a prior decision, they are far more prone to illusions of control. Gollwitzer found that it was enough to get subjects to focus either on an unresolved personal problem, or on a fixed personal goal, to get radically different results in the Alloy and Abramson set-up.[9]

The difference between deliberative and implemental mindsets is manifested in a host of further ways. Those in an implemental mindset are more likely to overestimate their other abilities in addition to control,[10] are more likely to focus on the advantages of achieving their goal than the disadvantages,[11] and are less receptive to new or peripheral information.[12]

These last features take us back to the idea of the stability of intention. For the idea there was exactly that agents are less ready

---

[8] See especially Taylor and Brown, 1988, and, for later review, Taylor and Brown, 1994.

[9] Gollwitzer and Kinney, 1989; for background to this piece and summary of subsequent work, see Gollwitzer, 2003. For a summary of the differences between deliberative and implementational mindsets more generally, see Gollwitzer and Bayer, 1999.

[10] Taylor and Gollwitzer, 1995.   [11] Taylor and Gollwitzer, 1995.

[12] Heckhausen and Gollwitzer, 1987.

to consider new information once an intention is formed than they would have been when they were in the process of forming the intention. However, we need to be a little careful before concluding that this provides empirical support for the stability of intentions. For stability was proposed as a feature of the intentions themselves, whereas Gollwitzer has shown that insensitivity to evidence is a feature of the mindsets of agents, something that can be then applied to other states that are in no way connected to an intention. When agents assess the control they have over the light, they are not implementing an intention. So how do the two pictures relate?

I think that there are two possible interpretations of Gollwitzer's findings. The first is that stability is a feature of the intentions themselves, but that the effect of contemplating such an intention is to cause agents to impute the stability to other states: there is a form of stability contagion from intentions to other mental states. The second interpretation is that stability is not a feature of intentions themselves, but is solely a feature of the mindsets that agents bring to intentions; however, the stable (i.e., implemental) mindset is one that is engendered by focusing on intentions. (A compromise sees stability in both the mindset and the intentions.)

I don't know which of these interpretations is right. Gollwitzer writes as though the second is, but, so far as I can see, his data are all consistent with the first. But interesting though the distinction is, I don't think that it need worry us. I will go on speaking of intentions as stable, meaning this to be understood as either that they have a degree of intrinsic stability, or that they engender a mindset that treats them as stable. Either way we will get much the same results.

Control

Let us turn now to the second characteristic imputed to intentions on Bratman's account, their controlling nature. The idea was that intentions can move agents to action *directly*; agents do not need to reconsider whether to perform the act.

If intentions were controlling in this way, one would expect to find that an agent who formed an intention to perform a certain action would be more likely to perform it than would a similarly motivated agent who had so far failed to form that intention. This is indeed the case, but to understand the findings here, and to see that they really do support the idea that (at least *some*) intentions are controlling in Bratman's sense, we need to understand a second distinction made by Gollwitzer, that between goal intentions and implementation intentions. Goal intentions are categorical in form: for instance, one intends to visit the Taj Mahal. In contrast implementation intentions are, explicitly or implicitly, conditional: one intends, if one sees a bus to the Taj Mahal, to get on it; or one intends to leave for the Taj Mahal at two o'clock.[13] Typically implementation intentions work in the service of goal intentions: having decided to go to the Taj Mahal one forms the further intention to get the bus to it, or to go at a certain time.[14]

Gollwitzer found that it is implementation intentions, rather than mere goal intentions, that increase the likelihood that subjects will act as they plan. Forming an intention to write a report of what they did on Christmas Eve sometime during the following forty-eight hours was enough to get a third of subjects to do so; but forming an additional implementation intention to write the report at some specific time within that 48 hours was enough to get three-quarters of subjects to do so. Similarly a simple goal intention to do breast self-examination was acted upon by half of the women in the study; where this was augmented with an implementation intention about exactly when to do it, all the women acted upon it. Numerous other studies have found similar effects.[15]

Clearly these results are very striking, but they should not be too surprising. If all one has is a goal intention, then this cannot be completely controlling: one will have to do more deliberation about how to implement it. And one may either forget to do that deliberation, or, having started it, one may decide to give up on the intention altogether. Alternatively, one may decide to procrastinate, and then, having procrastinated, one may never come back. In contrast

---

[13] That is, one intends, if it is two o'clock, to leave for the Taj Mahal.
[14] Gollwitzer 1993, 1996, 1999; for summary, see Gollwitzer, Fujita and Oettingen, 2004.
[15] Gollwitzer, Fujita and Oettingen, 2004, pp. 214ff.

an implementation intention, providing it is well chosen, does not require the agent to reopen deliberation. The relevant cue can simply serve to trigger the action. In Gollwitzer's phrase, one is 'passing the control of one's behavior on to the environment'.[16]

An array of further research confirms that this is what is happening. Implementation intentions cause the agent to be sensitized to the relevant cues; indeed the response can happen even if the cues are presented subliminally.[17] So they can certainly involve the short-circuiting of explicit deliberation. Nonetheless, the process is not blind. Implementation intentions have little effect if the goal intention that they serve is weak, and none at all if it has been abandoned.

So we have good evidence that intentions can be controlling. This is not in the mechanical sense that we are locked into an action come what may. Rather, provided we have formulated the implementation intentions in ways that tie them to perceptible cues, intentions enable us to act in ways that do not require us to deliberate further.

Resolutions

I have sketched the main lines of an argument for the utility of intentions, and have provided some empirical grounds for thinking that we actually have them. Once we have got this far it is easy to see that they might be useful in other roles too. Suppose that there is an act that I now believe I should perform at some time in the future; indeed currently I actively want to perform it. Suppose though that I know that when the time comes I shall not want to perform it. I shall be tempted to do something else. Then it would be useful to form an intention now, an intention that will lead me directly to act when the time comes, and that will provide some resistance to reconsideration in the light of the inclinations I shall have then. Similarly, suppose that I know that my future reasoning will go awry: after a few glasses of wine my confidence in my own abilities will be absurdly high. Then

---

[16] Gollwitzer, 1993, p. 173.   [17] Gollwitzer, Fujita and Oettinger, 2004, p. 213.

again it would be good to form intentions now that are somewhat resistant to reconsideration in the light of those beliefs. In short, it would be good to have a specific type of intention that is designed to stand firm in the face of future contrary inclinations or beliefs: what I shall call a *resolution*.

Philosophers have been keen on the idea that sometimes an intention will not be enough; that we will need to bind ourselves in some further way to fulfil our intentions, perhaps by placing temptation out of our reach, or by telling others of our plans so that fear of their disapproval should we fall short will provide an extra incentive.[18] But we should not let our interest in these exotic methods blind us to the fact that very often intention *is* enough. People get up on cold dark mornings, leave enjoyable lunches to return to work, give up nicotine, or alcohol, or other drugs; and they frequently use no mechanism other than an intention to overcome their contrary desires.

The use of intention to overcome desire becomes especially important in cases that involve repeated actions. I reason that since smoking forty cigarettes a day for the rest of my life will make a considerable difference to my chance of getting lung cancer, I should give it up. But should I deny myself the cigarette I was about to have? Smoking one cigarette will make very little difference to my chances of getting lung cancer, and anyway, that is all in the future. In contrast, one cigarette can give me considerable pleasure now. So why deny myself? Unfortunately the same argument will work just as well forty times a day for the rest of my life. What we need here is not just an intention to perform—or, in this case, to refrain from performing—a specific action. We need a general intention concerning a certain type of action; what Bratman calls a *policy*.[19]

---

[18] Elster, 1979. I suspect that very often the point of telling others of our resolutions is not to incur their scorn if we revise them. Rather it is simply to remind us of what our resolutions were, or of how seriously we made them. A midwife told me of the sole entry on one woman's birth plan: 'If I ask for pain relief in labour, show me this birth plan'. The woman did ask for pain relief, the midwife showed her the birth plan, and the woman decided against taking any. Presumably this was exactly a case in which the woman didn't want to publicize her resolution, but still wanted others to remind her of it.

[19] Bratman, 1987, pp. 87–91. If these 'one more won't hurt' arguments are not to be simply irrational, they will need to involve a degree of preference shift. See below, Chapter 6.

It is no easy matter to see quite how intentions can work to overcome future desires or beliefs. After all, although intentions are stable, they don't lock us in to a course of action. We can imagine a being that did work in this way: a being that, having formed an intention, would be inexorably moved to action by it. But we are not like that. We can revise an intention in the light of a changed desire or belief; so why do we not do so, even in cases where the intention was expressly formed in anticipation of such changes? Providing an answer to that question will be an ongoing theme of this book. But let me say a little here about the kind of structure that resolutions might have.

Clearly, if it is to work, a resolution has to be something that holds firm against temptation. At one extreme we could think of them simply as intentions with a specially high degree of stability. But that doesn't seem to get it right. It is no part of the nature of a resolution that it *will* be effective; the point is rather that it is *meant* to be. At the most intellectual level, resolutions can be seen as involving both an intention to engage in a certain action, and a further intention not to let that intention be deflected. Understood in this way they involve a conjunction of two simpler intentions, one first-order and one second-order (i.e., an intention about an intention). So, when I resolve to give up smoking, I form an intention to give up, and along with it I form a second-order intention not to let that intention be deflected.[20]

There is plenty of reason to think that we can and do form second-order intentions. For instance, on forming a goal intention to visit the Taj Mahal, I might form the further intention to make some relevant implementation intentions at a later time; that is a second-order intention. But it might seem that understanding resolutions as containing them is to make them rather too complicated. Can't children form resolutions without forming second-order intentions? Some clarifications here might help. To form a second-order intention children would not need the idea of a second-order intention; nor would they need to have the idea of a resolution. What they would need is the idea of a first-order intention, for only then could

---

[20] I am grateful to Alison Gopnik for discussion here.

they form intentions about intentions; but this idea need not be terribly complex or well-articulated. They certainly would not need to have any grip on the sort of account proposed here, the idea of intentions as states that are stable and committing (how many adults have a grip on that?). All they would need is the idea of what they are going to do, where this is distinct from what they want to do. And even this need not be a conscious idea; it would be good enough if their behaviour indicated that they could grasp it unconsciously.

Still it would certainly be evidence against the second-order construal of resolutions if it looked as though children could form resolutions before they came to understand the idea of an intention whether consciously or unconsciously; and it would be some evidence in favour of the construal if the ability to form resolutions came around the same time as, or subsequent to, the grasp of the idea of intention. We do not have overwhelming evidence on this point. But we do have evidence that children get much better at delaying gratification—that is, at resisting the temptation to take a small benefit when by waiting they can gain a larger one—at around the age of five: that is, at about the time that they come to understand the idea of intention.[21] Now, of course, there may be ways that one could delay gratification without forming a resolution to resist: one might simply distract oneself, as many of the children seemed to do. Nevertheless, it does appear that some of the children were forming resolutions, something that they will go on to do with increasing frequency as they get older. And the evidence is that that ability comes along with an understanding of the nature of intentions, just as a higher-order theory of resolutions would suggest.

Present-directed Intentions

The picture of intentions sketched so far is primarily a picture of future-directed intentions: intentions to do something at some future

---

[21] I discuss the delayed gratification literature in Chapters 5 and 6. For evidence of when children grasp the idea of an intention, see Schult, 2002.

time. But we might wonder whether there couldn't be present-directed intentions: intentions to perform an action *now*.[22] And, if there are, then it might seem that the account offered will not cover them. For some of the main advantages that were held to accrue from having intentions—curtailing deliberation, aiding inter- and intra-personal coordination, enabling resistance to temptation—do not seem to apply to present-directed intentions.[23]

A first thing to say is that if intentions are thought of as enduring states, then, for almost all intentions, there will come a point at which they are to be implemented. In that sense, then, they will be intentions to perform an action *now*. A future-directed intention will simply turn into a present-directed intention with the passage of time. So the issue is not really whether there can *be* present-directed intentions. The issue is rather whether, on the account proposed here, there can be reason for an agent to *form* a present-directed intention.

There can. It is simply not right to say that none of the advantages discussed so far apply to the forming of present-directed intentions. Indifference and incommensurability are problems that can affect present-directed action just as much as future-directed (I can be indifferent about what colour to paint the door *now*); and by hypothesis these are cases in which desires and beliefs are not sufficient to decide one way rather than another. So an agent faced with either of them would seem to have reason to form a present-directed intention to break the impasse.

Moreover, even if it were held that this on its own is too slight a reason to admit the existence of present-directed intentions, we might challenge the whole thrust of the argument that says that we should only concede their existence if we can find specific advantages to be had from forming them. It could be that they are there because of the advantages they bring in the future-directed case, and that then they get co-opted to do other work. If intentions are real psychological kinds, identified in the kind of empirical work that has been discussed, then it is an interesting empirical question whether present-directed

---

[22] See, for instance, the notion of proximal intentions in Mele, 1992, Part II.
[23] The criticism is made by David Velleman in his review of Bratman's *Intention, Plans and Practical Reason* (Velleman, 1991) and again in Velleman, 2007.

action works, very quickly, using them; or whether one can decide to perform an action and go on to perform it directly, without need of an intervening intention. I don't know of any empirical work that addresses this question, so for now I think that we should leave it open. Indifference and incommensurability give us some reason for admitting present-directed intentions, but not enough to be clinching.

Suppose it turned out that direct action were possible, without an intervening intention of the kind we have been discussing. Would that show that the account of intention I have offered is partial? It would only do so if we thought that there were some other kind of intention that obtained in cases of present-directed action, a kind that needed a further account. But why think that? The only reason I can see is that such actions would be naturally described as 'intentional'; and where there is intentionality, it might be thought, there must be intentions. That brings us to the complex issue of the relation between an action being intentional, and it being done on the basis of an intention.

Intentions and Acting Intentionally

There is a simple and straightforward theory that insists that an agent performs an action intentionally if and only if they act on an intention to perform that action. Some have proposed such an account because it provides the basis of a reduction: if acting on an intention is equivalent to acting intentionally, and acting intentionally can be reduced to acting on the basis of a certain belief and desire, then intentions can be reduced to beliefs and desires.[24] Others have simply assumed that two such closely related linguistic constructions as 'intention' and 'intentionally' should be equivalent in this way, or that one should be derived from the other.[25]

---

[24] See Davidson, 1963; in later work he identifies intentions with all-out evaluations, which, rather oddly, he identifies with the actions themselves. See Davidson, 1969 and 1978. For discussion, see Bratman, 1985, at pp. 22–3.

[25] Anscombe insists that the locutions should be treated together (Anscombe, 1963, §1), and is often seen as someone who wants to privilege talk of intentional action over that of intention. In fact, though, her position is rather complex. Her focus on intentional action

However plausible this might initially seem, there are good reasons for rejecting the equivalence. It has occasioned a great deal of discussion that I shall not repeat here.[26] Let me just point to two considerations. First, anyone struck by the linguistic proximity of 'intention' and 'intentionally' in English would do well to look to the complexity of translating those notions into other languages. In German or Spanish, for instance, one finds a number of different terms, and choosing the right one is a delicate business. If we started with those languages we might be more likely to think of a set of related but different notions, rather than the single notion that English idiom suggests.[27] Indeed, even in English the patterns of usage are more complex than one might expect if the simple equivalence held. Doing something *on purpose* is very close to doing something intentionally; but there doesn't seem to be a use of the noun 'purpose' that is quite the same as that of 'intention'.

Second, and more compelling, is evidence from Joshua Knobe that appears to show that 'intentionally' is a normative term in the way that 'intention' is not. Knobe asked one group of subjects to consider the following passage:

The vice-president of a company went to the chairman of the board and said, 'We are thinking of starting a new program. It will help us increase profits, but it will also harm the environment.'

The chairman of the board answered, 'I don't care at all about harming the environment. I just want to make as much profit as I can. Let's start the new program.'

They started the new program. Sure enough, the environment was harmed.

He asked the subjects whether the chairman had intentionally harmed the environment; 82 per cent thought that he had. Knobe then

is to some degree procedural (§§3–4); and she argues, via a series of rather strange thought experiments, that talk of intentional action cannot be understood in the absence of talk of intentions (§20).

[26] For discussion, see Bratman, 1987, Ch. 8; for a useful summary of much recent work, see Mele, 1997.

[27] Joshua Knobe and Arundra Burra, who develop this line, produce interesting data showing that the Hindi term corresponding to 'intentionally' is morphologically related to the term for knowledge rather than the term for intention; see Knobe and Burra, 2006.

asked a second group to consider an almost identical passage, except that the programme was said to *help* the environment. But here the judgement about whether the help was intentional was radically different; 77 per cent *denied* that the chairman had intentionally helped the environment.[28]

Other experiments have brought similar results. Ask people about an intentional action that has a *bad* consequence as a foreseen side effect, and Knobe found that most of them will say that that side effect was brought about intentionally; ask them about a parallel case in which the side effect is *good*, and a majority will say that it was not brought about intentionally. In contrast, in both cases a majority will say that there was no intention to bring about the side effect.[29]

So normally people are more likely to see an action as intentional if its consequences are bad than if its consequences are good. It turns out that the full picture is more complicated than this suggests. There are a few cases in which attributions of intentionality are made even when the act is judged good, and working out quite why is a tricky business.[30] And it can be seen that the moral status of the side effect has an impact on some people's judgements not just of whether an act is performed intentionally, but of whether it is performed on the basis of an intention. A minority apparently use the term 'intention' much as the majority use the term 'intentionally'. Nonetheless, there are very good grounds here for thinking that there are two different notions in play: one, normally denoted by the noun 'intention', that is a psychological notion; and one, normally denoted by the adverb 'intentionally', that combines the psychological with the normative in some rather complicated way. To say this is not to say that the terms are utterly distinct: it is not to say that 'intention' only occurs in 'intentional' as, say, 'bus' occurs in 'business'. Of course they come from the same root, and have a great deal in common. It is just to say

---

[28] Knobe, 2003.

[29] For summary of Knobe's results, and some others, see Knobe 2006.

[30] See Knobe, 2007. Knobe suggests that the full account requires a distinction between spontaneous unconscious attributions of goodness or badness, and those that are more measured; it is the former rather than the latter that are operative in attributions of intentionality. I suspect rather that it turns on a difference between actions that involve the violation of a requirement and those that don't; but I shall not develop this here.

that, by a process of lexicalization, a process that is familiar for words that have been in the language for a very long time, they have come to have different meanings in standard English.[31] We see that with many other terms: consider, for instance, the connections and differences between 'awful', 'awesome' and 'awe-inspiring'. My concern in this book is with intentions, not with intentional actions.

Reduction

I mentioned at the beginning that the third element of Bratman's account was an argument that the role of intention cannot be played by beliefs or desires. I hope that what I have said so far shows that intentions have an important role to play; we cannot just give them up and talk in terms of beliefs and intentions instead. But that leaves open the possibility that intentions can be analysed in terms of beliefs and desires, so that ultimately those two can do all of the work.

Certainly the intention to ϕ does not look like either the simple belief that one will ϕ or the simple desire to ϕ. One can believe that one will succumb to a temptation without intending to do so; and equally one can want to perform some forbidden act without thereby intending to perform it. Moreover, cases of indifference are ones where, by hypothesis, one lacks the desire to perform either action, and the belief that one will. So if intention is to be reduced to belief and desire some more complex analysis must be given. Several authors have tried to give one, and they do indeed become very complex. For instance, David Velleman argues that the intentions consist in 'self-fulfilling expectations that are motivated by a desire for their fulfillment, and that represent themselves as such'.[32] And on the desire side, with even greater complexity, Michael Ridge contends that:

A intends to ϕ if and only if (a) A has a desire to ϕ, (b) A does not believe that ϕ-ing is beyond her control, (c) A's desire to ϕ is a *predominant* one, which

---

[31] The evolution of the terms is actually quite complex. The *OED* gives a number of other meanings for 'intention' that are now obsolete, including some notion of mental application or effort, as in Locke's *Essay*: 'When the Mind with great Earnestness, and of Choice, fixes its view on any Idea . . . it is that we call Intention or Study' (Locke, 1690, II xix §1).

[32] Velleman, 1989a, Chapter 4.

is just to say that there is no desire ψ, such that A does not believe ψ-ing is beyond her control, she desires to ψ as much as or more than she desires to ϕ, and she believes that a necessary means to her ϕ-ing is that she refrain from ψ-ing, (d) A has a desire not to deliberate any more about whether to ϕ unless new, relevant information comes to light.[33]

I doubt that either of these accounts work, but I will not say much to defend this doubt.[34] I want to raise a more fundamental question: why should we want to reduce in the first place? Ridge contends that a reduction will allow us to maintain the 'attractive Humean view that a full, rationalizing, explanation of an agent's intentional actions always can be had without appealing to anything other than beliefs and desires'. Insofar as the Humean account is supposed to provide a contrastive explanation of an agent's actions, so that it explains why they performed one action *rather than* another, I think that there are other reasons for rejecting it, reasons that will be discussed in Chapter 4. But, independently of that, why should we prefer an account that offers explanations of agents' actions in terms of beliefs and desires rather than one that makes use of beliefs, desires and intentions?

An obvious response is the Ockhamist one: an account with fewer ontological commitments is, *ceteris paribus*, better that one with more. But if this is to be plausible the *ceteris paribus* clause will need to do a lot of work. Reducing our ontological commitments by reduction should not be an end in itself. To take an example from Kripke: when describing a population of married people, we could quantify only over the women, reducing all that we wanted to say about their husbands to statements about the wives. Of course the predicates

---

[33] Ridge, 1998.

[34] In brief: against Velleman I doubt that we can form entirely self-fulfilling beliefs prior to having reasons to believe that they are true. Compare: I tell you that there is a handkerchief inside the box before you, and that, by some complex process, it is whatever colour you believe it to be. Knowing this, and having no independent reason for thinking it is any particular colour, can you just come to believe that it is, say, red? I think not. For similar worries, though stressing the normative inappropriateness of forming self-fulfilling beliefs as well as their impossibility, see Langton, 2004. Against Ridge I take it as evident, his protestations notwithstanding, that if I desire to do something but intend to resist this desire, I do not intend to do it. And the general recipe for creating Humean analyses that he proposes seems to me to beg the question.

would become more complicated—each woman would now have both a wife-weight and a husband-weight, and so on—but we would have halved our ontological commitments. Still, clearly the approach is absurd. Reduction is good if it brings greater explanation, and this does not. The women are different from the men, and reducing the latter to the former only brings confusion.[35]

I suspect that something similar is true of intentions. A reduction of intentions to beliefs and desires only confuses things. Certainly the accounts that we have seen from Velleman and Ridge bring a great deal of complexity. If they are to justify this, they need to bring some explanatory advantage beyond a mere claim of ontological reduction.

Velleman does indeed argue that his account brings such an advantage. Treating intention as a form of belief explains some otherwise puzzling features that it has. In particular it explains: (i) why it is that intending to perform a certain action entails a belief that one will perform that action; and (ii) why it is that intention is governed by a consistency requirement that makes it irrational to intend to do two things that one believes to be inconsistent.

That would be all to the good if intention had these features. But they are controversial. I contend that the first is simply illusory: intention does not entail belief. The second is more complicated. Whilst there are consistency requirements on intention, I contend that they are quite weak, and give no support to the thesis that intention is a form of belief. These issues are the topic of the next chapter. I start with the question of whether intention entails belief.

---

[35] The example was given in a seminar in Princeton in the late 1980s.

2

Belief

Does intending to do something entail that you believe you will succeed in doing it?[1] Let us consider some examples.

(i) Last night's storm brought down a tree, which now lies across your driveway, penning in the car that you urgently need to use this evening. You are not sure whether you will be able to move the tree yourself, having never confronted something quite this big before. Three possibilities have occurred to you. You might lever it out of the way with a crowbar (though you are not sure how much force you can exert with that). You might saw it into manageable pieces with a chainsaw (though you are not sure that you will be able to get the chainsaw started). Or you might put a rope round it and drag it out of the way with your car (though you are not sure, given the way that the car is penned in, that you will be able to manœuvre it into a position from which this would work). Alternatively, and at considerable cost, you could get the local tree company to move it; but the storm brought down a lot of trees, so to stand any chance of getting them out in time you would certainly need to phone them first thing. In the end you telephone the tree company, making a (cancellable) arrangement for them to come late in the afternoon. Then you walk down to the shed and load up the wheelbarrow with your biggest crowbar *and* the chainsaw *and* a

---

[1] The literature on the question is large. For pieces arguing that intention requires a corresponding belief, see Hampshire and Hart, 1958; Grice, 1971; Harman, 1976; Velleman, 1985, 2007; and Setiya, 2007. For argument that it does not, see Bratman, 1987, forthcoming; and, plausibly, Anscombe, 1963: note her examples, at p. 94, of St Peter, and of the man who knows he is to be tortured. I discuss these below.

rope: all in preparation for a morning attempt to move it, one way or another, yourself.

(ii) You have some library books that are badly overdue; in fact so badly overdue that your borrowing privileges are about to be suspended (a major inconvenience) if you do not return or renew them by the end of the day. Since you have finished with them, the best thing would be to drop them off at the library on your way home; but that is after the departmental seminar, and you know that, once you get on your bicycle with your head full of ideas from the discussion, you are all too likely to cycle straight home. Alternatively, you could renew them online; but that would require your library password, which is scribbled on a piece of paper lying somewhere on your desk at home. If you renewed them online you would not need to take the books home with you, but you would need to take your laptop, which you would otherwise leave at work. In the end you head for the seminar with your bag weighed down by both the library books *and* your laptop, moved by the thought that you will avoid suspension one way or another.[2]

I take it that in the first case you do not believe that you will move the tree on your own. But, contrary to what some authors seem to have assumed, you are not wholly agnostic on the matter; clearly you think that there is some chance you will.[3] Similarly, in the second, you do not believe that you will take the library books back, though again you think that there is some chance that you will. What should we say about your intentions?

Linguistic Intuitions and Their Limits

We can start, in time-honoured analytic fashion, by consulting our linguistic intuitions. Here, it seems to me, the two cases are rather

---

[2] I take the examples from Bratman, 1987, pp. 38–9. Bratman's examples concern a log and a bookshop, not a tree and a library; but since I have modified the examples, I thought it best to modify their objects to keep them distinct.

[3] For instance, David Velleman writes as though in such cases, lacking all-out belief, agents simply have no opinion about whether they will succeed or not; see Velleman, 2007. I discuss this below.

different. In the first case we would naturally say, not that you intend to move the tree by yourself, but only that you intend to *try*; and that datum might be taken to lend support to the thesis that intention requires belief in success.

But what of the second case? We surely would not say that you intend to *try* to take the library books back; it is not as though the library is currently under siege, and you are sceptical about your abilities to get through the defences. No—if you get home and find to your annoyance that the books are still in your bag, it will not be true that you even tried to take them back.

Forgetfulness is not the only failing that can give rise to such cases. Weakness of will can generate them too. Suppose that you arrive at the library steps, and, seduced by the lovely glint of gold tooling on the books' smooth cloth-covered boards, you decide that, suspension notwithstanding, you simply will not give them up. An unlikely event perhaps, but possible. Then once again it would not be true that you *try* to take the books back; we are not supposing some strange compulsion forces your hand back as you endeavour to place them in the return chute. And once again this is an outcome that you might foresee even as you form the intention to take the books back; you can form the intention in the knowledge that you might not succeed.

So what do we say of such cases? One perfectly natural description is that you intend to take the books back, but are unsure whether you will do so. So long as we add the qualification, the direct statement of intention is quite acceptable.

If what I have said about the library case is right, this should make us reconsider the tree case, for the two are very similar. In each you can see different ways of achieving the same end; and in each, whilst you prefer one of these ways (moving the tree yourself, returning the books on the way home), you are unsure that you will be successful in it. (To make the cases closely parallel, we can assume that the probability that you assign to success is much the same in each.) So in each case, whilst making preparations for acting in the preferred way, you simultaneously make preparations to achieve the end in other ways. (Again, to keep the cases parallel, we can assume that your assessment of the chances of achieving the end in these other ways is much the same in each.) But if the two cases are so similar, and we would naturally say that in the second you have an intention to return the book coupled with doubt that you will succeed, why should we restrict our description of the first to talk of trying? Why not say straight out that you have an intention to move the tree yourself, coupled with doubt that you will succeed?

An obvious suggestion here is that the explanation is *pragmatic*: it is not that it would be false to say that you intend to move the tree yourself, but rather that it would be misleading to say so when there is something more informative that we could say, namely that you intend to try to move it. The difference between the two cases is just in what is available to be said. In the tree case there are actions that you are confident that you will perform, and these actions constitute trying to move the tree even in the absence of success in moving it; so these are the actions that you can mention. In contrast, in the library case there is no action of trying to take the books back that you are confident of performing but that falls short of actually taking them back; so there is no such alternative thing that we could say.[4]

This suggestion is very plausible, though it is a little complicated to say quite why the statement that you intend to try to move the tree is more informative than the statement that you intend to move it. Presumably it adds the information that you lack confidence that you will succeed; but how does it do this? The best explanation I can see draws a parallel between our statements about our own future actions and our statements about our intentions. I see you strolling purposefully towards the tree, crowbar in hand, and ask what you are doing. Suppose first that you do not make explicit reference to your *intentions*, but just talk about what you are *going to do*. You would be

---

[4] An alternative suggestion about what distinguishes the cases is this: only in the tree case are you doubtful of your *ability* to perform the action; in the library case you simply doubt that you *will* perform it. So it might be suggested that a necessary condition on intending to perform an action is confidence that one will be *able* to perform it. This strikes me as implausible. There are alternative versions of the library case in which you would be unable to return the book, but in which I think our linguistic intuitions would be unchanged. Suppose that exciting seminars have a tendency to provoke epileptic seizures in you; if you were to suffer such a seizure you would be unable to return the book the same day. Could we not still say that you intend to return the book but are uncertain whether you will do so, even though in this case you are uncertain of your ability?

in no position to say that you were going to move the tree unless you were confident that you were going to be successful. Lacking that confidence, you might rather say that you were going to *try* to move it; at least you could be sure of that.[5] But then plausibly the same considerations come into play even when you do explicitly describe your intentions: rather than saying (truthfully) that you intend to move the tree, you say that you intend to try to move it, since this description of your intention conveys the information, by analogy with the earlier descriptions of your action, that you lack confidence that you will succeed.

As I said, I think that there is much plausibility to this pragmatic account, but it is clearly not conclusive. The main lesson that I want to draw is negative: when it comes to cases like these it is not obvious what we should say. Certainly there are no compelling grounds for saying that we lack intentions to do anything more than try; and there are some grounds for saying that we have intentions, provided that we add a rider to indicate our lack of confidence in success. What we need then, if we are to make any progress, is not just an examination of intuitions regarding these cases, but a developed account of them.

Such an account, I suggest, should contain two elements. It will need to say something about the attitude, an attitude falling somewhat short of all-out belief, that we have to the proposition that we will succeed. And it will need to say something about the attitude, an attitude falling somewhat short of all-out intention, that we have towards the action that we might perform. The first topic has been much discussed in philosophy, under the heading of *partial belief*. I want, however, to understand it in a novel way, and it is with this that I shall start. The account of partial belief will set things up for the second notion, that, to maintain the parallel, I shall call *partial intention*.[6]

---

[5] Lacking confidence, one does not simply *say* that one will try; one actually *thinks* of one's action in a different way, typically by focusing on the proximate mechanics of the movement rather than on the final goal. For research on our tendency to focus in this way in the face of difficulty, see Vallacher and Wegner, 1987.

[6] Terminological point: Bratman also talks of intentions being partial, but he means by this the very different idea that their details are not filled in. I hope that my very different

The Surprising Absence of Credence from the Discussion

We have assumed that you lack the all-out beliefs that you will be successful in moving the tree or in dropping off the books. But in assuming this we have not assumed that you have absolutely no clue about how things will work out. On the contrary: you think that there is some chance that you will succeed, and some that you will not. Indeed, in order to make the cases parallel I added the assumption that you give equal weight to the chance of success in each case. The standard way of understanding such attitudes is as *credences,* attitudes assigning a value between zero and one to each proposition in ways that, normatively at least, conform to the axioms of the probability calculus (so that, for instance, the credence assigned to p should be equal to one minus the credence assigned to not-p).

The idea of using credences is so well established that we might expect other authors writing about intentions to have framed their discussion in terms of them; yet they have not. We need to pause to ask why, since it is clearly not just an oversight. Admittedly, some of the early discussion of intention took place before the notion of credence had become so familiar; perhaps it did not occur to the initial authors to work with anything other than all-out belief. But in more recent work the restriction has been deliberate. The terms of the recent debate were largely set by Bratman's book *Intention, Plans, and Practical Reason*; and there Bratman explicitly rejected any discussion of credences, in favour of all-out belief.[7]

Although Bratman does not say much about his motivation for this, it is easy to see the kinds of considerations that moved him. First, it looks as though, as a matter of descriptive fact, we typically work with all-out beliefs rather than credences. Certainly in most ordinary common-sense attributions of cognitive attitudes to ourselves and to others, what we attribute are all-out beliefs. Of course this may just

usage does not lead to confusion. I considered using another term (Graded intention? Uncertain intention?) but none seemed right, and the parallel with the well-entrenched notion of partial belief was too strong to resist.

[7] Bratman, 1987, pp. 36ff.

be a mistake: it could be that we are working with a crude ungraded notion in our folk theory, when the reality is graded. But it would be surprising if our ordinary notions were so far adrift from the states that we actually have. Even when we move to a more partial notion, we do not normally ascribe specific numerical credences to agents. The psychological findings show that we are far happier making qualitative probability judgements ('I think it pretty unlikely that p' 'There is a good chance that q') rather than giving our judgements numerical values, even vague ones.[8] That is unsurprising. Maintaining large numbers of credences leads to enormous complexity, especially if our updating is by conditionalization, since this requires us to have a prior conditional probability for every pair of propositions.[9] And there are widely known results indicating that when we do try to make probabilistic calculations we often make terrible mistakes, ignoring base rates, reacting differently to the same information presented in different ways, and so on.[10]

This is not to deny that there are areas of action and belief formation in which our behaviour seems to be well described by assuming that we act as Bayesian agents that form fairly precise credences and update by conditionalization; and the same is true of other animals.[11] But such areas typically involve unconscious judgements, or unconscious manipulation of conscious judgements, about the kinds of things for which we might well expect specific cognitive competences to have evolved, such as our ability to identify causal dependencies. Such competences no more suggest that we are able to engage in conscious Bayesian reasoning than the fact that some aspects of vision are well modelled by Fourier series shows that creatures who can

---

[8] Budescu and Wallsten, 1995.

[9] For this criticism, see Harman, 1988, pp. 25–7. Put as I have put it, the complaint is overstated. Rather than assigning prior conditional probabilities to all pairs of propositions, we might use Bayesian Networks, representations that implicitly assume that many factors are independent, and so drastically reduce the number of priors needed. For an introduction to Bayesian Networks, with clear discussion of this point, see Charniak, 1991. Nevertheless, the computational complexity remains outside our conscious ability.

[10] The classic study here is Kahneman and Tversky, 1973; there has been much more since. See the articles collected in Kahneman and Tversky, 2000.

[11] For review, see Chater et al., 2006, and the articles that follow it in the same journal.

see are competent with harmonic analysis.[12] However much we might want consciously to entertain sets of credences that conform to the axioms of the probability calculus, and manipulate them by methods like conditionalization, it looks as though we simply cannot do it, any more than wanting to swim like a dolphin enables us to do that. And the situation would not change if we were to understand what would be involved in entertaining sets of credences, and were to learn to perform some of the appropriate manipulations in isolation—just as we still would not be able to swim like dolphins even if we were to understand the biomechanics of dolphin swimming, and were to learn to ripple parts of our bodies in the appropriate manner.

A second reason for wanting to eschew credences concerns the issue of how to relate them to all-out belief. A natural first thought is that all-out belief is just high credence. But, for familiar reasons, such an approach is hopeless. How high does an agent's credence need to be before we ascribe them an all-out belief? We might require complete certainty, but then almost all of our attitudes to contingent propositions (and to some necessary propositions) would not count as belief. Alternatively we might try to establish a threshold which credence must pass to count as belief: 0.9, say. That does no better. One problem is that any particular threshold will seem arbitrary. Another is that we normally expect belief to agglomerate: if an agent believes A and believes B, then they will believe A *and* B. But if credences obey the rules of the probability calculus, then we will not in general get this result. If A and B are independent beliefs that are just on the threshold of 0.9, then the agent's credence in A *and* B will be the product of the two individual credences: in this case 0.81, which will fall below the threshold, and so not count as belief.[13] A related problem, the Lottery Paradox, confirms that the threshold view and a rule of agglomeration do not fit together. Suppose that there are 1,000 tickets in a fair lottery. We reasonably assign a credence of 0.999 to any given ticket that it will not win. Since such a credence takes us over the threshold for belief, it follows, on the threshold view, that

---

[12] The comparison is from Chater et al, 2006, p. 288.
[13] For these two worries, see Stalnaker, 1984, pp. 91–2.

we believe of each ticket that it will not win. In itself that sounds wrong. Add an agglomeration rule and it would follow that our belief is that no ticket will win. Yet we surely do not believe that: we know that one of them will win.

Of course, problems in relating credence to all-out belief do not by themselves tell against credences; in fact they have more often been used by proponents of a credence account for explaining why they should have no truck with all-out belief. But once we accept that we do have all-out beliefs, then these considerations provide further reason for not blithely adding credences in as well.

I take it that these are the sorts of consideration that led Bratman to avoid talk of credences; and they are powerful. But they should not lead us to try to work exclusively with all-out belief. Clearly the tree and library examples can only be handled by introducing some attitude that falls short of that. The most that we can conclude is that this attitude is not well modelled by the classical credence account. I think that implicitly Bratman concedes this. Bratman thinks that one can rationally intend to ϕ iff *either* one believes that one will ϕ, *or* one neither believes nor disbelieves that one will ϕ. All that is ruled out is that one disbelieves that one will ϕ.[14] In proposing this I think that he is not just working with two attitudes, believing that p and disbelieving that p. He is implicitly working with a third: neither-believing-nor-disbelieving that p. This is not simply the state that agents are in when they do not believe that p and do not disbelieve that p. One could be in that state as a result of never having raised the question whether p. Yet if disbelieving that one will ϕ is incompatible with intending to ϕ, then surely failing even to have considered whether one will ϕ is incompatible with intending it. Rather the attitude of neither-believing-nor-disbelieving that p looks to be a distinct attitude that one can take to p, an attitude that assigns it a degree of belief less than that assigned by believing it, and greater than that assigned by disbelieving it. But once we admit three attitudes we no longer have an all-out account of belief; we have a very coarse-grained version of a graded account.

---

[14] Bratman, 1987, p. 38.

Belief, Partial Belief and Credence

So can we give an account of partial belief that is psychologically more realistic than that provided by the credence account, and that can be integrated into an account of all-out belief? I think that we can. In this section I want to sketch the outlines of such an account, and to say something about how it relates to the idea of credence.

We saw how hard it is to arrive at all-out belief by starting with credences: the threshold account is clearly hopeless. So let us try to move in the other direction. Let us start by getting clearer on the nature of all-out belief, and then inquire how it might be made more partial.

A number of recent authors have argued that the central feature of all-out belief concerns its relation to practical deliberation. For instance, in distinguishing belief from credence, Timothy Williamson has suggested that one all-out believes a proposition if and only if one is willing to use it as a premise in practical deliberation.[15] The proposal echoes some earlier comments of Bratman who, in discussing his original log case, wrote:

> To believe something is not merely to assign a high probability to its occurrence. I might assign a high probability to my failing to move the log without believing that I will fail... what seems distinctive about believing that I will fail is that it puts me in a position to plan on the assumption of failure.[16]

As it stands the proposal is over restrictive. Mightn't I have all-out beliefs about certain things (things in the distant past, for instance) where the question of action does not arise? And, conversely, seeing no other possibility of getting what I want, mightn't I act on a supposition even though I do not fully believe it? Moreover, all-out

---

[15] Williamson, 2000, p. 99.
[16] Bratman 1987, p. 40. Elsewhere Bratman is keen to distinguish the idea of acceptance, which is what is needed for reliance, from belief; see Bratman, 1990. For other interesting accounts of all-out belief that tie it to the idea of action, see Frankish, 2009, and Weatherson, 2005. Weatherson is also adamant that all-out belief is not a distinct state from partial belief, but that the distinction stems only from our different descriptions of it. I am inclined to think that the distinction is psychologically real; see below.

belief surely has connections with other attitudes that are independent of action. To take a nice example from David Owens: my feelings of guilt, or pride, or anger only really come in when I all-out believe that I have done badly, or well, or have been badly done to.[17] Nevertheless, I think that the central idea, that all-out belief is at heart a practical attitude, is right.[18] We are cognitively limited creatures. Maintaining and manipulating large numbers of credences would overload our capacities, and our reasoning would get nowhere. So as a practical matter it makes sense to accept certain premises as given, and to do our reasoning on the basis of them, even though we acknowledge that there is some chance that they will be wrong. In making my plans this morning I took it as a premise that the philosophy department would be functioning, that my route to it would be open, that my computer would not have been stolen, and so on; and this is so even though I would give to each of these propositions a credence of less than one. I even took it as a premise that the lifts would be working, pressing the button and waiting patiently for one to come, though the credence I would assign to that proposition is quite considerably less than one.

On this picture, the role of all-out beliefs is in many ways parallel to the role that, in Chapter 1, I ascribed to intentions. Just as intentions enable us to resolve deliberative uncertainty in order to facilitate action, so all-out beliefs enable us to resolve epistemic uncertainty in order to facilitate action. They allow us to reduce an unmanageable amount of information to a manageable amount by excluding certain possibilities from our practical reasoning. They provide us with a relatively simple description of what the world is like, to which straightforward non-probabilistic reasoning can be applied, around which plans can easily be built, and which can easily be communicated to others.[19]

---

[17] Owens, forthcoming.

[18] Here I am especially indebted to conversations with Agustin Rayo.

[19] There is a further way in which beliefs are similar to intentions, in that they too have a certain inherent stability. This can be best understood, once again, in terms of differing thresholds for formation and for revision. Some considerations that would have been enough to stop me forming an intention will not be enough to lead me to revise it once it has been formed. Similarly, some evidence that would have been enough to stop me forming a belief will not be enough to get me to revise it once it has been formed. Though obviously such tendencies can lead to irrationality, I think that it is quite rational

Note how this approach to all-out belief differs from that suggested by Williamson and Bratman. Deliberating with all-out beliefs is an attitude dictated by practical considerations. But the deliberation that we do is not then limited to practical matters. I can deliberate about what happened in the distant past, or what will happen in the distant future, or about what I would have done if things were very different from how they are, even though none of this will affect my behaviour. The approach offered here thus plausibly entails that if someone believes a proposition they will use it in their practical deliberation insofar as it is relevant; but it does not identify belief with such a use.[20]

If this is right, we can see why it makes sense to deliberate with all-out beliefs wherever possible. But of course we cannot always do so. Sometimes it is clear to us that we do not know what did or will happen; this is true of the tree case and of the library case. In such situations we have to make use of a more partial notion. But this does not take us all the way to credences, for two reasons. First, as we have seen, we do not normally assign anything like numerical values to the possibilities.[21] We just talk of one outcome being likely or unlikely, or being more likely than, or equally likely as, another. Sometimes we do not even do this, but simply think of a number of possibilities as being live, without trying to rank them.

Second, and more importantly, even when we do assign non-zero credences to a range of propositions, we need not accept each of them

to have them to some degree. I suggest that they work by placing different thresholds for initial consideration and for reconsideration.

[20] The proposal has a similar subsuming relation to various other proposals in the literature. Thus, for instance, Mark Kaplan has argued that the defining characteristic of all-out belief in p is, roughly, the agent's preparedness to assert that p if they are restricted to asserting either p or not-p. See Kaplan, 1996, ch. 4, for details. This feature plausibly follows from the account proposed here, but again I do not think that it captures the essence of belief.

[21] Exception: cases in which the uncertainty is not primarily epistemic, but can be thought of as deriving from a chance that is in some sense objective: the chance of rolling a six on a fair dice for instance. Here people are quite prepared to assign numerical probabilities. But exactly because of this objective construal, it is plausible to think that the probability assigned is part of the *content* of an all-out belief, rather than a measure of the *attitude*: one all-out believes that there is a one-sixth chance of rolling a six. Certainly our standard ordinary language locutions suggest this. No one who is not a theorist talks of having a one-sixth degree of belief.

as what we might call a *live possibility*. In the tree case I attributed to you a partial belief that you would succeed in moving the tree using one of three methods, and a further partial belief that you would fail with all three and that the tree company would move it. But unless your view was remarkably blinkered, this would not exhaust your credences; or, at least, it would not exhaust the credences that you would be inclined to entertain, given the right prompting. You might give a non-zero credence to the tree being moved by a helpful gang of passing weightlifters, or to it being blown out of the way by a freak local tornado; and you would give a much higher credence to the tree not being moved at all, either because both you and the tree company tried and failed, or, more likely still, because you failed and the tree company did not show up. So, on reasonable assumptions, your credences over the four options would not sum to one. Nevertheless, it is a very normal case in which you narrow your focus to these four, as we have assumed that you do. These are your live possibilities. They are the only four upon which you base your reasoning and, in this case, your plans.[22] You do not consider what to do if the tree is not moved. Or, at least, if you did initially consider this possibility, you do not continue to do so, and you certainly do not make plans around it. It is not live. You thus do not make plans around the possibility that you will be unable to move the car: you do not telephone those you should meet this evening to warn them that you might not make it, do not ask to see if someone can pick you up, do not start finding out about taxi services. So there is something special about the four options that you believe partition the ways in which the tree will be moved. You have an all-out belief in their disjunction, even though your credence in that disjunction remains less than one. It follows that the attitude you take to each of the disjuncts is not simply credence.[23]

---

[22] We do not require that live possibilities always give rise to plans. In thinking about the distant past we can equally treat some possibilities as live (Mary Queen of Scots was in the pay of the French), and others not (she was in the pay of the Russians), even though we would assign each a credence of greater than zero. So the approach does not collapse back into that of Bratman and Williamson.

[23] It remains open whether or not we are sufficiently competent to take an attitude of credence to the disjunction; even here we could still be trying to be dolphins.

I conclude then that there is a practical stance that one can take towards a proposition that is rather like all-out belief, but is partial. We might call it *partial all-out belief;* but, since that has an air of oxymoron, I shall somewhat stipulatively call it *partial belief.*[24] Then we can summarize the discussion in a pair of definitions, taking the notion of a live possibility as primitive:

All-out Belief
One all-out believes p iff one takes p as a live possibility and does not take not-p as a live possibility.

Partial Belief
One partially believes p iff one takes p as a live possibility and takes not-p as a live possibility.[25]

Although I have been keen to emphasize the ways in which partial belief differs from credence, there is an important way in which they are alike. Like credence, partial belief involves a distinctive (partial) attitude to a normal content, rather than a normal attitude to a distinctive (partial) content (one partially believes that p, rather than all-out believing that p is probable). Given that partial belief and credence share this structural feature, we might ask whether credence can be accommodated within the partial belief account. I suggest that we think of credences as the partial beliefs that an agent would have if they were quite unconstrained by cognitive limitations; or, more plausibly, as the partial beliefs that they do have when their cognitive limitations are irrelevant. One obvious

[24] Williamson discusses the idea that all-out belief comes in degrees whilst remaining distinct from credences, but he means to measure something rather different by it, namely how readily one would abandon one's reliance if the stakes were to go up (Williamson, 2000, p. 99).

[25] It is an interesting question, one that will not be properly pursued here, how we determine which possibilities are live and which are not. I certainly would not want to suggest that one can simply choose which options to regard as live. More plausible is the idea that they will be determined by some sort of rules. An obvious place to start would be by looking at the rules that contextualist accounts of knowledge use to determine relevant epistemic possibilities, for instance, like those given in Lewis, 1996. One plausible difference, though, concerns Lewis's rule of attention, by which the mere mention of a possibility makes it epistemically relevant. It does not look as though the mention of a possibility should make it live (though it is debatable whether this rule is correct even for the case of knowledge).

circumstance in which these limitations are largely irrelevant is in simple betting behaviour. When you are asked the odds that you would give to a certain outcome—the odds that a gang of passing weightlifters will move the tree—this does not require much from you. It does not require you to formulate complex plans contingent on that outcome, since it doesn't require further action on your part; if you win the bet, the winnings will be delivered to you.[26] So in such circumstances there is typically no need to exclude the possibility from your reasoning: you just come up with an answer. Typically it is not a very good one (we tend, for instance, to overestimate small possibilities and underestimate large ones), and serious work would be required to make it better; but nonetheless we are unconcerned about saying something. So we can concede to the orthodox approach that in certain circumstances we can form attitudes that are very like credences,[27] and that betting behaviour provides the touchstone for them, whilst insisting that this is really a very particular phenomenon, one that provides a bad model for our cognitive attitudes more generally.

Clearly there is much more that would need to be said in making precise this account of partial belief, and in explicating the notion of a live possibility on which it rests. But it should be clear enough for us to return to our main topic, that of partial intention.

Partial Intention

Consider again the tree example. We supposed that you acknowledge four live possibilities: that you will move the tree with the crowbar (which you will try first); that you will fail with the crowbar and move it with the chainsaw (which you will try next); that you will fail with the chainsaw and move it with the car (which you will try last); and that you will give up and let the tree company move it. And let us say that you think that success in each of the first three

---

[26] Things would be very different if you were required to ascertain whether you had won, and then to claim the winnings yourself. For the extra cognitive load that this would impose would make it rational to avoid getting involved in much betting behaviour.

[27] I leave open the question of whether even here we are good enough at manipulating them for us to say that they are credences.

possibilities is rather unlikely, but that overall you think you are about as likely to move it yourself as to have to wait for the tree company to move it.

You have then a set of partial beliefs; that is enough to start planning and acting on them. That is what you do when you phone the company and fill up your wheelbarrow with the various tools. In so doing you exhibit various attitudes that are intention-like. It is not clear that we would ordinarily call them 'intentions'; but equally we would not ordinarily call your partial beliefs 'beliefs'. The attitudes are certainly like all-out intentions in many respects. They play the same roles of curtailing deliberation, resolving indeterminacy and enabling coordination that intentions play: you fix on a small number of plans from the many that occurred to you and that you might have pursued, and as a result of this you can coordinate around your other plans (the plan to go out in the evening), and with other people (the people at the tree company). What distinguishes the states you are in from normal intentions is simply that they are partial: they stand to all-out intentions much as partial beliefs stand to all-out beliefs. You do not all-out intend to move the tree by means of the crowbar; but you do *partially intend* to do so. Moving it with the crowbar is one component—a subplan—of your larger all-out intention of moving it before the evening.

There are two ways to understand the idea of a partial intention. We might say that an agent has a partial intention whenever they have merely a partial belief in its success. Or we might say that it is essential to partial intentions that they be only a proper part of an overall plan, i.e., that they be accompanied by alternative partial intentions to achieve the same end. As we saw, in agents' partial beliefs the analogues of these two different features come together: if I have a partial belief in p, I will automatically have an accompanying partial belief in its complement, not-p. With intentions the result does not come automatically. If I have only a partial belief that I will achieve my end by succeeding in a certain intention, it does not automatically follow that I have an alternative intention designed to achieve the same end. I might have no backup plan: I might simply have a partial belief that I will achieve the end at all.

So we need to make a choice of how to define partial intentions, in terms of partial belief in success or of the presence of alternative intentions to the same end. I take the second path:

Partial Intention
An intention to F is partial iff it is designed to achieve a given end E and it is accompanied by one or more alternative intentions also designed to achieve E. If an intention is not partial it is all-out.

After all, it does seem that if something is partial there should be other parts that make up the whole; that is the idea the definition captures. As defined here, the crucial aspect of partial intentions is that, like partial beliefs, they involve a division in the agent's consideration. An agent with partial beliefs considers two or more competing live possibilities. An agent with partial intentions is working with two or more competing plans.

Note, though, that since all-out intentions are in turn defined as those that are not partial, the lack of an alternative intention is enough to qualify an intention as all-out. The definition thus leaves open the possibility that there may be all-out intentions in whose success the agent has only a partial belief; in other words it does not follow from the definition that all-out intention entails all-out belief. Of course there may be other reasons for believing in that entailment; we shall examine some later. But it does not follow by fiat.

It might look as though this definition makes the partiality of an intention sensitive to the way in which the end is described. The worry is that if my end when wielding the crowbar is to *move the tree*, then clearly the intention is partial, since I have other intentions aiming for the same end; but if my end is rather to *move the tree with the crowbar*, then it is not partial. So let us be clear: given the definition, an intention is partial if and only if there is *some* description relative to which it is partial. The intention to move the tree with the crowbar is thus partial *simpliciter*. This raises a worry from the other direction. Mightn't it be the case that, at some level, all of our intentions are directed at the same end: our *eudaimonia*, for instance? The worry is misplaced. Even if all of our intentions were ultimately directed at our *eudaimonia*, it is very unlikely that they would represent *alternative* ways of achieving it as the definition requires; rather they are *contributory*.

One intention is an *alternative* to another in achieving an end if and only if, were it successful, there would be no possibility of using the other to achieve the end. A partial intention need not be half-hearted. When you set to work with the crowbar, it does not follow that you push more gently than you could, on the grounds that your intention is only partial. You may: you may want to hold some energy in reserve for the other options, or, knowing that you have them in reserve, you may be more careful not to risk your back. But that is not essential to the endeavour. Although your intention is partial, you may execute it with everything at your disposal. A partial intention is only partial because of the presence of alternatives. Does this bring a disanalogy with partial belief? It may seem that, in contrast to this whole-heartedness, the state of partially believing requires one's belief to be half-hearted. But I doubt that that is an apt parallel. It is the *action* that results from the partial intention that can be whole-hearted, and this is equally true of an action that results from a partial belief. My confidence that the chainsaw will start may be very low, but that doesn't mean I pull the start cord with any less vigour.

To sum up this section: I propose that we should admit a notion of partial intentions, standing to all-out intentions much as partial beliefs stand to all-out beliefs. Whether we call them 'intentions' or not is of little importance: after all, ordinary usage is unclear on the parallel issue of whether partial beliefs should be classed as a form of belief. In the light of the earlier considerations, I suggest that much of the reluctance we have to call them intentions is merely pragmatic, triggered by the availability of mentioning instead a distinct action that is a trying. Where no such action is available (as in the library case) we have less reluctance. But I am not too concerned if I am wrong about that; ordinary language is no infallible guide to psychological kinds.

Do We Need Partial Intentions?

Perhaps, though, we could live without partial intentions; perhaps we could account for the kinds of cases that I have discussed with just the normal framework of all-out intentions. I have already explained, by means of the library example, why we cannot in general think of them as all-out intentions to try. We might instead try to understand them as *compound* all-out intentions. Presumably they are not conjunctive: you do not all-out intend to move the tree by yourself *and* have it moved by the tree company, since you know that that is impossible. But mightn't they be disjunctive: could we not simply say that you all-out intend *either* to move the tree yourself, *or* have it moved by the tree company?

Of course we could say that; but to say only that would be to lose explanatory force. For we need to break compound intentions down into their elements if we are to understand quite what explains what. Consider a parallel example with ordinary all-out intentions. Here presumably conjunction is permissible: if I intend to hear a concert and intend to buy some whisky, then I intend to hear a concert and buy some whisky. But we would not want to be constrained to use only the conjunctive sentence. It is my intention to hear the concert that explains why I buy a ticket; it is my intention to buy some whisky that explains why I divert to the off-licence. It is only if we break the conjunction down into its consistent atoms that these explanations become available. The same is true when we try to give all-out disjunctive surrogates for partial intentions. It is my partial intention to get the tree company to move the tree that causes me to phone them; if we are limited just to all-out disjunctive intentions, we can give no explanation of this.

A more plausible approach uses *conditional* all-out intentions: you all-out intend, *if* your attempt with the crowbar fails, to cut up the tree with the chainsaw; and so on. This avoids the problem raised for the disjunctive approach, since in place of each partial intention we get a separate conditional intention. Nonetheless, I do not believe that the proposal will work. Of course it is true in a trivial sense that you intend each subplan to work if the others fail; to that extent your partial intentions are conditional. That, however, is just to say that they are partial intentions; it does not explain how they are to be characterized as a class of all-out conditional intentions. What gives some support to this latter claim is the idea, made explicitly in the tree case, that each of the later stages in your plan will be triggered by the failure of earlier stages. But that does not provide a general recipe for reducing partial intentions to conditional intentions. First it is not true of the first stage: moving the tree with the crowbar is a partial intention but not a conditional one. Nor, in the library example, is your intention to return the books on the way home a conditional intention. But we want to register that these are not normal all-out intentions: they are already enmeshed in further intentions that would have no place if they were. Second, one may formulate a set of partial intentions without yet deciding how to integrate them; perhaps when you place the tools in the wheelbarrow you have not yet decided which to employ first. So there is not yet a set of conditional intentions in place. Of course in this case there is a compound intention: to start with either the crowbar or the chainsaw or the rope, and if that fails, to proceed to one of the remaining methods, and so on. But we have already seen that compound intentions of this form cannot do the work that is needed of them. Third, whilst it is true that the subplans in the tree-moving example and the library example are basically sequential—I go through one subplan after another—not all cases will be like this. Again we can use an example from Bratman to illustrate the point.[28] I am faced with two identical video games. Success in either involves hitting a target with an electronic missile. This is a difficult feat that will probably require many attempts. Ambidextrous as I am, I decide to start shooting in both games at once, one per hand, despite my knowledge that the games are linked, so that were I to be about to hit both targets simultaneously (a chance I rate as very slim), both would shut down.[29] In this case I do not intend to hit both targets; I know that to be impossible. Rather, I partially intend to hit a target with each missile. But these are not conditional intentions; I do not fire the missiles sequentially, but simultaneously.

So all-out intentions to try will not do all of the work required of partial intentions, nor will all-out disjunctive intentions, nor will

---

[28] (Bratman 1987) pp. 114ff. Bratman denies that there are intentions involved here, for reasons that I discuss below.

[29] Perhaps being ambidextrous is not enough; perhaps I would need independent eyes if I were to aim each of the missiles independently. Still, that is possible, though it may require severing my corpus callosum (compare the case of Kim Peek, the model for the central character in the film *Rain Man*, who, born without one, can reputedly read the left and right pages of a book simultaneously).

all-out conditional intentions. But I have responded to each with a different counterexample. A worry thus remains that a patchwork of different strategies might do the work: replace some of the partial intentions with intentions to try, some with disjunctive intentions, and some with conditional intentions. Such a response certainly seems inelegant; but can it be refuted? I suggest that the initial library example provides a refutation. I have already argued that that cannot be seen as an intention to try. But nor can it be seen as simply a disjunctive intention to either return or renew the books (I need separate explanations of why I take the books with me, and why I take the laptop). Finally it is not a conditional intention: since it is the first in the series, it will not be triggered by the failure of some other intention. I conclude then that we need a separate notion of partial intentions.

Consistency Requirements

Bratman rejects the idea that there are states like partial intentions. But this is not on the grounds that they are unnecessary. Rather, he holds that they infringe a plausible consistency requirement on intention. My aim in this section is to rebut this argument, and then to explore consistency requirements on partial intentions more generally.

There is a minimal consistency requirement that everyone can concede, so let us start by getting it out of the way. It should never be the case that your total set of intentions and partial intentions puts you in a practically impossible situation: it should never require you to do two inconsistent things (or, at least, two things that you believe inconsistent) at the same time. Call this the *execution requirement*. Though the intuitive idea is clear, the requirement is rather hard to formulate. Sometimes a perfectly rational plan will require you to try to do two things that are in a sense inconsistent at the same time: that is just what happens in the video-game case. The point is rather that the demands on your immediate, proximate actions should be consistent: you should not have to stand up and sit down at the same time, to shoot the gun and not shoot the gun, to turn simultaneously to the left and the right, and so on. What is consistent here is a highly contingent matter: perhaps an intention to rub my stomach and pat my head is consistent for me, perhaps not; perhaps the only way to find out is to try.

The execution requirement poses no threat to the existence of partial intentions. But this is not the kind of requirement that interests Bratman. Rather, he is interested in the consistency of our intentions with our beliefs in their success. A weak requirement of this kind is:

Weak consistency
If an agent forms an intention, then they must not believe that they will fail to realize that intention.[30]

This is an *atomic* requirement: it places a constraint on each intention individually. We might want something stronger, a *holistic* consistency requirement that places a constraint on the agent's intentions and beliefs all taken together. The obvious candidate is the constraint that Bratman endorses, namely:

Strong consistency
If an agent forms an intention, then the realization of that intention must be consistent with their beliefs and with the realization of all their other intentions.[31]

Clearly the weak consistency requirement follows from the strong, since if an agent believes that they will fail to realize their intention, then the realization of that intention is inconsistent with their beliefs. The strong requires, in addition, a holistic coherence. For those who endorse the intention-entails-belief thesis, the strong consistency follows from the requirement of consistency on beliefs. But for those, like Bratman, who deny this thesis, it is an independent constraint.

Strong consistency leads Bratman to deny partial intentions, or states like them, the status of intentions. Consider, for instance, the mental

---

[30] Bratman endorses such a principle (1987, p. 38).

[31] That is, the proposition describing the realization of that intention must be consistent with the propositions that form the content of their beliefs, and the propositions that describe the realization of their other intentions (Bratman, 1987, p. 31).

states involved in the video-game example described above, where I simultaneously shoot at two targets, one with each hand, knowing that I cannot hit both (or the games would shut down). It follows, by both weak and strong consistency, that I cannot intend to hit both targets with both missiles for I believe that this is impossible. Further, since neither missile is privileged, any intention I have regarding one I must have regarding the other. So, by strong consistency, it follows that I cannot intend to hit either, for if I intended to hit one, I would also intend to hit the other, and the realization of both intentions is not compatible with my beliefs. In consequence, following Chisholm, Bratman classes them as mere *endeavourings*, states that resemble intention in being action-guiding, but that are otherwise very different.[32]

I think that Bratman's response here is mistaken. As we have seen, partial intentions are like intentions in that they enable agents to coordinate, to curtail deliberation and to resolve indecision. Thus the only ground for denying them the status of intentions is that they fail the strong consistency requirement. Yet whilst simple consistency is a plausible constraint on all-out intention, as it is on all-out belief, it is not a plausible constraint on partial intention. Rather, the consistency constraint that we place on our partial intentions should be like the one that we place on our partial beliefs; otherwise we are not treating like with like. We do not require that partial beliefs be consistent, in the sense that everything that we partially believe must be compossible; so we should not require this of our partial intentions. Instead, we should require of our partial intentions at most the same kind of consistency that we require of our partial beliefs.

So how can we reformulate analogues to the consistency conditions on partial beliefs? A natural reformulation of the weaker requirement is:

Very weak consistency for partial intentions
If an agent forms a partial intention, then they must not all-out believe that they will fail to realize that intention.

---

[32] Bratman, 1987, pp. 129ff.

Or, slightly stronger, we might require them to have, not just an absence of all-out belief that they will fail, but at least a partial belief that they will succeed:

Weak consistency for partial intentions
If an agent forms a partial intention, then they must have a partial belief that they will succeed in realizing that intention.

After all, if they are partially intending to do something, then they will have a subplan in which that partial intention figures. But if they lack a partial belief in success, and yet do not all-out believe that they will fail, this must be because they have failed to consider whether they will succeed; in which case it is surely irrational to have formed that subplan.

The move from very weak consistency to weak consistency looks an innocuous one, but it brings an interesting consequence. Very weak consistency clearly places only an atomic requirement on our intentions. Weak consistency appears to do the same. But since it requires a partial belief for each partial intention, it follows that if we have a consistency condition on partial beliefs, it will be transformed into a global requirement on partial intentions. For if each partial intention must bring with it a partial belief, and there is a global consistency requirement on partial beliefs, that in turn will provide a global consistency requirement on the partial intentions.

However, placing a global consistency requirement on partial beliefs is no trivial task. If we were dealing with credences, it would be clear how to proceed. We have a notion of consistency for sets of credences that is provided by the axioms of the probability calculus: a set of credences is consistent if and only if it conforms to those axioms. Can we make use of a similar approach for partial beliefs? The problem, of course, is that it was precisely one of the features of partial beliefs, part of what distinguished them from credences, that they did not get numerical values.

There are two ways to go. One is to retreat from the position that an agent will frequently only have partial beliefs. Let us suppose then that, in addition to their partial beliefs, an agent, at least a rational agent, will go on to establish precise credences in ways that correspond to the axioms of the probability calculus. Then we might say, plausibly enough, that the partial beliefs will inherit their values from the corresponding credences in a way that preserves the ratios between them. Thus if your credence that you'll do something yourself is 0.45, and your credence that you'll get someone else to do it is 0.45, and you all-out believe that you'll get it done in one of those two ways, then your partial belief in each of the two possibilities will be 0.5.

The alternative, far more in keeping with the account of partial belief that I originally proposed, is to try for a weaker test of consistency. It would be analogous to the requirements of the axioms of the probability calculus, but applying, where it does, in an ordinal way. Treating one possibility as likely would require treating its negation as unlikely; the conjunction of two possibilities must be treated as no more likely than either of them, and so on. Such a requirement would be more easily satisfied—in particular, it would place no constraints at all in cases in which probabilities were not even ranked—but it would still provide a global constraint.

Still, it might seem too weak. Suppose, to vary our example, that you think that moving the tree by sawing it up is very likely to succeed, whereas moving it with the car or the crowbar is almost certain to fail. But suppose that, despite this, you plan to put almost all of your effort into the latter two plans. And suppose that there is no independent justification for this: it is not as if the latter two plans require more effort, or have to be tried first, or that there is something immoral or offensive or otherwise undesirable about sawing up the tree. Then there are some grounds for saying that you would be behaving in a practically irrational way. Yet the weak consistency requirement, even with a consistency requirement on partial belief, says nothing against it.

To rule out this kind of imbalance we would need a stronger global measure of coherence akin to that given by the strong consistency requirement. That requirement works by demanding consistency between all the agent's beliefs and the realization of all their intentions. We might try to do likewise. Suppose then that, in addition to placing a value on partial beliefs, we could place a value of between zero and one on each partial intention. Then we could impose a consistency requirement between the beliefs and the intentions by insisting that these states should, when taken *together,* conform to the axioms of the probability calculus. To see how to do this, imagine replacing each occurrence of 'has a partial intention of degree n that he will F' with 'has a partial belief of degree n that he will F' as these occur in the full description of the agent's intentions. Then one needs to check that putting the class of such statements together with the class of statements fully describing the agent's beliefs gives a class that is consistent with the axioms of the probability calculus. Calling this the 'extended probability calculus test' we could now define a strong consistency requirement for partial intentions (all-out intentions now becoming the special case where $n = 1$):

Strong consistency for partial intentions
If an agent forms a partial intention, then that intention must be consistent with the agent's other intentions, and with the agent's beliefs (partial and all-out), as this is established by the extended probability calculus test.

Or, slightly stronger (and following parallel reasoning to that which took us from very weak consistency to weak consistency):

Proportionality requirement
For each partial intention of degree n the agent should have a credence of degree n that it will succeed; and the agent's total set of credences, including those that result from this requirement, should conform to the axioms of the probability calculus.

How, though, should we place a measure on partial intentions? It is no good saying that a partial intention has degree n if and only if one has a credence of degree n that it will be successful; that makes the proportionality requirement trivial and so does nothing to rule out the cases of imbalance. Instead we need a truly independent measure of the strength of a partial intention. At a first pass we might say that one partial intention is twice as strong as another if and only if one relies on it twice as heavily. This in turn we can gloss by saying that one relies on one intention twice as heavily as on a second if and only if one plans to invest twice the resources into the first as into the second. That still hasn't got us a cardinal scale, but we can achieve this by adding that the values of the different partial intentions that one has for achieving the same all-out intention sum to one.

This is rough; how, for a start, do we measure the investment of resources? Still, it is hopefully clear enough to give some sense to the proportionality requirement; enough, I think, to see that it is not plausible. For it may be that one option will simply require more resources to be successful, however resources are measured; you are not irrational if you give it what it needs to have a chance of succeeding, even though you think it no more likely to succeed than the less demanding option. Alternatively you might simply prefer one of the options, even if you think it less likely to succeed; again you are not irrational if you put more resources into it than into the others.

Indeed, I suspect that the whole attempt to place a measure on partial intentions is wrong-headed. I do not mean just that they need not receive values, in the way that partial beliefs need not. More fundamentally, when it comes to partial intentions, there is no role for values to play. Our preferences can receive values, and so can our partial beliefs, and these are important for the intentions that we form. But once we have formed a partial intention, we add no explanatory advantage to our account of it if we also ascribe it a value—this is one important way in which partial intentions differ from partial beliefs. I conclude then that there is no place for anything like strong consistency for partial intentions, or the proportionality requirement. Insofar as there is need to preserve some degree of proportionality, it should rather come as a constraint on the intentions that one forms: given one's beliefs and preferences, one should all-out intend to put this many resources into this partial intention, and that many into that.

One reason that I have spent so long investigating these various coherence requirements is because they will be important to us in considering whether partial intention entails partial belief. But before we turn to that, let me briefly conclude this section by mentioning a further normative constraint on intentions that has been much discussed. This is what Bratman calls the constraint of *means–ends coherence*: roughly, we must intend the means to our intentions. This goes beyond a simple consistency requirement in that it can require us to add new intentions if these are needed to provide the means to our existing intentions; it is thus the intention analogue to dynamic requirements on belief formation, rather than to static requirements of consistency. The requirement as I have roughly formulated it is a very strong one; almost certainly too strong, though I shall not argue that here.[33] Here we need only observe that the introduction of partial intentions by itself forces no substantial revision on the requirement of means–end coherence. It is just that the intention to achieve the means to a partially intended end may itself be partial. Given that partial intentions from different subplans need not be consistent, you can partially intend the means to one partial intention, whilst at the same time partially intending something inconsistent with that means: one requirement for the success of your subplan that involves getting the tree company out is that you do not phone to cancel. So that subplan had better not contain any such intention. Yet it is exactly part of the other subplans, those in which you do move it, that you do phone to cancel.

Intentions and Belief

We are finally in a position to return to the question with which we started, that of whether intention entails belief in success. That has now fractured into a set of three questions depending on whether the belief is all-out or partial, and similarly whether the intention is all-out or partial. I take them in turn.

Does partial intention entail all-out belief? The answer to this question is obvious: a partial intention does not entail all-out belief in success. If one had all-out belief in success, one would have no need of a merely partial intention.

[33] It may, for instance, be more rational to abandon one's intention, than to go on to intend the means to realize it. This suggests the idea that 'oughts' in these contexts typically have wide scope: it is not that, if one has an intention, one ought to intend the means, but rather that one ought, if one has the intention, to intend the means; and this latter obligation can, and sometimes should, be discharged by abandoning the initial intention. For discussion of the plausibility of this move in application to intentions, see Setiya, 2007.

Does all-out intention entail all-out belief?   The answer to this second question, although it has been much discussed, is, I think, almost as obvious. All-out intention does not entail all-out belief. An all-out intention is simply one that is not accompanied by an alternative intention, and that is quite compatible with a merely partial belief in success. One might, for instance, be simply resigned to a high chance of failure in achieving one's end, having no idea of any alternative intentions that one might pursue. Of course, I could have defined an all-out intention as one that is accompanied by an all-out belief in success; but then the claim that all-out intention entails all-out belief would have been trivial. Once it is understood as a substantial claim, we have no grounds for believing it.

To say this is, as we saw, to disagree with David Velleman, to whose arguments, mentioned at the end of the last chapter, we can now turn. His first contention is that it is only if one believes that one will do something that one will be able to coordinate one's plans around it, and that others will be able to do likewise. He writes: 'If I am agnostic as to whether I will be in Chicago on Tuesday, why should anyone plan or act on the assumption of my being there?'[34] Here he gives simple agnosticism as the alternative to belief, which is unsurprising since he is working in an all-out belief framework. But once we move to the kind of framework that I have proposed, the alternative to an all-out belief in success need not be agnosticism. Instead it can be a partial belief. Of course, an all-out belief in success will engender greater confidence that I will coordinate successfully. But even a partial belief can provide enough structure to enable defeasible intra-personal coordination—after all, what else am I to do if I can see no other options? And defeasible inter-personal coordination is equally possible, though we would expect a warning of my uncertainty to my collaborators.

Velleman's second claim about intention picks up on Anscombe's observation that the natural expression of an intention to do something is the simple assertion that one will do it. It may well be true that in cases when we have an all-out intention and an all-out belief in success we typically do report an intention to perform some act by

---

[34]   Velleman, 2007, p. 206.

saying that we will perform that act. But, as we have seen, where that belief is lacking, intention is more naturally reported by saying that one intends to act (or that one will try to act, if the act of trying can be separated out), often with a qualification that one is unsure of success.

Velleman's third contention concerns coherence requirements on intention. He writes: 'Why, for example should an agent be rationally obliged to arrange means of carrying out an intention, if he is agnostic about whether he will in fact carry it out?'[35] A first response is again that the alternative to all-out belief is not agnosticism but partial belief. If the answer to our remaining question—whether intention entails partial belief—is positive, this may be enough to ground the normative constraints. So, before addressing Velleman's point fully, let us turn to consider that issue. We can do so by considering partial and all-out intentions together.

Does intention (whether partial or all-out) entail partial belief? Here, at last, a positive response has some plausibility. If I intend to do something, then it might seem that I must regard success as a real possibility. If I did not, then I would be in no position to plan and coordinate around it; and it is only if I plan and coordinate around it that we can really see it as an intention. I raise two worries, though.

The first concerns the strength of this claim. If it is only the claim that an intention entails a partial belief, then the claim is very weak. Indeed it is just the weak consistency requirement for partial intentions that was discussed in the last section, now elevated from the status of a normative requirement to that of a necessary truth. We might hope to make it stronger, but the only way to strengthen it that I can see is in the direction of the strong consistency or proportionality requirements of the last section, again transformed from normative requirements to necessary truths. But, as we saw there, it is very hard to make them plausible even as defeasible normative requirements; I see little hope of establishing them as necessarily truths.

We should stick then with the weaker claim that intention entails partial belief in success, that is, as seeing success as a live possibility,

---

[35] Velleman, 2007, p. 205.

though perhaps one to which little confidence is given. My second worry concerns even this weak claim. It may be true that if one intends to perform an action, it follows that one will take the performance of that action as a live possibility in one's deliberations about what to do *up until* that action. But is it so clear that it requires one to take it as a premise in what to do *subsequent* to the time at which the action will or will not have been performed? Take Anscombe's example of the man who is to be tortured, who believes he will break down, but who is determined not to. Might he not be sure that he will break down? (This does not mean that he has a credence of zero that he will fail; only that he does not treat it as a live possibility.) Or take Anscombe's other example of St Peter, determined not to betray Christ, but convinced, since he has it on Christ's own authority, that he will. Again, this seems possible.[36]

It is not easy to get into the mind of either of these agents, but let us focus on the man who is to be tortured, since here at least we can avoid distracting issues of divine foreknowledge. His planning for what to do up until the torture takes it as a live possibility that he will not break down. We can imagine that he prepares himself in whatever way he can to resist (it is wise not to try to imagine this too far). But at the same time his thought about, and plans for, the period subsequent to the torture all involve the premise that he will have broken down. Such a state of mind, admirable though it is, is perhaps *rationally* criticizable; if he is convinced he will break down, should he not rationally give up his resolve to hold out? But we have yet to see a reason for denying that it is possible.

In this case perhaps it will be countered that he has not so much an intention as a hope that he will not break down; after all, it may seem that there is little that he can do to plan for it. But that is surely incidental to the form of the case. In general it seems that there may be cases in which agents have plans to achieve certain ends, but in which they are sure that they will fail. We might wonder why, if they are really not prepared to formulate partial intentions contingent on their success, they are even bothering to try. There are answers that one might give: perhaps they superstitiously fear that entertaining the

---

[36] Anscombe, 1963, p. 94.

possibility of success will doom them to failure; perhaps they think that they will be rewarded for having the intention;[37] perhaps, as in the torture case, they think that it is right to have the intention, even if they are sure that they will fail. All of these do seem to involve grounds for having or not having an intention that are, in some sense, non-standard: the value is there whether or not one achieves the end. We might then try to embrace the restricted claim that agents' *standard* intentions entail the corresponding partial beliefs that they will succeed; but it is quite unclear that we will be able to define 'standard' in a way that makes this interesting. And even if we could, since intentions are typically arrived at on a variety of grounds, we would risk excluding too much.[38]

So I am sceptical even of the weak hypothesis that intention entails partial belief. The thesis is better kept as the normative one that intentions rationally require partial belief. If this is right, though, it brings us back to the third of Velleman's arguments, discussion of which we postponed above. Velleman asks how we are to understand the source of the normative constraints on intention—most obviously the various coherence requirements discussed above. He argues that, if we understand intention to entail belief, then the normative constraints on belief will be inherited by intention. As we might put it, practical rationality is premised on theoretical rationality.

One response to this is to insist that the normative requirements on practical rationality are *sui generis*.[39] But the considerations raised here suggest another. Velleman's approach has much plausibility when we consider just all-out belief and all-out intention, for there we clearly have a better take on the coherence constraints

---

[37] Imagine a Kavkaesque case in which I am to be rewarded if I can somehow intend to do something that I believe impossible. I discuss such cases in Chapter 7.

[38] Such counterexamples are lent some support by a clinical literature that seems to show cases of subjects with frontal damage maintaining intentions in the knowledge that they are acting against them. For various such cases, see Luria, 1966, ch. 5; for discussion of these and others, see Monsell, 1996. I say that these only lend support, since the findings are somewhat unclear. In particular, most of Luria's cases involve agents who have been given commands but fail to act on them, whilst nevertheless acknowledging that they should be doing so. An alternative but equally plausible explanation is that they have failed to form the right intentions, or that, whilst they have formed them, they are failing to realize that they are not acting on them.

[39] This is the approach taken in Bratman, forthcoming.

on theoretical rationality. In particular, we have a very good take on (static) consistency for belief, which we might hope will provide a basis for consistency of intention. But matters are rather different when we turn to the partial case. We have no obvious analogue of consistency when it comes to credences or partial belief. The best that we have is the idea of conformity to the axioms of the probability calculus. And the standard arguments for the rationality of that commitment rely on arguments that themselves appeal to practical rationality: Dutch Book arguments, that aim to show that agents who fail to meet the commitment will accept bets that they will be bound to lose; and Representation Theorem arguments, that aim to show that agents will meet the commitment on the assumption that they have certain preferences, and that they will seek to maximize utility. Some have claimed that here theoretical rationality is grounded in practical rationality.[40] But one does not have to go that far. We might say instead that the distinction between theoretical and practical rationality is less clear. Rather than grounding one on the other, we should see them as forming a package that will stand or fall together. And once we think this about partial intentions and partial beliefs, maybe we should explore the idea that this holds for all-out intention and all-out belief too.

Conclusion

In this chapter I have argued for a novel interpretation of partial belief, and for the existence of partial intentions. I have argued that we should be sceptical of the intention-entails-belief thesis in any of its forms. And I have argued that the consistency requirement on intentions is a very weak one. That removes the only motivation that I can see for reducing intentions to beliefs. Beliefs and intentions are distinct existences, characterized by distinct features. We should not expect necessary connections between them. Let us turn now to ask how intentions are formed.

---

[40] For an effective response to that, see Christensen, 1996.

3

Choice

If intentions are real, and irreducible, we should ask how we come to have them. Some we form automatically. Seeing the stationary traffic ahead I form the intention to change lane, and start scanning the mirror for an opportunity to do so. If you ask me what I am doing I can tell you, but I have given no conscious thought to the matter. According to much contemporary social psychology most of our mundane actions are like that.[1] Indeed, even when the stakes are high, there need be no conscious consideration of alternatives. Gary Klein, in his study of various kinds of experts (nurses, fire commanders, missile operators, etc.), writes:

> We asked people to tell us about their hardest cases, thinking that these would show the most decision making. But where were the decisions? The commander sees a vertical fire and knows just what to do . . . He never seems to decide anything. He is not comparing a favorite option to another option, as the two-option hypothesis suggests. He is not comparing anything.[2]

Experienced agents frequently just know what to do; they do not need to make a choice. Klein argues that they use a number of methods to arrive at this knowledge, of which the most important involves a form of stereotyping: new situations are recognized as similar to situations that have been encountered before, and so the actor knows what to do on the basis of what worked in the past.

But not every case is like that. Sometimes the situation may be in some way novel—a new situation, or a new option in a familiar one—so that our stereotypes do not readily fit. Or it may be significant in other ways, so that we pay special attention even though

[1] Bargh and Chartrand, 1999; Bargh, 2002.   [2] Klein, 1998, p. 16.

our stereotypes do apply. Or we may simply have been prompted to think about it. In these cases, cases in which the question of what to do arises explicitly, we have to make a choice. This is my topic in this chapter.

The distinction I am drawing between the acts that we choose to perform, and those that we perform without choice, suggests some kind of two-level system. One—standardly known as System I—is the level of automatic heuristic-based responses. These are fast, cognitively economical, typically very limited in scope. We pick up on a certain cue and respond to it. The second level—System II—involves conscious consideration and choice: it is slow, demanding, but more flexible. Though the details are contentious, such an approach has become increasingly influential in psychology, and I do indeed presuppose it here.[3] But I shall not do anything to defend or elucidate it; the main questions that remain can only be answered by empirical psychology.

In contrast there is much philosophical work to be done in elucidating the notion of choice. I suggest three central features. First, choice is an act.[4] It requires time, concentration and a certain amount of effort. This has been well documented: subjects making choices become *ego depleted*: that is, they become less able to exercise subsequent self-control, a sign that their executive resources have been used up.[5] And it is the choice itself that has this effect: mere deliberation doesn't do it, nor does implementing the choices made by others. This in turn helps explain how we can resent having to make a choice, and can feel jaded and fatigued when we do: shoppers faced with many options are more likely not to buy anything, and are less contented

---

[3] For a good overview, see Stanovich, 2004, ch. 2. For some application to the experience of action (though not specifically choice), see Haggard and Johnson, 2003. They stress the idea that even automatic actions can be brought under conscious control. Similarly, activities that start out under the control of System II can become automatic as agents become more experienced: driving is the classic example. In general I think that the two systems should not be thought of as radically isolated; indeed we may have something more like a continuum than two discrete systems.

[4] This feature of choice has been well emphasized by Thomas Pink (1996). In subsequent work, though, he has taken this to militate in favour of libertarianism; not the conclusion I shall draw. See Pink, 2004, ch. 7.

[5] Vohs et al., forthcoming. I talk more about ego-depletion in Chapter 6.

with what they do buy.[6] We can choose (a higher-order choice) whether to choose, and when. We can put off a choice, perhaps to gain more information, or perhaps just because we are reluctant to make it. Or we can bring a choice forward, convinced that we already know enough, keen to make it, or keen to get it over with.[7]

Second, choice is not determined by our prior beliefs and desires. It is quite compatible with a given set of beliefs and desires that we choose one way or we choose another. That, of course, is part of what makes choice an action: we are not pushed along by our beliefs and desires.

Third, choice has effects. Once the question of what to do arises, choice is typically *necessary* for action. In order to move to action, we need to make a choice about what to do. The other psychological states that we might have, in particular, our beliefs and desires, are not, on their own, enough. Just as they do not determine our choices, they do not determine our actions either. In contrast, choice typically is enough. Once the question of what to do has arisen, choice is not just necessary but *sufficient* for action: it gives rise to an intention, and the intention leads to the action.

It is our ordinary experience that provides us with evidence of these effects. It is merely evidence, defeasible in ways that we shall examine shortly. But in this it is parallel to so many other ordinary cases. We have matches, kindling and plenty of oxygen. Is this enough to give us a fire? No. One of the matches needs to be struck. Our evidence for this is simple: in standard circumstances we don't get a fire without striking a match, and we do get a fire if we do. Likewise for choice. Once the question of what to do has arisen, if we don't choose, then typically we don't act; once we do choose, then typically we do.

I say that these effects are typical, not that they always obtain. In some cases, even when the question of what to do has arisen, an act

---

[6] Iyengar and Lepper, 2000. For a nice general discussion of the costs of excessive choice, see Schwartz, 2004.

[7] Note that there is no regress here. There would be if every choice were an act, and every act required a prior choice. But I do not say that every act requires a prior choice; only that (normally) a choice is required for every act *for which the question of what to do arises*. We do not normally choose whether to choose. We virtually never choose whether to choose whether to choose.

of choice will not be necessary for action: automatic actions will take over. Conversely an act of choice will sometimes not be sufficient for an agent to act in the way chosen. Again automatic tendencies can override an intention arrived at by deliberate choice; or the intention might be forgotten; or one might change one's mind. Such considerations need not worry us any more than the observations that fires can be started by lightning hitting a match that no one has struck, or that matches can be damp, or badly made, or can blow out after they are struck.[8]

Compatibilism and Choice

I am leaving a proper discussion of freedom to Chapter 8. But it will help to put my account of choice in perspective if I contrast it with standard compatibilist accounts of freedom, that is, with accounts that hold that freedom is compatible with causal determinism. It is sometimes said that such accounts leave the agent out of the picture; where the agent should be we get a passive vessel.[9] This is what drives some to libertarianism, to the denial that human actions are caused. I will not be driven so far, but I think that there is something in the charge. The problem is clearest with accounts like that of Hobbes', who, very roughly, took freedom to consist in the ability to get what one wants. His model of decision is that of the scales:

The objects, means, &c are the weights, the man is the scale, the understanding of a convenience or inconvenience is the pressure of those weights, which incline him now one way, now another; and that inclination is the will.[10]

Here we can see clearly the sense in which the decision-making process is passive: there is nothing more to the process of decision than letting the weight of one's understanding of the desirability of

---

[8] Some sceptics go further, arguing that choice is never necessary or sufficient for action. Daniel Wegner (2002), for instance, argues that choice is epiphenomenal. It seems to me that the burden of proof is very much against such a position: one would need very good argument to deny the efficacy of choice. I briefly sketch what I think wrong with Wegner's argument in a review of his book (Holton, 2004). For some fuller like-minded responses, see Nahmias, 2002, and Bayne, 2006.

[9] For a compelling articulation of the worry, see Velleman, 1992.

[10] Hobbes, 1656, p. 326.

the various options press upon one. Indeed it is tempting to think that the decision machinery has no role at all. But that would be a mistake. To press the analogy: we need well-working scales if we are to weigh fairly. The point then is not that the scales are redundant; it is rather that they fail to make any *discretionary* contribution to the output. This is the sense in which the inputs *determine* the output: once we know that the scales are true we know how the scales will move simply by knowing the weight of the objects put upon them. Things are parallel on the simple Hobbesian model of action. Assuming that agents are well-functioning, their actions will be determined by the force of the inputs, where these consist of the agents' understanding of the utility of the various options. There is no place for an independent contribution from an act of choice. There is just the risk of malfunction.

The same is true when we turn to the other main class of compatibilist models and add in a more substantial role for deliberation and belief. Such accounts characterize freedom as consisting in one's ability to get one's actions into line with one's beliefs about what is best.[11] So we might invoke a four-stage model that characterizes a typical exercise of freedom of the will unfolding as follows:

(i) *Deliberating:* Considering the options that are available, and their likely consequences; getting clear on one's own desires, and one's own prior plans and intentions; seeing how the options fit in with these desires and plans; establishing pros and cons.

(ii) *Judging (deciding that):* Making a judgement that a certain action is best, given the considerations raised in the process of deliberation. The upshot of the judgement is a belief.

(iii) *Choosing (deciding to):* Deciding to do the action that one judged was best. The upshot of this decision is an intention.

(iv) *Acting:* Acting on the intention that has been made, which involves both doing that thing, and coordinating other actions and intentions around it.

---

[11] Frequently they also require that one's beliefs about what is best be true, or that one have the ability to get true beliefs—that one be, in John Martin Fischer's phrase (weakly) reason-responsive (Fischer, 1994, pp. 164–8). I don't think that this affects the substance of what I am arguing here.

This might look to give a certain place for choice in the third positions, but it is an unhappy one. What is the relation between the second and third stages? On one account the choice is constrained by the judgement: the decision *to* perform an action will amount to no more than an echo of the prior decision *that*.[12] So, if we want to give a more substantial role to choice, we will need to say that the decision *to* is independent of the decision *that*. But now it seems that choice has become a liability: to give a substantial role to choice is just to say that we retain the possibility of failing to do that which we judge best. Once again choice consists in the possibility of malfunction. Wouldn't we be better off if we moved directly from judgements to intentions, cutting out choice altogether?

The upshot is that on the standard compatibilist picture, choice can be given no rationale. In naturalistic mode, we find that we have no explanation as to why we might have evolved the capacity to make choices. And, more broadly, we can see no reason why we should value having that capacity. So let us ask what might be good about an ability to choose that is not determined by a prior judgement—which is not, of course, to say that it is undetermined *simpliciter*.

Three Unsuccessful Rationales

(i) *Choice as a test*: There is a well-established Christian line of thought that sees choice as a test: God gives us choice so that in failing to err we can pass. Even in a Christian framework there are familiar problems with the argument. In a secular context I can see no way of developing it.

(ii) *The rationale for choice derived from the rationale for intentions*: In Chapter 1 I charted some of the advantages of intentions. They enable us to curtail over-long deliberation, to coordinate and to resist temptation. If that is right, then, given that the upshot of a choice is the formation of an intention, we might try to argue backwards. Since there is a rationale for intention, and intentions stem from choices, perhaps that rationale extends to choice. The

---

[12] What we might call an internalist account; see, for instance, Watson, 2003, pp. 177 ff.

problem with the argument is that choice is not the only way of forming intentions. It is easy to imagine an agent whose intentions are determined directly by their judgements about what is best, cutting out any need for choice. Choice would then only serve to divert the intentions in other directions; again it ends up looking like a liability.

(iii) *Choice as resolving indifference and incommensurability:* A further advantage of intention that was mentioned in Chapter 1 is that it enables us to overcome indifference and incommensurability. So does this give us a rationale for choice?[13] It points us in the right direction, but, as normally understood, I doubt that either will give us quite what we want. We confront indifference daily: a trip to the supermarket with its stacks of identical products provides many instances. Yet we hardly think of this as a paradigm of choice. It is more like random picking than like choosing.[14] In contrast, incommensurability does bring us situations where we have to choose. The problem here is that it is a contentious phenomenon on which to build a theory; many have quite reasonably doubted that it exists.[15] We need a somewhat different approach.

Choice as Enabling Action in the Absence of Judgement

Let us think more carefully about the supposed cases of incommensurability. How often are agents really sure that two options are incommensurable? What evidence do they have? Isn't it more plausible to think that they are unable to compare, without adding the

---

[13] Raz (1997) suggests something like this picture.

[14] For the contrast, see Ullman-Margalit and Morgenbesser, 1977. Such cases were used in Antiquity to argue that the will could not be determined. See Sorabji, 1988, pp. 149ff.; Bobzien, 1998, pp. 34–5.

[15] In particular, if A and B are truly incommensurable, then shouldn't an action that is clearly much worse than A (and hence commensurable with it) be incommensurable with B? Yet that is not what we typically find. There are things that might be said to try to explain this (see the Introduction to Chang, 1997), but clearly the notion is more complicated than it initially appears.

conviction that there is no comparison to be made? That is a good part of what makes such situations so troubling: one is constantly looking for the argument that will give one a handle on what is best. I do not dogmatically deny that there may be some truly incommensurable options; it is just hard to think that one could ever be in a position to know that one had found one.[16]

This is to make incommensurability into a problem that is primarily epistemic: we do not know how to compare. Once we think that way we can see that a similar phenomenon is at the heart of choice. We choose, I have claimed, when the question of what to do has arisen. That question has in turn arisen because we don't yet know what to do.[17] When we think about what to do, we may come up with a judgement that one option is best. But we may well not. We may instead come up with a judgement that certain options are equally good; that is indifference. More likely, we will see various reasons in favour of one option, and others in favour of another, without arriving at a judgement of which reasons are most important. This may be because we have no idea how, in principle, to go about ranking (incommensurability); or because we know how to do it in principle but can't in practice; or because, whilst we can do it in practice, we don't think any benefits that might be gained are worth the effort. Maximizing, as choice theorists have been telling us for a long time, is a difficult, cognitively expensive business. Coming to a judgement about what is best is a form of maximizing.

I suggest then that in very many cases we choose what to do without ever having made a judgement about what would be best—we decide *to* without deciding *that*. Now, though, we are back to our second problem: for if there is no judgement that one option is better than another, how can choosing ever be any more than arbitrary picking?

---

[16] Even where we think we have an argument for incommensurability we should be cautious. The notion dates to Pythagorean mathematics, and to the supposed finding that the diagonal of a square was not commensurable with its side. The Pythagoreans were right that they cannot both be assigned rational numbers, but of course it doesn't follow that they are incommensurable. They are fully commensurable when assigned elements of the reals. The Pythagoreans simply lacked the means to measure them.

[17] Which is not to say that when it does not arise we do know what to do.

The answer lies in the fact that we can be good at doing something without making any judgements. The psychology literature is full of examples; particularly striking is an experiment by Lewicki, Hill and Bizot.[18] Subjects were asked to play a rather basic computer game: the screen was divided into four, a cross would appear in one of the quadrants, and their job was to press the button corresponding to the quadrant. As time went on they got much quicker at responding. Why was this? We might speculate, as the players themselves did, that they were getting more skilful, reacting more quickly. The real answer was far more interesting. The location of each of a sequence of crosses was determined by a fairly complicated algorithm. The subjects had, quite unconsciously, learned to use this algorithm to predict where the next cross would appear. Change the algorithm, as the experimenters did, and their newly acquired skills evaporated, much to the players' bemusement. They had acquired predictive skills that worked in the absence of any conscious judgements.

The players in the quadrant game didn't make choices about which button to press; they were reacting faster than their conscious processes could track. In other cases agents do make choices, but still with no realization of why they are being made. Consider a series of experiments by Bechara and others.[19] Subjects were confronted with four decks of cards; they were informed that they would make a number of plays (in fact 100, but they were not told this), each of which would consist in choosing a card from one of the decks. Each card would give a reward, but in addition a few cards would also bring a penalty. Subjects soon discovered that two decks, A and B, gave large rewards and large penalties; the other two, C and D, gave smaller rewards but smaller penalties. What was much harder to discover, as was shown by the subject's comments, was that in the long run C and D, with smaller rewards but smaller penalties, gave the greater net return. Subjects were interviewed about the game after 20 card turns, and subsequently after every 10. They were asked if they understood how the game worked. In addition, their skin conductance responses

[18] Lewicki, Hill and Bizot, 1988. I learned of this experiment, together with several others that I cite in this chapter, from the excellent Wilson, 2002.

[19] Bechara et al., 1997. See also Bechara et al., 1994, 1996.

(SCRs), indicators of emotional arousal, were measured. Initially (until about card 10, when they suffered their first losses) normal subjects chose cards predominantly from decks A and B. Then came a period (until around card 50) where their behaviour changed so that they were slightly favouring decks C and D. During this time they began to show stronger anticipatory SCRs in the moments immediately preceding the choice of a card from decks A and B than they did prior to choosing a card from C or D: they were picking up on the fact that decks A and B were more risky. However, when interviewed they reported that they had no idea what was going on. Next came a period, from around card 50 to card 80, which Bechara describes as the 'hunch' period: here their behaviour changed so that they were choosing cards from decks C and D far more frequently than from A and B; their anticipatory SCRs before picking a card from A and B remained high; and they reported *liking* C and D, and *guessing* that they were safer, whilst remaining unsure whether they were. In the final period (typically from around card 80 on, though never reached in some subjects) they were ready to say that they knew which decks were the risky ones.

It appears that the emotional response was guiding behaviour before the judgements were made. As Bechara et al. put it, 'Our experiment indicates that in normal participants, the activation of covert biases preceded overt reasoning on the available facts.' Further evidence for this comes from the fact that subjects whose prefrontal cortices had been damaged did not show the anticipatory SCRs, and, though they eventually came to realize that decks A and B were more dangerous, they continued to choose more cards from those decks than from C and D. Not only does the emotional response influence behaviour before judgement is made; it appears that without the emotional response, judgement is powerless.

Other cases can be understood in a similar light. Here is one reported by Gary Klein:

It is a simple house fire in a one-storey house in a residential neighborhood. The fire is in the back, in the kitchen area. The lieutenant leads his hose crew into the building, to the back, to spray water on the fire, but the fire just roars back at them. "Odd," he thinks. The water should have more of an impact. They try dousing it again, and get the same results.

They retreat a few steps to regroup. Then the lieutenant starts to feel as if something is not right. He doesn't have any clues; he just doesn't feel right about being in that house, so he orders his men out of the building—a perfectly standard building with nothing out of the ordinary. As soon as his men leave the building, the floor where they had been standing collapses. Had they still been inside, they would have been plunged into the fire below.[20]

It turned out that the source of the fire was in a basement. The lieutenant had picked up on various indicators of this—the great heat of the fire and the lack of noise relative to this heat—which gave him an emotional response to the situation that influenced his action. But he didn't realize that he had picked up on these factors. He put his action down to ESP. It was only when Klein's team analysed what must have happened many years later that he came to see why he had chosen to act as he had.

I suggest that cases like this are very common, whether we have to act quickly, or we have plenty of time for reflection. Very often when we make a choice, and can see no compelling reason why we should act one way rather than another, our choice will turn out to be effectively random.[21] But very often it will respond to features that we have registered but of which we are unaware. It will not be mere picking, though we shall be in no position to know that it is not. So, although the process of choosing (i.e., the process that meets the three conditions outlined earlier) is conscious, the mechanisms that determine that choice are frequently not.

It might be objected that these are cases in which we do make a judgement about what is best, but this is an unconscious judgement, influenced by unconscious beliefs. To this I have two replies. First, in many cases I doubt that the unconscious states that influence our choice should be classed as beliefs at all. Perhaps someone might think that the fire lieutenant had unconscious beliefs that guided his actions, but the states involved in the gambling game are surely too modular, too unavailable to the agent's other thought processes, to properly

---

[20] Klein, 1998, p. 32.
[21] 'Effectively' in that it may be controlled by some non-random mechanism that should have no bearing on the choice, as in the case of right-bias discussed below.

count as beliefs.[22] I doubt even more that they give rise to unconscious judgements of what is *best*, since to judge something best is in fact to rank it as better than the other options: exactly what modularity prevents one from doing. This is true in the fire case just as much as the gambling game. The lieutenant would not have chosen differently if someone had told him that his hearing had become impaired, because he didn't realize that the lack of noise from such a hot fire was determining his choice. It is easy to think that we have unconscious beliefs that are just like conscious beliefs—except, of course, that they are unconscious. (Perhaps this is the legacy of Freud.) The reality appears to be rather different. Many of the unconscious states that influence our actions are very unlike beliefs as we normally think of them.[23]

These claims about modularity are controversial, and it may well be that our notion of belief is too elastic for us to come to a definitive resolution of the debate. My second response does not trade on them. Even if it is true that the agents in these cases are moved by unconscious judgements, that does not undermine my main point. I have been arguing that choice in the absence of judgement is not essentially random; but I am happy to restrict that to the claim that choice in the absence of *conscious* judgement is not essentially random. My inquiry has been into the experience of choice; that is, into the nature of a conscious process. So what is of interest is choice in the absence of conscious judgement. My contention has been that that need not be random.

Judgement as Not Prior to Choice

'Still,' a critic might object, 'it would be foolish to deny that there are conscious judgements around: the lieutenant surely judges that he should get his crew out.' It would indeed be foolish to deny it, so I don't. What I say instead is that very often the judgement *follows* from

---

[22] More precisely they are, in Fodor's terminology, informationally encapsulated (knowledge from outside cannot get in) and cognitively impenetrable (not under the control of central processes); see Fodor, 1983.

[23] See Wilson, 2002, for discussion.

the choice. Or, at least, let us start with that strong version of the claim. I shall qualify it later to the claim that very often the judgement *doesn't precede* the choice. We have seen something like this already in the Bechara experiment. There the judgements come at the end of a sequence of choices, where the consequences of the choices can be understood as providing evidence for the judgements (the agents got to see how they fared when they chose from the C and D packs). But I want to argue that the phenomenon arises even in the case of a single choice, and where the consequences of the choice provide no further evidence for the judgement. If there is evidence here, it is just that provided to the agent by the knowledge that they have chosen. The basic idea is that agents can come to find out something about the world—in particular about which choice is best—by looking at what they have chosen.[24]

Consider the discussion of right-bias in Nisbett and Wilson's seminal article on self-knowledge. Their exact wording is revealing. Under the heading 'Erroneous Reports about Position Effects on Appraisal and Choice', they write:

[P]assersby were invited to evaluate articles of clothing—four different nightgowns in one study (378 subjects) and four identical pairs of nylon stockings in the other (52 subjects). Subjects were asked to say which article of clothing was the best quality and, when they announced a choice, were asked why they had chosen the article they had. There was a pronounced left-to-right position effect, such that the right-most object in the array was heavily over-chosen. For the stockings, the effect was quite large, with the right-most stockings being preferred over the left-most by a factor almost four to one. When asked about the reasons for their choices, no subject ever mentioned spontaneously the position of the article in the array.[25]

Are we talking here about judgements ('appraisals', 'evaluations')—the judgement that a particular pair of stockings is best? Or are we rather talking about choices—the choice of a particular pair of stockings?

---

[24] Note that I am not saying that the choices come to be best for them because they have chosen them; I am merely making the more modest epistemic claim that choosing can be a way of discovering what is best. I remain open minded as to whether there are circumstances in which the ontological claim is true. For discussion, see Winch, 1972, esp. pp. 165ff.

[25] Nisbett and Wilson, 1977, pp. 243–4.

Nisbett and Wilson's prose moves, quite naturally, between the two. Did the subjects have a brute tendency to judge the right-most best? Or did they rather have a brute tendency to choose the right-most, from which they inferred that the item they had chosen must be the best? The latter explanation is surely more plausible. The subjects behaved like shoppers faced with a choice of what to buy. As Nisbett and Wilson conclude, 'It is possible that subjects carried into the judgement task the consumer's habit of "shopping around," holding off on choice of early-seen garments on the left in favor of later-seen garments on the right.' Then, having made that choice, they inferred that it must have been made for a reason, and so judged what they had chosen to be the best.

It is easy to think that such judgements are just rationalizations; that is clearly so in this case, and it is the approach that has dominated cognitive dissonance theory.[26] But in other cases it might be held that they provide a path to knowledge. Certainly it has long been recognized that they may provide a path to *self*-knowledge: agents can come to discover something about their attitudes and emotions as a result of looking at their own choices.[27] I am arguing, though, for something stronger: if the competences described above are characteristic, agents can also come to know something about the world from looking at their choices, and so they can *form*—rather than just *discover*—their judgements on that basis. It is some procedure like that, I suggest, through which the fire lieutenant went. He was picking up on cues that were not available to consciousness. Other evidence suggests that choosing that is not done on the basis of conscious judgement can be better in some cases even if the factors are available to consciousness. The cases arise when there are many factors to consider. Thus subjects choosing a car on the basis of twelve attributes did better if they were distracted for the period before making their choice than if they were allowed to concentrate on it.[28]

---

[26] I say more about cognitive dissonance theory in Chapter 5.

[27] See Bem, 1972. Note that this is not a modern-day behaviourism: although the stress is on publicly observable behaviour, there need be no hostility to mental states and acts. On Bem's view one can gain self-knowledge by looking at one's choices even if one has not yet done anything.

[28] Dijksterhuis et al., 2006.

I conclude then that judgements often follow, rather than precede, choices. Or, at least, that is in the spirit of what I will conclude. I said that I would sketch the position starkly and then retreat a little. So now the retreat.[29] I have spoken as if choices were sudden: we make an abrupt transition from having no intention to having the intention fully formed. Often, perhaps normally for important choices, things are not like that. We contemplate an intention, try it on, see what it feels like. At the beginning of the week it is a fanciful idea, by the end a firm resolve; even if the stages of the shift were conscious, there is no point that we recognize as the decisive shift. In tandem, we see a change in our judgement of what is best: we start with nothing, or perhaps with the kind of hunch that Bechara found in his subjects, and end with a full-blown judgement. In such cases, intention and judgement interact, each reinforcing the other. At other times, rather than providing reinforcement, one can undermine the other. It is exactly the impossibility of making the corresponding judgement that kills the nascent intention, or the inability to form the intention that kills off the hunch.

The formation of an intention involves a host of complex inter-actions, not just between intention and judgement, but also between conscious states and the unconscious reactions and abilities that I spoke of before. A growing intention provokes an emotional response, which modifies the intention, which triggers an unconscious pattern recog-nition, and so on.[30] Forming an intention can sometimes seem more like a rolling ball finding its equilibrium settling point, than like the tripping of a switch. Even though the choice is something of which we are conscious (it is not like the process involved when an action is performed automatically), the mechanism by which we arrive at it can involve a drawn-out process of which we are not aware. Sometimes

---

[29] Thanks to Ken Winkler for pointing out the need to make it.

[30] The Bechara experiments, mentioned above, make clear the importance of emotional responses in choice. For a more general discussion, see Damasio, 1994. Damasio discusses a patient, Elliot, who, as a result of damage to his ventromedial region, is unable to make choices. After laying out a set of options, Elliot remarks, 'And after all this, I still wouldn't know what to do' (p. 49). What is unclear from Damasio's discussion is whether Elliot is unable to make judgements ranking options, or unable to make a choice one on the basis of a ranking. On the account I am suggesting the unclarity is unsurprising, since the two come together.

we will be responding to important features, as in the card-game case. At other times the choice will be random, or influenced by irrelevant considerations, as in the right-bias case. We do not know which.

None of this, however, undermines my main contention. My point is not to establish that judgement is frequently subsequent to choice. It is rather to establish that, in many cases, it is not prior to it.[31]

Choice Generalized

Earlier I sketched a four-stage model: a model that involves deliberation, judgement, choice and action. My argument in the last few sections has been that we are frequently in no position to take the second of those steps: we are frequently unable to form a judgement about what is best, not because we come to a judgement that no one thing is best, but because we come to no judgement. As a result I concluded then we must be able to move directly from deliberation to choice. So the model is flawed as a general account.

But what of the cases in which we do form a judgement about what is best? Do we retain the ability to choose even there? We could imagine beings like that: beings who, once they formed a judgement that a certain option was best were compelled to act on that judgement, even though they could make choices in the absence of such a judgement. But we are not like that. The faculty of choice that I have argued is essential in the absence of judgement is also available to us in the presence of judgement.[32] That is why akrasia is possible; though, given our tendency to form and revise our judgements in the light of our choices, a tendency that will be

---

[31] There are empirical reasons for taking this kind of approach for desires too. As Shafir and Tversky put it, 'the experimental evidence suggests that preferences are actually constructed, not merely revealed, in the elicitation [i.e., decision] process, and that these constructions depend on the framing of the problem, the method of elicitation, and the available set of options' (Shafir and Tversky, 1990, p. 97).

[32] Interestingly there is some empirical evidence that people feel less free when they make a choice between two apparently equal options than they do when one option is clearly better. See Westcott, 1988, and discussion in Nahmias et al., 2005, and Nahmias, 2006. I take this as evidence of just how many things are bound up in our ordinary notion of freedom. I should be very surprised if the subjects questioned had thought that the close calls involved less of a choice.

discussed further in Chapter 5, I suspect it is rarer than philosophers think.

To this extent, then, we might think of our *generalized* choice as a liability. If that is right, then it is perhaps best explained as the price we pay for the times when we need it. On this view it would have been optimal if we had evolved into creatures that could choose only in the absence of judgement. But the outcome of evolution is rarely optimal: just as our immune system makes us vulnerable to hay fever, so the system of choice that we have makes us vulnerable to akrasia.

However, even here, things are far from clear. Sometimes our choice to act akratically might be governed by the same unconscious registration of reasons that can occur when we act without judgement. So sometimes we may do better if we are moved by those reasons than if we do that which we judge best.[33] It is a difficult empirical question whether, overall, our capacity for *akratic* action is a liability or not.

Further, we can exercise choice in circumstances in which we would normally act without choice. Once we focus on habitual or unthinking actions we can raise the question of whether to do them; a question that we do not normally ask. And once we have asked that question, choice is available. In sum then, the model I am proposing is a complex one. Sometimes we form a judgement first and then choose. Sometimes we choose and then form a judgement. Sometimes we do both together. And sometimes, as in the case of habitual action, we act without choice at all. We should not pre-judge, of any action, into which class it is going to fall.

---

[33] A point that Nomy Arpaly has made well; see Arpaly, 2000.

4

Weakness of Will

In the last chapter I was concerned with how we form our intentions. In this, and those that follow, I shall be concerned with how we implement them. It often helps to get clear on something by looking, not at the cases where it works, but at those where it fails. So I start by examining weakness of will. But when one turns to the philosophical literature on the topic, one finds that it is not as one might expect. Even David Wiggins, in a discussion that has much in common with that to be given here, starts out by claiming:

Almost anyone not under the influence of theory will say that, when a person is weak-willed, he intentionally chooses that which he knows or believes to be the worse course of action when he could choose the better course.[1]

I do not agree that this is the pre-theoretical view. Whenever I have asked non-philosophers what they take weakness of will to consist in, they have made no mention of judgements about the better or worse course of action. Rather, they have said things like this: weak-willed people are irresolute; they don't persist in their intentions; they are too easily deflected from the path that they have chosen. My aim in this chapter is to pursue this line of thought. I shall develop the idea that the central cases of weakness of will are best characterized not as cases in which people act against their better judgement, but as cases in which they fail to act on their intentions. To say this is not to say enough. Not every case of a failure to act on one's intentions is a case of weakness of will. Sometimes we realize that our intentions were ill-judged, or that circumstances have changed to make them inappropriate. When, in such cases, we fail to act on

[1] Wiggins, 1978, p. 239.

our intentions, we need not display weakness of will. So a large part of this chapter will be concerned with saying what kind of failure to act on one's intention does constitute weakness of will. The basic idea is this. Just as it takes skill to form and employ beliefs, so it takes skill to form and employ intentions. In particular, if intentions are to fulfil their function, then, as we saw in Chapter 1, they need to be relatively resistant to reconsideration. Weakness of will arises, I shall suggest, when agents are too ready to reconsider their intentions.

In taking this approach I depart from almost all of the literature on the subject.[2] Since I find the approach obvious, this calls for some explanation. I suspect that there are three factors at work. First, as we have seen, there has been widespread philosophical suspicion of intentions, as something that should be, at best, reduced, and at worst eliminated. If intentions are under suspicion, then it is no wonder that philosophers have been unwilling to account for weakness of will in terms of it. I have already given my grounds for thinking that the suspicion is misplaced.

[2] Since writing the article on which this chapter is based, I have found there are rather more exceptions than I had realized. I apologize to those authors I did not acknowledge there. Gilbert Ryle defines weakness of will much as I do, though in the context of an attack on the very idea of the will (1949, pp. 72–3). M. McGuire (1961) sketches an approach that is similar to mine in the course of responding to Hare. Gwynneth Matthews (1966) argues that weakness of will can be constituted by, amongst other things, a failure to act on one's resolutions or decisions when one has insufficient grounds to revise them. Donald Davidson raises failure to act on an intention, decision or choice as a possible form of weakness but does not go on to discuss it (1969, pp. 23–4). David Wiggins, in the article mentioned above, goes on to sketch an account of weakness of will that does tie it to failure to persist in one's intentions. Amelie Rorty insists in various articles that weakness of will should not be identified with akrasia; and in an unpublished piece outlined a distinction like that pressed here (it is mentioned in Stocker, 1979, at p. 738). She also charts a number of places at which the 'akratic break' can take place, including at the point between forming an intention and acting on it (Rorty, 1980). I discuss some of the issues raised by this paper below. Thomas Hill (1986) similarly argues that weakness of will should not be identified with akrasia; focusing on weakness of will as a character defect, he discusses a number of ways in which it can be manifested, amongst which the failure to persist in one's intentions is central. Alfred Mele (1987) discusses cases of weakness of will in which one acts against one's intention, but he still treats this as a special (and specially problematic) case of action against one's best judgement; that is, these are cases in which one judges a particular course as right, and then forms the intention to pursue it, and then fails to act on it. In contrast, I suggest that action against one's judgements about what is right need not enter into examples of weakness of will at all.

The second, related, factor that has plausibly been at work is a form of motivational internalism: this doesn't deny the existence of intentions, but denies any independent interest to them. If one thinks that intentions are so closely linked to judgements that they are bound to follow them, so that any change in intention must be occasioned by a change in judgement, then it might seem that it is judgement that is the real focus of interest. So an account of over-ready intention revision will just collapse back into an account of bad judgement formation. Such views find it hard to accommodate the possibility of action against one's better judgement, and this in itself should count against them. But my objections go further. Even if it is right that intentions and judgements typically line up, often the direction of influence goes in the opposite direction: as I shall argue in Chapter 5, agents frequently change their judgements because they change their intentions. The ability to maintain one's intentions is a skill that is distinct from the ability to form good judgements. It needs its own account.[3]

The final factor that has influenced the lines of the discussion is the impetus given by Plato and Aristotle. Both clearly were concerned with the question of whether it is possible to act against one's best judgement; and much of the contemporary literature has been concerned with assessing and responding to their arguments.[4] Let us grant the term 'akrasia' to refer to action voluntarily undertaken against one's best judgement; it is, after all, scarcely a term of ordinary English.[5] Then my contention will be that weakness of will is not akrasia.[6]

---

[3] Thanks to an anonymous referee for raising this point.

[4] It is far less clear that this was *all* that they were interested in. There are many passages in Aristotle that at least seem to be concerned with weakness of will as I shall understand it (for instance, *Nichomachean Ethics*, 1145 and 1151 *passim*).

[5] Though there is a now obsolete English term, 'acrasy', meaning 'intemperance' or 'excess'; it is used by Spenser in *The Faerie Queene* as the name for intemperance personified as an enchantress (Spenser, 1590, II.xii.362). Though it stems from a different Greek root than the Aristotelian notion of akrasia (from ἀκρᾱσία, meaning 'bad mixture', rather than ἀκρᾰσία meaning 'ungoverned'), the *OED* suggests that the two terms have become confused.

[6] It is an interesting question when philosophers first started to translate, or gloss, Aristotle's term 'akrasia' as 'weakness of will'. In the nineteenth-century literature it is either left in the original Greek, or else translated, following the Latin, as 'incontinence'. See,

Weakness of Will

I have argued that we have a need for intentions, that is, that we have a need for action-guiding states that are not readily revised. My suggestion now is that this gives the basis for an account of weakness of will. For a first attempt, let us say that a person exhibits weakness of will when they revise an intention in circumstances in which they should not have revised it. This 'should' is not meant in a moral sense. Rather it is the 'should' which is generated by the norms of the skill of managing one's intentions. A person is weak-willed if they revise their intentions too readily.

What is it to be too ready to revise an intention? Clearly not every case of a revision is a case of an over-ready revision. If you and I intend to go for a picnic, and it starts to rain, we might be quite right to revise our intention, and in doing so we need not show weakness of will. (I only say we *need not* show weakness of will in such a case, for I have left it under-described; if we had vowed to go, whatever the weather, then we probably would have been weak-willed in giving up when it rained.) It might be thought that we can accommodate cases like these by invoking conditional intentions. Even if we did not say so explicitly, it might be thought that our intention was the conditional one of going for a picnic provided it did not rain. But not every reasonable revision of an intention can be understood as the triggering of an escape clause in a conditional intention. We would be equally right to abandon our intention in the face of a freak plague of frogs falling from the sky; but neither of us considered that, even implicitly. We need then some general account of when it is right to revise our intentions.

---

for instance, Grant, 1857; Cook Wilson, 1879; Stewart, 1892; Fairbrother, 1897. Sidgwick (1893) refers to it as 'want of self-restraint' and then as 'unreasonable action'. The first place I have found it translated as 'weakness of will' is in Ross, 1923, p. 221, though this is just a parenthetical gloss: his primary translation, both there and in his translation of the *Ethics* is 'incontinence'. It is only with Hare that 'weakness of will' starts to become the standard term (Hare, 1952, p. 169, 1963, p. 77). Perhaps this should not be surprising, since the expression 'weakness of will' appears to be a fairly recent one. The earliest citation in the *OED* is from 1885. Earlier writers spoke of agents being faint-hearted, or weak-kneed, or of lacking fortitude.

Nietzsche seems to have held that it is *always* wrong to revise an intention:

To close your ears to even the best arguments once the decision has been made: sign of a strong character. Thus an occasional will to stupidity.[7]

Perhaps this is good advice for football referees. But as a general attitude it is surely a recipe for disaster. Moreover, it isn't even true that such intransigence is a sign of a strong character. One is reminded of Somerset Maugham's jibe against the Vicar of Blackstable: 'Like all weak men he laid an exaggerated stress on not changing one's mind.'[8] Nevertheless, if our account of intentions is correct, there is something right about the idea that there should be a real reluctance to revise an intention, and that at times this might lead one, if not to stupidity, at least to a less than optimal outcome. To see this, let us return once more to Bratman, and to his account of the circumstances in which we rationally should reconsider our intentions. Bratman's idea is that it is rational to reconsider an intention just in case doing so manifests tendencies that it is reasonable for the agent to have; similarly it is rational to fail to reconsider an intention just in case this manifests tendencies that it is reasonable for the agent to have.[9] This means, of course, that sometimes it will be rational not to reconsider an intention even when reconsideration would, in that instance, have been in the agent's interests. In general once we've decided which restaurant to eat in, it is a good idea to let the matter rest, without endlessly discussing the pros and cons; and this is true even though it occasionally means that we'll go to a restaurant that, with some more discussion, we could have realized was not the best choice.

Presumably the converse of Bratman's criterion also holds: it is not rational to reconsider something if the reconsideration manifests

---

[7] Nietzsche, 1886, §107; cited also in Watson, 1977, p. 328.

[8] Maugham, 1915, ch. 39. Note that Maugham doesn't ascribe weakness of will to the vicar. There is more than one kind of weakness; what is at issue here is more like weakness of character. For a further distinction, consider Austin's complaint about the 'grotesque confusion of moral weakness with weakness of will' (Austin, 1956, at p. 146 n.1).

[9] Bratman, 1987, p. 68. Bratman actually talks in terms of habits rather than tendencies. But for something to be a habit, it must be habitually exhibited. In contrast it is possible for a tendency to be only rarely exhibited, if at all. I want the latter notion.

tendencies that it is not reasonable for the agent to have. Adding this to the account proposed here, we arrive at the following: actors show weakness of will when they revise an intention as a result of a reconsideration that they should not have performed; that is, when their reconsideration exhibits tendencies that it is not reasonable for the agents to have.

As it stands this will seem horribly vague. Which tendencies of reconsideration is it reasonable for an agent to have? I would suggest rules of thumb like the following:

- it is reasonable to have a tendency to reconsider intentions if one believes that circumstances have changed in such a way that they defeat the purpose of having the intention;
- it is reasonable to have a tendency to reconsider intentions if one believes that they can no longer be carried out;[10]
- it is reasonable to have a tendency to reconsider intentions if one believes that they will lead one to great suffering when that suffering was not envisaged at the time of forming the intention;
- it is reasonable to have a tendency not to reconsider intentions in circumstances that prevent clear thought if those intentions were made in circumstances that allow clear thought;
- it is reasonable to have a tendency not to reconsider intentions that were expressly made in order to get over one's later reluctance to act.

This is still pretty vague: the principles themselves are vague, they are doubtless incomplete, and I have said nothing about which of them should take precedence over which. But I shall not try to eliminate this vagueness, at least not at this point.[11] Vagueness is a problem when we try to determine the extension of a concept: when we try to provide a means of telling for each particular act whether it does or does not display weakness of will. My concern here is rather with giving an account of the concept itself. If the concept is vague,

[10] Note that this rule needs careful application if it is not to trivialize the whole account. For what if my reason for thinking that the intention cannot be carried out is my belief that I lack the willpower to see it through? That had better only count as a reason for thinking that I *will not* see it through, not that I *cannot*.

[11] I return to discuss these rules of thumb in Chapter 7.

then the account had better be vague too, and along just the same dimensions.[12] I hope that we shall see that the account proposed here provides just the right sort of vagueness.

However, the account is not plausible as it stands. I need to make a clarification and an amendment. First, the clarification. Suppose I intend to perform a rash and dangerous act: leaping from a high cliff on an untested home-made hang-glider. Would I show weakness of will in revising my intention? That rather depends on why I revise it. If I reassess the chances that the hang-glider will fail, and decide on a programme of more cautious preliminary testing, that is surely a reasonable revision. If, on the other hand, I simply suffer a failure of nerve, backing off from the edge of the cliff at the sight of the drop before me, a failure I would have suffered no matter how good the hang-glider, then that is plausibly a case of weakness of will. That is why I did not phrase the account in terms of whether or not it is reasonable to reconsider my intention; instead it is phrased in terms of whether or not the particular reconsideration I perform is one that exhibits tendencies that it is reasonable for me to have. Note further that these tendencies need not be all-or-nothing. Someone might well be very resolute when it comes to dangerous hang-gliders, but very irresolute when it comes to alcohol. So we should not talk of individuals being weak-willed *simpliciter*, but of them being weak-willed with respect to a particular class of intentions, where this class might be very tightly circumscribed.

Now for the amendment.[13] Some people go in for a lot of low-level intention revision. They decide to go to one restaurant, change their minds in favour of another, switch back to the first, again to the second, and so on. Now it is not reasonable to have such tendencies; much time and effort is wasted, and inter-personal coordination becomes a nightmare. But, whilst we might describe such people as fickle or capricious, we would not normally describe them as weak-willed. So the account offered so far is too broad. We need to know what is

---

[12] I have authority on my side: 'It is the mark of the trained mind never to expect more precision in the treatment of any subject matter than the nature of that subject permits' (Aristotle, *Nichomachean Ethics*, 1094b23−5).

[13] Jeanette Kennett pointed out that I needed to make an amendment here. Lloyd Humberstone showed me how to make it.

distinctive about weakness of will, what it is that distinguishes it from caprice.

In Chapter 1 I introduced the distinction between simple intentions and resolutions. Resolutions serve to overcome the desires or beliefs that the agent fears they will form by the time they come to act, desires or beliefs that will inhibit them from acting as they now plan. (Often the two will be muddled up in ways that we shall examine in the next chapter: the strong desire for a cigarette may bring the irrational belief that it won't actually do any harm; the drunken belief in one's own capacities may engender a new desire to climb the public statue.) To cover both cases, and perhaps others—fear, panic, lethargy—that are neither beliefs nor desires, let us talk of resolutions being *contrary inclination defeating*.

The distinction between simple intentions and resolutions provides us with what we need to distinguish weakness of will from caprice. If someone over-readily revises a resolution, that is weakness of will; if they over-readily revise a simple intention, that is caprice. Consider again the vacillating diner. Suppose he has become concerned about his tendency to keep changing his mind, and so resolves to go to a particular restaurant even if another seems more attractive later on. In other words, suppose he forms a resolution to go to that restaurant. Then if he revises his intention once again, he would not merely be capricious; he would display weakness of will.

Thus we can think in terms of a genus with two species. The genus is that of unreasonable revision of intention. The two species, weakness of will and caprice, are distinguished by whether the intentions revised are resolutions or not.

Defeating contrary inclinations might be only part of the reason for forming a particular intention, and not a very important part at that. Indeed, sometimes this aspect might be merely implicit in an intention, and might only emerge if we asked the person what they would do if they were to change their preferences or beliefs in certain ways. So it will not always be easy to identify which intentions are resolutions. However, the notion is not vacuous, since some clearly are not. Thus I might form an intention which has the content: I will go to The Red Lion tonight, providing I still feel like going, and still think it a good idea to go. This is clearly not a resolution, but nor is it otiose. Such an intention can still have an important role in inter- and intra-personal coordination (we can know that it is very likely that I will not change my mind), despite its conditional nature.

We have arrived at the idea that weakness of will then is unreasonable revision of a resolution. But that is still not quite right.[14] Suppose that I spend rather too much time reading various Dadaist tracts. As a result I decide that I am far too rule-governed; I need to be more spontaneous. And as a result of that I abandon some of my resolutions. We might suppose that this is an utterly ridiculous, romantic gesture, one that is clearly not reasonable. But do I thereby show weakness of will? I think not. The problem is that the intentions have not been revised in the right way: they have not been revised in response to the pressure of the very inclinations that the intentions were supposed to defeat. We thus need to amend again: weakness of will is unreasonable revision of a contrary inclination defeating intention (a resolution) in response to the pressure of those very inclinations.

This is not a fully reductive account: what is it to say that a revision comes *in response* to the pressure of an inclination? That it is caused by it? That surely won't do: it would be easy to come up with deviant causal chains, in which the inclination causes the revision, but in the wrong sort of way. If we persist with causal talk we will probably have to end up saying that the revision is caused by the inclination in the *appropriate sort of way*, and, whilst we can give plenty of examples of this, we will have no reductive analysis of what it means. But I don't think that we should let this detain us. We have a good enough grasp on the account that is being offered, certainly one that is sufficient to enable us to distinguish it from the traditional account, and to see which does best. It is to this task that I now turn.

Advantages of the Present Proposal

I shall present six reasons for believing the account of weakness of will that is offered here; or, to be more precise, six reasons for preferring it

---

[14] Thanks to Alison McIntyre for raising this point; see McIntyre, 2006, at n.16.

to the traditional account that understands weakness of will as a failure to do what one judges to be best.[15]

1. Accommodating Weakness of Will in Cases of Indifference or Incommensurability

We can form resolutions in cases where we treat the options as incommensurable. When we do so, and revise our resolutions, we can show weakness of will. That is just what the account proposed here would predict. But the traditional account can make no sense of such cases; for, by hypothesis, the agents involved do not judge one option to be better than the other, and so cannot be acting against their better judgement.

To see the possibility of such cases, consider again the example of incommensurability mentioned in Chapter 1. I am caught between the conflicting demands of fighting fascism and of staying to look after my mother. Unable to compare them in any meaningful way, yet knowing I must choose, I resolve to go and fight. But then, when the moment to leave comes, I revise my resolution and stay with my mother. If the account of my revision is filled out in the right way, that will be an example of weakness of will. (Note that to generate such a case we need not say that the options really are incommensurable; only that the agent judges them to be so.)[16]

2. Explaining the Relation of Weakness of Will to Strength of Will

One would expect the property opposed to weakness of will to be strength of will. And strength of will is something that shades off into stubbornness. The account I propose explains this in a straightforward way. A person shows strength of will when they

---

[15] Some of these considerations also, I believe, provide reasons for preferring it to the accounts offered in Jackson, 1984, and Bigelow, Dodds and Pargetter, 1990; but I shall not argue for this contention here.

[16] Can we generate parallel examples of weakness of will in cases of indifference? I see no reason in principle why not, but in practice it is hard to see why one would form *resolutions* in such cases, and hard to see why one would then be tempted to switch to other options.

stick to their resolutions in circumstances in which they are right to do so; that is, when they do not reconsider them, and not doing so exhibits tendencies that it is reasonable for them to have. Strength of will turns to stubbornness when they stick by their resolutions even when it is reasonable to reconsider and revise them. And, of course, the boundary between these two is vague; reasonable people will disagree about which tendencies of intention revision it is reasonable to have, just as they will disagree on when strength of will moves over into stubbornness. (One way of understanding the quotation from Nietzsche is to see him placing the boundary at one extreme.) Here then is one place where the vagueness in the *analysans* mirrors the vagueness in the *analysandum*.

In contrast, the traditional account has real problems in explaining strength of will. Indeed, typically, defenders of the traditional account have contrasted weakness of will with self-control, where this is understood as the ability to do what one believes to be best. But self-control is not continuous with stubbornness, in the way that strength of will is. It is perhaps possible to have too much self-control; but the worry there is that one lacks spontaneity; and lacking spontaneity is very different from being stubborn.

3. Accounting for Cases of Oscillating Weakness of Will

Consider this example from Thomas Schelling:

As a boy I saw a movie about Admiral Byrd's Antarctic expedition and was impressed that as a boy he had gone outdoors in shirtsleeves to toughen himself up against the cold. I resolved to go to bed at night with one blanket too few. That decision to go to bed minus one blanket was made by a warm boy. Another boy awoke cold in the night, too cold to retrieve the blanket and resolving to restore it tomorrow. But the next bedtime it was the warm boy again, dreaming of Antarctica, who got to make the decision. And he always did it again.[17]

Let us suppose that the cold Schelling ineffectually tried to retrieve the blanket without leaving his bed. How would we describe the

---

[17] Schelling, 1980, p. 59.

situation? Would we say that Schelling displayed weakness of will when he reached for the blanket despite his earlier resolution to leave it off? Or would we say that he displayed weakness of will in leaving the blanket off again the following night, despite his resolution to leave it on? I think that we might well want to say both (we would need to fill out the details in the right way; he must form each resolution seriously, having given it real consideration, and so on). The account I am offering enables us to do so. We say that in each case, in overturning his previous resolution, Schelling displays tendencies that it is not reasonable for him to have. But on the traditional account of weakness of will it is not easy to see how we can get this result.

On the traditional account, the normal case is one in which the agent maintains a view about which action is the right one, and then acts contrary to this belief. But that cannot be the case here, since if the young Schelling maintained a view, then it would have been either that it is best to leave the blanket on, or that it is best to take it off. But if he maintained either of these views, then it is not possible for *both* actions to display weakness of will, since it is not possible for both actions to be contrary to the view maintained. Alternatively proponents of the traditional account might think that the young Schelling changed his mind about which course was the best. Then, in order to characterize him as doubly weak-willed, they would have to say that in the middle of the night, shivering beneath one blanket too few, he believed that what was best was to keep the blanket off, and his weakness stemmed from reaching for it; and they would have to say that when going to bed, warm and dreaming of the Antarctic, he believed that it was best to keep the blanket on, and his weakness stemmed from his leaving it off. But that is completely implausible; if there were any reason for thinking that, in the middle of the night, he believed it best to keep the blanket off, that would be because he believed this when he went to bed, and had not changed his mind; and, similarly, if there were any reason for thinking that, at bedtime, he believed it best to keep the blanket on, that would be because he believed this in the middle of the night, and had not changed his mind.

4. *Allocating the Stigma of Weakness of Will*

There is a considerable stigma attached to being weak-willed. I think that the account offered here correctly predicts the times that it is deserved, and the traditional account does not. I have a friend who believes that all the arguments point to the same conclusion: he should not eat meat. But he is not moved. 'I am', he says disarmingly, 'inconsistent.' Now there is something very odd about that, but, although he is akratic, and he attracts the stigma that goes with that, he doesn't attract the stigma that attaches to weakness of will. Indeed, I would never call this friend weak-willed. Suppose, however, that he were to announce that he has decided to give up meat; his resolve is firm. If I were then to find him roasting himself a suckling pig in a pit, I should say that he was weak-willed, and quite rightly. It is the failure to persist in the resolution that makes all the difference.

We can make the point in another way. Suppose my friend tells me that he will give up eating meat on the first day of January; it is his New Year's resolution. I find him ruefully eating sausages on New Year's Eve; I cannot scorn him for his weakness of will. Yet, were I to find him eating the same meal the following day, I could. His views about what is best have not changed over the two days; the difference stems from the date built into the resolution.

These considerations are relevant to one of the binding strategies mentioned above. If I fear that I shall not persist in my resolution, then one thing I can do is to make it public; for the scorn that I will suffer if I revise the resolution will provide me with an incentive to keep with it. The important point here is that if I want to enlist the potential scorn of others in this way, it is not much use simply announcing my opinion of what is best; I need to announce my resolution.

5. *Explaining Cases of Weakness of Will without Inner Conflict*

Some people say that in cases of weakness of will there must be an inner conflict: the agent must feel the pull of the course that they are weakly abandoning. And they take this as an argument for the traditional account.[18] That strikes me as quite wrong. Of course, when

---

[18] For instance, Cordner, 1985.

we self-ascribe weakness of will we will typically feel some tension; otherwise we wouldn't know to self-ascribe it. But we can ascribe weakness of will to a third party in whom there is no conflict. We surely can ascribe weakness of will to a person who has vowed to give up smoking, and who blithely starts up again straight away, saying that they have changed their mind (again we would need to fill in the details in the right way). We can make perfect sense of this on the view proposed here: we simply say that they gave up their resolution too easily. We need to be sure that the initial resolution really was formed, and too sudden a change might make us doubt that; and the revision itself might be seen as involving a kind of conflict. But there need be no internal conflict at all at the point at which they smoke the cigarette.

Thus it seems that rather than being a point in the traditional account's favour, its requirement that there be internal conflict actually counts against it. For it is hard to see that the traditional account could count our recidivist smoker as weak-willed unless there was, deep down and repressed, a belief that smoking was the wrong thing to do. Yet we do not need to attribute such self-deception in order to attribute weakness of will.

Note that I have not said that cases of akrasia are impossible. Suppose that I were tempted by the arguments of Socrates and Aristotle and their latter-day followers, arguments to the conclusion that a person cannot choose other than that which they judge best. Then I might try to exploit the account given here to say that what appears to be akrasia is really just an unreasonable revision of resolution. But I am not tempted by those arguments. So I can happily accept that there are cases of akrasia, and that they do give rise to internal conflict. I simply claim that unless they also involve an unreasonable revision of a resolution, they are not cases of weakness of will.

6. Accommodating Cases of Both Akrasia without Weakness of Will, and Weakness of Will without Akrasia

So far we have considered cases of weakness of will without akrasia, and we have considered cases of akrasia without weakness of will.

There are some cases that display both. Consider the following three examples:

(a) Ravi has devoted his life to his poetry and considers it the most important thing in the world. But he has fallen in love with Una, an English schoolgirl. She finds herself pregnant, and, fearing that her father will force her into an abortion, they elope. Despite his ongoing view that poetry is what is most important, Ravi vows that no one will harm the child. However, his commitment is short-lived. They are found, and the police threaten him with prison. Faced with the choice between standing by Una and the unborn child, or leaving her to a forced abortion and going free to pursue his poetry once again, he shamefacedly chooses the latter.[19]

(b) Christabel, an unmarried Victorian lady, has decided to embark on an affair that she knows will be disastrous. It will ruin her reputation, and quite probably leave her pregnant. Moreover, she considers it morally wrong. So she thinks it not the best option on either moral or prudential grounds. Nevertheless, she has resolved to go ahead with it. However, at the very last moment she pulls out: not because of a rational reconsideration of the pros and cons, but because she simply loses her nerve.[20]

(c) The President has his finger on the nuclear button and his threat is simple: if the enemy invade, he will retaliate in massive fashion. That will be a catastrophe for everyone, for the President and his people as well as for the enemy. But he reasons that such a threat is needed to deter; and that in order for the threat to be credible it must be genuine: he must really form the conditional intention to retaliate if the enemy invade. Then the unthinkable happens: the enemy invade. Enraged, the President prepares to retaliate. But then, faced with doing what he takes to be morally

---

[19] Godden, 1975.

[20] Thanks to Rae Langton for this example. It is adapted from the story of Christabel LaMotte in A. S. Byatt's novel *Possession* (1989)—Byatt's Christabel, however, does *not* lose her nerve. In thinking about the case it is important to recall the distinction, applied above to the hang-glider example, between a revision that it is rational to make, and a revision that is made rationally.

and prudentially appalling, he hesitates, revises his resolution, and desists.[21]

All three examples have a similar form. At some point each agent either forms, or finds themselves with, a resolution that is in some sense akratic: a resolution to do other than what they judge best. Ravi resolves to stand by Una; Christabel resolves to have the affair; the President resolves to push the button. None at this point seems to show weakness of will, notwithstanding the gap between what they have resolved and what they judge best. So here we have akrasia without weakness of will; or, at least, we would have if the agents had acted on those intentions. Then the agents revise their intentions, bringing them into line with what they judge best. Ravi now intends to abandon Una and pursue his poetry; Christabel now intends to forgo the affair; the President now intends to take his finger off the button without pushing it. But in each case it is precisely the revision that leaves them open to the charge of weakness of will. So here we have weakness of will without akrasia.

For Ravi and Christabel, I think it is clear that revising the intention constitutes weakness of will. There are, however, important differences between the two examples. Ravi has a guilty conscience about what he is doing; whilst he does judge it the best option, all things considered, he doesn't judge it to be the morally best option. So we might try to save the traditional account by arguing that weakness of will consists in failing to do what one judges to be morally best. Christabel's case shows us that this defence will not work. She does think that the best option, all things considered, is the morally best option, yet in revising her intention she too shows weakness of will.[22]

The case of the President is more complicated. It is not clear whether we should ascribe weakness of will to him; but that is because it is unclear whether or not it is reasonable for him to have a tendency

---

[21] I am grateful to David Lewis for this example. I am not sure that he intended it for quite the use to which I have put it.

[22] Advocates of the traditional account have typically insisted that the judgement of what is best, all things considered, is not the same as the judgement of what is morally best; and that the account of weakness of will should be framed in terms of the former notion, not the latter. See Davidson, 1969, p. 30.

to change his mind in this case. Let us return to the point at which the President was still trying to make the deterrence policy work. Then, at least according to the logic of deterrence, it was reasonable for him to form the resolution to retaliate if the invasion happened. At that point we could surely have expressed a conviction that he would stick with this resolution by describing him as strong-willed; and, equally, we could have expressed a doubt that he would stick with it by describing him as weak-willed. That is what the account predicts. But once things have gone wrong, it's not obvious what he should reasonably do, even if we accept the logic of deterrence. On the one hand, he reasonably judged that he should retaliate in case of invasion, and he is now in such a case; on the other hand, triggering an all-out nuclear war is madness. If we incline to the second of these considerations (as we surely should) then we won't describe him as weak-willed if he revises his resolution. But the memory of what we said before the invasion should make us uneasy with that judgement. In cases like this we get ourselves into a very real and very dangerous muddle over what it is reasonable to do; our confusion over applying the notion of weakness of will reflects that muddle.

Responses to Objections

I have given my six reasons in favour of the account that I propose. I shall conclude this chapter by responding to six possible objections.

1. Why Be So Strict?

Amelie Rorty, in her enlightening paper 'Where does the Akratic Break Take Place?' answers her own question by providing a multitude of candidates.[23] I have suggested that weakness of will consists in just one kind of failing. Why should I be so strict? The English language is a plastic instrument. It seems overwhelmingly likely that sometimes people have used the expression 'weakness of will' to describe other

---

[23] Rorty, 1980. Note that Rorty is here giving a discussion of akrasia, not of weakness of will; like me she denies that the two are the same. See her note on p. 333. For an enlightening discussion of the different forms that weakness of will can take, see Hill, 1986.

failings, such as some of the others that Rorty mentions. In particular, isn't it very likely that sometimes it has been used to describe the case in which a person fails to form an intention to do what they know to be best, and as a result does what they know not to be. In short, isn't it very likely that the traditional account captures one of our uses of the expression?

Perhaps that is right. If so I should rest content with the claim that many cases of weakness of will are captured by the account proposed here; I should offer it as a supplement to the traditional account, not as a replacement. But I cannot help thinking that the traditional account is not simply inadequate, but straight-out wrong. First, we have seen a number of cases in which people appear to be akratic without being weak-willed. Second, I doubt that there are any clear cases of weakness of will that can be captured by the traditional account and not by mine.

Consider this example concerning Jim Dixon, hero of Kingsley Amis's novel *Lucky Jim*.[24] Dixon, a junior and untenured lecturer, is staying with Professor Welch, his head of department and arbiter of his future in the university. He awakens after a night of heavy drinking to discover cigarette burns through his bedclothes.

Had he done all this himself? Or had a wayfarer, a burglar, camped out in his room? Or was he the victim of some Horla fond of tobacco? He thought that on the whole he must have done it himself, and wished he hadn't. Surely this would mean the loss of his job, especially if he failed to go to Mrs. Welch and confess what he'd done, and he knew already that he wouldn't be able to do that.

Wouldn't we say that Dixon displays weakness of will here? Yet he never forms an intention to tell Mrs Welch. So mustn't we accept that there can be weakness of will that does not consist of a failure to do what one intends? This might seem like good evidence that the traditional account is at least sometimes correct.

I am not so sure. Why doesn't Dixon resolve to tell Mrs Welch? Presumably because he knows that he wouldn't be able to go thorough with it if he did: 'he already knew that he wouldn't be able to do that'.

<hr>

[24] Amis, 1956.

So he knows that if he did form such a resolution he would display weakness of will, where this is understood in terms of the present account. It is because he knows that he is someone with a tendency to weakness of will that he acts as he does. So, on the account given here, his weakness of will explains his action (or rather his inaction). It seems to me that is good enough. Once we have said that we feel no compelling need to insist that Dixon actually exhibits weakness of will here.

If we are to get a really compelling counterexample, we need a clear case of weakness of will in which a person knows that, if they were to form the resolution to do what they judge best, they would stick to that resolution; but they fail to form it. Perhaps I am blinded by partiality to my account, but none comes to mind.

So I doubt that the traditional account captures a natural sense of our talk of weakness of will. However, I should concede that there is at least one common use which does not conform to my account either. I have been talking about an intra-personal phenomenon, in which agents do or do not abide by their own intentions. But there is also an important social use of the expression. Thus we say of individuals who habitually manage to impose their wills on others—whether in a boardroom or a pre-school class—that they are strong-willed; and those who too easily agree to the imposition we readily describe as weak-willed. We might try to treat this as simply requiring a generalization of the account that I have offered: the weak-willed person is someone who gives up on their intentions too easily, whether in the face of their own desires, or in the face of pressure from others. But I doubt that this line can be maintained: there is no requirement that the socially weak-willed person abandons their prior intentions (perhaps they are so weak-willed that they never think to form them); and, even when they do, there is no requirement that they be contrary inclination defeating. Better to concede that this is a different, though related, use.[25]

---

[25] There are doubtless others. For instance, we read in *The New York Times* that Jonathan Edwards criticized Barack Obama 'by portraying him as weak-willed for voting "present"—rather than yea or nay—on scores of bills as an Illinois state senator' (Patrick Healey and Jeff Zeleny, 'Obama and Clinton Tangle at Debate', 22 January 2008). Here it seems to mean something like 'cautious' or 'over-ready to avoid commitment'.

2. Can the Account Accommodate Disagreement?

I said that one plausible way of filling out the story of the young Schelling and his blankets is to say that he displayed weakness of will twice over. But there are other things we might say. Knowing Schelling's subsequent career as an economist rather than an explorer, we might say that the real Schelling (the rational, realistic, Schelling) is the one who wanted to keep the blanket on; hence it was only the fanciful dreamer who displayed weakness of will when trying to get it off. (Contrast this with Sir Francis Chichester, who, true to his real self, stripped his childhood bed down to just a sheet, seems never to have been tempted to pile on extra blankets, and became a fearless adventurer.[26]) Alternatively we might say that the weakness of will occurred only in the middle of the night; the real Schelling was the one who made his decisions in the light of day, not tempted by the lure of the warm blanket. We can imagine that debate about this could go on for some time. We can imagine the kinds of evidence that would be relevant. And we can even imagine that, when all the available evidence was in, people might still disagree.

It is easy to see how the traditional account of weakness of will can try to explain this disagreement. The debate would be over what Schelling really judged best: his comfortable sleep or his training as an explorer. Can the account offered here explain it as well? I think it can; indeed, I think it can actually do better than the traditional account. The account offered here employs both a descriptive and a normative element. To display weakness of will agents must have formed a resolution that they then revise in response to the very inclinations that it was supposed to defeat; that is the descriptive element. And their revision must have been something that, by the standards of a good intender, they should not have done; that is the normative element. Disagreements about whether or when agents manifest weakness of will typically result from disagreements about the second of these two factors. So we might argue that Schelling should have kept to resolutions that were formed when he could think

---

[26] Chichester, 1964, p. 26.

clearly (such as in the daytime) rather than when he could not (such as when he was tired at night). Or we might argue that he should have kept to resolutions that were realistic (the resolution to get a good night's sleep) rather than romantic and unrealistic (the resolution to become an Antarctic explorer).

Here we have the second way in which the vagueness in the account mirrors the vagueness in the concept. I doubt that there will in general be agreement on when an agent shows weakness of will; and I suspect that this disagreement is actually better captured by the account on offer here than on the traditional account. On the traditional account the answers will depend on what the agent thought best, and that is a purely descriptive question. On the account on offer here the answers will depend on which resolutions he should have stuck with as a rational intender. That is a normative question. I suspect that the deep-rootedness of the debate gives us some reason for characterizing it as normative, but I cannot think of a way of resolving the issue with any degree of certainty.

There is an alternative course here, once urged on me by Alison McIntyre.[27] We might say that *every* instance of the kind of resolution revision that I have been talking about is an instance of weakness of will. The normative considerations simply determine whether or not the weakness of will is reasonable. So, in the case we have been discussing, Schelling shows weakness of will twice over; disagreement would be only over which, if either, is reasonable.

This would certainly simplify the account, and it is far from obvious that it is wrong. Nevertheless, I am disinclined to accept it. I tend to think that there is a more pejorative element in a charge of weakness of will than McIntyre's proposal allows. If we really think that a revision is justified, we would not think of it as weakness of will. Consider this case. I have formed a resolution to give up drinking tea. It is not that I think drinking tea is bad for me; quite the opposite, I think that it is probably beneficial. But a friend has recently claimed that I am becoming dependent on tea, and I decide to demonstrate, both to her and to myself, that I can stop if I choose. I anticipate

---

[27] She no longer holds such a view; see McIntyre, 2006, pp. 299ff.

that there will be some withdrawal symptoms and I steel myself to endure them. When it comes to it, there are indeed withdrawal symptoms: a nagging headache that persists despite not having had any tea for some weeks, and that I am now using codeine to dislodge; a craving for tea that stops me concentrating on other things; and a general sense of misery in the mornings. I decide to go back to drinking tea.

It seems clear that my decision to go back to drinking tea is reasonable. Indeed, persisting with the resolution comes close to infringing the third of the rules of thumb that I sketched earlier: do not persist if this involves great suffering that was not envisaged at the time the resolution was formed. Nevertheless, the resolution has been defeated by exactly the kind of inclinations that it was designed to overcome. Is this a case of weakness of will? I am inclined to say that it is not, and so to stick to my original account. Those who think it is, even if a justifiable one, should embrace McIntyre's revision.

3. Does the Account Work for Policy Resolutions and for Procrastination?

It might be thought that the account cannot accommodate weakness of will with respect to policy resolutions. Suppose I intend to get up every morning at six. Then can't I show weakness of will by lounging in bed today till nine, even though I have not revised my resolution? The right answer is that I have revised the resolution. I haven't abandoned it altogether, but I have revised it. I have inserted a let-out clause: I intend to get up every day at six, *except today*. (The case brings out a feature of my use of the word 'resolution' that deserves remark. I understand resolutions as a species of intention. But they can also be thought of as a species of rule. It is only in the former sense that the exception requires a revision; I can break a rule without revising it.)

A similar thing should be said about procrastination. I resolve to start on some tedious task, yet every day put it off. This surely might be a case of weakness of will, even though I haven't abandoned my intention to do it. The explanation is that I have revised it. I intended to start *some time soon*, and I have failed to do so.

4. Can the Account Accommodate Actions Performed without Intentions?

I have written as though there is a tight link between intentions and actions: as though we do not get actions without intentions. But, as I conceded in Chapter 1, that might be wrong; there may be direct actions that work without the need for intervening intentions. Then it seems that the following is possible. I form a resolution to perform some act, and then do something else. But I don't revise my resolution; I simply act without an intention. Couldn't that be a case of weakness of will that doesn't fit the account offered here?

If there were such cases I doubt that they would pose too much of a problem; we could extend the account to embrace certain failures to act on intentions as well as revisions of intentions. (Not all such failures should be included: I do not typically display weakness of will if I *forget* my intention.) But I am not convinced that there are any cases of this kind. Let us consider one of Bratman's examples of action without intention. Suppose you throw me a ball and, without thinking, I just reach out and catch it. That is perhaps an intentional act; but it is not clear that I formed an intention to catch it. I acted quite without reflection.[28] But now suppose I form the resolution not to catch the ball; I have had enough of your games. You throw it, and again I just reach out and catch it. Have I shown weakness of will? I rather doubt that I have. I suspect that insofar as the act really is one that is done without an intention, it is one that falls outside my immediate control, and so outside of the area in which weakness of will can be shown. I might resolve not to faint when the incision is made, not to duck when the jets fly low overhead, not to smile when my friend inadvertently makes a clown of himself. However, if I cannot help myself doing these things, my failure to stick by my resolution does not manifest weakness of will. Certainly these are failures of self-control. But this is just another reason for not equating such failure with weakness of will.

5. Can the Account Distinguish Weakness of Will from Compulsion?

It is a commonplace in the philosophical literature that weakness of will should be distinguished from compulsion. On the traditional

---

[28] Bratman, 1987, p. 126.

account, the distinction is made as follows: one displays weakness of will when one *freely* acts against one's own best judgement; one is compelled when one's action against one's own best judgement is *not free*.[29] But it might seem that the account offered here can make no such distinction. For consider a compulsive person—a kleptomaniac, for instance—who intends never to steal again, but who revises that intention and does. Won't his revision be one that he rationally should not have made? Yet if so he will count as weak-willed.[30]

I shall talk about compulsion more fully in the next chapter, where I will question the traditional account. But, even leaving it in place for now, I have two things to say. First, it is not obvious to me that it would be a disaster if the account did classify compulsive acts as weak-willed. For it is not obvious to me that they are not. Certainly we would not normally *say* that a compulsive person was weak-willed, but that could be because it would be inappropriate rather than false to say so—in the way that it would be inappropriate to say that sadistic torturers are unkind. Are we really averse to saying that compulsives are *pathologically* weak-willed?

Second, it is not obvious whether the account offered here would classify compulsives as weak-willed. Certainly one can imagine cases for whom the compulsive action is so automatic that there is no need of an intention, and hence no need to revise any contrary intention: for the kleptomaniac who simply finds himself placing objects in his pocket, intentions to steal or not to steal are quite beside the point. So such cases will not be classed as weak-willed. But what of the kleptomaniac who consciously but compulsively does revise his intention not to steal; that is, who is simply unable to refrain from making the revision? Will he count as someone who has an unreasonable tendency to revise, and hence as someone who is weak-willed? This depends, of course, on how we determine what is reasonable. We could use internal criteria, criteria which always restrict what it is reasonable for an agent to do to that which it is

---

[29] See Watson, 1977; Kennett and Smith, 1994. Watson argues that the relevant notion of a free action is one that the agent could have performed had they developed in themselves the kinds of skills and capacities that we expect them to develop.

[30] Thanks to Linda Barclay and Michael Smith for making me think about this issue.

in the agent's power to do.[31] Such criteria would not classify the kleptomaniac's revision as unreasonable, and hence would not classify him as weak-willed. Alternatively, we could use external criteria, criteria which do not restrict what it is reasonable for an agent to do to that which it is in the agent's power to do. Such criteria probably would class the kleptomaniac's revision as unreasonable, and hence probably would classify him as weak-willed. I have not come down in favour of one or the other of these criteria of what is reasonable; indeed, I suspect that whilst I am trying to give an account of our ordinary notion of weakness of will I should remain uncommitted. For I suspect that this is another place where our ordinary concept is vague.

So the present account of weakness of will has difficulties with compulsion only if two further claims are met: if it is right to use external criteria of what is reasonable, *and* if the compulsive should certainly not count as weak-willed. I have questioned both of these claims; but even if they were true, a simple amendment to the account would fix things up. Rather than saying that weakness of will consists in over-readily revising an intention, say that it consists in over-readily revising an intention *when it is in the agent's power to desist from that revision.*

6. Are We Working with Too Simple an Account of Akrasia?

I have characterized akrasia as simply doing other than that which one judges best. In an unpublished paper, Jamie Swann objects that in order to avoid akrasia, it is not enough just to do what one judges best; one must do it *because* one judges it best.[32] He points out that this will, in turn, have repercussions for some of my cases that purportedly involve weakness of will without akrasia: the cases of Ravi and Christabel. For, in these cases, whilst the agents do that which they judge best, they do not do it because they judge it best; rather, they do it because their nerve fails. Swann goes on to suggest

---

[31] In the agent's power in some broad sense; we could follow Watson in thinking that what is important is what would have been in the agent's power if the agent had developed the capacities that they would normally be expected to develop.

[32] Swann, unpublished.

that my failure to give cases of weakness of will without akrasia in this revised sense is not accidental: if one unreasonably revises a resolution (which is what is required for weakness of will) one will never be doing something which one judges best because it is best: one can never judge an unreasonable revision to be the best thing. So a case of weakness of will cannot be a case in which the agent avoids akrasia.

I think of akrasia as a technical term. So I could respond by insisting that what I mean by akrasia is what is meant by it in the philosophical literature, and here one finds only the simple account that I have worked with, and not the more involved one that Swann proposes. But that would be a superficial response. For, even if that is indeed what is meant in the literature, there is a clear sense in which it is inadequate. The interesting idea is that of doing what one judges best *because* one judges it best; and one should still count as deviating from this even if, by chance, one happens to end up doing what one judges best for some other reason.

Let us concede then that Swann's revised definition of akrasia is the more interesting one. Can we come up with examples of actions that are weak-willed but are not akratic in this sense? I think we can. But we will need to pay a little more attention to the issue of whether it is the revision that is unreasonable, or the reconsideration itself. Recall that I mentioned two different (though frequently entwined) reasons for forming a contrary inclination defeating intention: the expectation that one's desires will change, and the expectation that one's beliefs will change. Consider first an example of the second of these sorts of reasons. Suppose that I know that I am going to be drinking, and I know that this will radically inflate my confidence in my physical abilities. I therefore resolve not to contemplate performing various pranks that might present themselves, for were I to deliberate about them I know that I would reach dangerous conclusions. Weakness of will here consists in allowing myself serious deliberation at all: in allowing the pranks to become real possibilities for me. If I do, weakly, allow myself to deliberate, I will do what I then judge best, and for the very reason that I judge it best. So the ensuing foolhardy action will not be akratic, even in Swann's revised sense. Yet it will exhibit weakness of will. The crucial point is that, given my drunken confidence, revising my resolution will not be unreasonable, in the sense that it will not be contrary to my current best judgement; but it will be unreasonable to let myself perform that revision in the first place.

A parallel phenomenon can arise in cases in which the resolution is aimed at overcoming a change in desire. Consider again the blithely recidivist smoker mentioned earlier. Comfortable in the café, surrounded by his smoking friends, the earnest desire to give up, and the attendant resolution, have melted away. They are replaced by the desire for a cigarette. Once he thinks it through, he becomes convinced that taking a cigarette is the best thing to do; and he forms an intention to do so. The mistake comes in allowing himself to think it through. Again we can have a case of weakness of will without akrasia. I will have much more to say about such cases in the ensuing chapters.

5

Temptation

I have talked about weakness of will. Before talking about its contrary, strength of will, it will be useful to get clearer on what it is that strength of will resists. So in this chapter I look at temptation.

Some temptations merely tempt. Others, it can seem, do more. If a person is addicted, then the temptation can look irresistible. Taking that idea seriously gives rise to the familiar philosophical distinction that contrasts standard cases of weakness of will, and of akrasia, with cases of compulsion. In the standard cases one succumbs to a temptation whilst retaining the ability to resist. As a result one maintains one's agency. In contrast, in cases of addiction—and perhaps in other cases like obsessive–compulsive disorder and kleptomania—one's ability to resist, and hence one's agency, is lost.[1]

I want to accept that what happens in addiction is different from what happens in standard cases of temptation. But I want to disagree with much of the philosophical discussion about the nature of each case. First, I argue that temptation frequently works not simply by *overcoming* one's better judgement, but by *corrupting* one's judgement. It involves what I call *judgement shift*. I don't mean this as an essential claim: I am not endorsing the Socratic thesis that one could never act against one's better judgement. It is rather that, as a matter of empirical fact, temptation normally induces judgement shift. This in turn gives rise to the problem of understanding how one can resist it: the impetus to resist cannot come from the judgement that resistance is best.

---

[1] I say that this is a familiar philosophical conception, but in fact several writers have recently challenged the idea that addiction is compelling. See, for instance, Watson, 1999, and Wallace, 1999.

Second, drawing on recent empirical work, I argue that addiction should not be *defined* as a state in which an agent cannot resist temptation. Addictive behaviour is clearly compulsive, but that is not to say that the desires are irresistible. What is distinctive about addiction is that it involves a specific form of decoupling between, on the one hand, one's judgements, and, on the other, one's desires. Normally if one judges that one would get no pleasure from satisfying a desire, its force is automatically undermined; a similar effect arises when one judges that one ought not to satisfy it. Addiction undermines these links. It is then an interesting question whether or not an addict will be powerless to resist temptation. Perhaps there are cases where they are. But in many cases it simply means that resistance will have to come in a different way: not by undermining a desire's force, but by resisting it directly. As in the case of standard temptation, we are then faced with the problem of understanding how this resistance can work.

So whilst I argue that ordinary temptation does differ from addiction—the first involves judgement shift, the other involves a decoupling of judgement from desire—one consequence of my account is to bring them more closely together than in the standard philosophical picture. For a start, whilst the two phenomena are different, they are not incompatible, so that cases could involve both processes happening at once. In particular, if decoupling comes in degrees, which looks very likely, then it is plausible that very many cases of ordinary temptation will involve it to some extent.

More significantly for our concerns, in both cases the strategy needed to resist temptation will be much the same. Since judgement is typically either corrupted or powerless, it cannot be the motor for resistance. That, though, is the topic of the next chapter. The concern of this one is to spell out more fully these rather sketchy characterizations of ordinary temptation and of addiction.

Ordinary Temptation

Let us start with some empirical work by Rachel Karniol and Dale Miller.[2] Eight year-old children are shown marshmallows and chewing

---

[2] Karniol and Miller, 1983.

gum and asked which they prefer. Half the children are then told that they can have their first choice, but only after the experimenter returns from some tasks she has to do. The other half are told the same, but are told in addition that at any point they can ring a bell to summon the experimenter, in which case they will get their second choice. The marshmallows and chewing gum are left in plain sight.

After ten minutes the experimenter returns (the few children who rang the bell in the meanwhile have been excluded). She says that she is not yet in a position to give the rewards, but that she needs to ask a further question, one that she forgot to ask before. The question concerns the value, on a scale of one to five, that the children place on the two options. And here is the interesting finding: the group who had the chance to ring the bell give a value to their preferred choice that is significantly lower than that given by those who did not have the chance to ring the bell.[3] Moreover, it is the group who had the chance to ring the bell whose valuations are anomalous. The valuations of those who had no chance to ring the bell are the same as those of a third control group who did not have to wait; and the same as those of fourth and fifth groups, who were treated just like the first and second group respectively, with one difference: the marshmallows and chewing gum were not left in their sight.

So what is happening? It seems that children who (i) have the chance to ring the bell, and (ii) have the options in sight, come to devalue the option that is initially preferred. But that is just the case in which there is maximum temptation: the children have the possibility of giving up a later, greater benefit for a lesser, more immediate one; and that possibility is made very salient by the visual presence of the options. Moreover, it really does seem to be the temptation that is doing the work. In a subsequent experiment Karniol and Miller found that the phenomenon does not occur when there is a large difference in the initial valuation: if something is not attractive enough to be a real temptation, it does not lower the value placed on the thing it is competing with.

So this is a case of judgement shift. The temptation causes the agent to re-evaluate: the value of what will be gained by holding out goes

---

[3] There is no difference in the value of their less preferred choice.

down, and so the relative value of what will be gained by succumbing goes up.[4] By the time agents succumb their action will typically not be akratic, since their judgement about what it is best to do will have followed their judgement of which outcome is most desirable. Of course this will seem a trivial example (though perhaps not to eight-year-olds). But there is nothing special about the experimental set-up; we have good reason to think that this is a very general phenomenon. When we succumb to temptation we tend to judge that that is the best thing to do.

The most obvious explanation of what is going on comes from cognitive dissonance theory. In general we work very hard to ensure that the picture we have of ourselves is coherent: that it is not 'dissonant'. Moreover we want—are *driven*—to come up with a picture that puts us in a good light.[5] Achieving this involves us in all kinds of change of attitude: among other things, people can reinterpret how interesting something is, how much it hurts, how good it is, and how much they want it; all of this can change if the change makes for a more coherent, flattering picture. And, importantly for the case at hand, reinterpreting a state frequently leads to a real change in the state being reinterpreted. People actually come to want something less—they will sacrifice less to get it—because they interpret themselves as valuing it less.

So here is the proposed understanding of the Karniol and Miller finding. The children who undergo judgement shift are tempted to ring the bell to get the less desirable option, rather than the waiting for the more desirable option. They are aware of the temptation growing, and aware that they are likely to act on it. So they start to tell themselves a story that will make sense of this behaviour. One story would be of the kind that economists tell, one involving, implicitly at

---

[4] But not the absolute value, which remains significantly unchanged; see Karniol and Miller, p. 938.

[5] Establishing how the desire for coherence and the desire to look good interact—in particular, assessing which one is dominant in those cases in which they conflict—is controversial. It is further complicated by the question of what the standards are against which individuals want to look good: their own, or those of the group around them. For a useful history of the cognitive dissonance approach, see Cooper, 2007. Following his own 'Self-Standard Model', Cooper argues that a desire to look good by community standards is particularly central. For details, see Stone and Cooper, 2001.

least, discount rates. They could come to think that they prefer the lesser good now, rather than the greater good later, because they add in the unpleasantness of waiting. But that is a complicated story, and, besides, it leaves them open to later regret. For they will later think that if only they had not had such a steep discount curve—had not been so impatient, in ordinary talk—they would have got something they liked more. Better to simply re-evaluate the two options themselves, independently of the wait, so that the one available is the one that is preferred. Then one will be able to have now what one most wants, and there will be no later regret. This, I suggest, is what is happening here.[6]

Assuming that this is right, then the change in valuation is not the *origin* of the process that leads to the subjects yielding to temptation: it is rather itself caused by the children's awareness that they are likely to yield. Nevertheless the change in valuation is real. Indeed, although Karniol and Miller did not do the experiment, there is some circumstantial evidence for thinking that, at the point at which the children would succumb to taking what they formerly viewed as the second-best option, they would actually choose it over the other option if offered a free choice between the two (though it is also possible that a free choice would lead to a reconsideration that would restore the original valuation). My reason for saying this is that it has been shown: (i) that reducing subjects' resolve, so that they take a tempting but otherwise less preferred option, leads them to choose that option even for circumstances in which their resolve would not be reduced;[7] and (ii) that once a choice has been made, subjects come to strongly prefer the thing they have chosen, even if at the time of the choice the preferences were very close.[8]

If the change in valuation is not the source of the process that leads to yielding, what is? What causes the subjects to yield is desire,

---

[6] Oddly Karniol and Miller seem to give the first interpretation (p. 936); but the children are evaluating the things themselves, not the packages of the things *together* with the wait. Of course, it could be that they are unconsciously factoring in the wait; but we would need evidence that this was so.

[7] Wang et al, forthcoming.

[8] This was one of the core early findings of the cognitive dissonance approach (Brehm, 1956).

in one sense of that rather broad term. It is the desire for the sweet that is available now. We can get some purchase on its nature by recalling that the change in valuation does not occur when the sweets are covered—when, out of sight, they can be kept out of mind. In contrast, when something is visually present it is much more likely to come incessantly into one's thoughts, and this is an important factor in desire. Incessant presence, of course, is not enough to constitute desire. Thoughts of a dreaded thing will occupy one's mind. Nevertheless, it is central. We get closer to characterizing the state we are after if we turn to Scanlon's notion of *desire in the directed-attention sense*: this happens, he says, when the thought of an object 'keeps occurring to him or her in a favorable light, that is to say, if the person's attention is directed insistently toward considerations that present themselves as counting in favor'.[9]

Yet that still is not quite right. In a guilty state of mind, the things that count in favour of the virtuous but forsaken course of action may come insistently to my attention; but that does not mean that I want to take it. What is missing in Scanlon's characterization is the idea that desire *pulls* me to a course of action: that I have an *urge*, or, in more extreme cases, a *craving*, something that moves me to do it. Such a feature cannot, I think, be reduced to more cognitive talk of focusing on an object or seeing things in a certain light. These cognitive features may be necessary for desire to arise; but they do not constitute it. Desire in the sense we are after is a state that preoccupies an agent's attention with an urge to perform a certain action.

So, to sum up, what I think is happening in the Karniol and Miller experiments is this: the tempted children find their attention focused on the immediately available sweet; as a result they find themselves with a strong urge to ring the bell to get it; and, as they become aware that they are likely to succumb to this urge, they change the evaluation of their options so as to avoid cognitive dissonance.

I do not want to say that this happens in every case of temptation. And I am certainly not making the (implausible) analytic claim that whatever an agent chooses simply is what they value most highly. Rather I am describing a causal process. So there are surely cases of

---

[9] Scanlon, 1998, p. 39.

ordinary temptation (i.e., cases not involving addiction) in which this process does not take place: cases in which agents choose an option whilst, even at the time, valuing that option less than some other that is available. I suspect, though, that the power of the cognitive dissonance mechanism is so great that such cases are unusual. Even where agents act in ways that they initially know to be morally wrong, the ability to reinterpret what is happening to put themselves in a reasonable light is remarkable.[10] As a result, cases of akrasia are rarer than most philosophers have supposed.

Addictive Temptation

So much for standard cases of temptation. I turn now to cases of addictive temptation. People sometimes speak as though addiction hijacks the body: as though one's intentional systems are simply by-passed as one moves to take the drug. But whilst there may be some movements that are like that—reflexes such as being startled, and perhaps, more interestingly, certain actions performed in response to emotions like fear[11]—addiction typically works *through*, rather than *against*, our intentional systems.[12] It is not surprising that this should be so. Meeting an addiction, especially an addiction to an illegal drug, will typically require some real planning on the agent's part. The agent will need to obtain the funds, find a dealer, negotiate a price, prepare the drug, all whilst avoiding arrest. This is not the kind of thing that could be achieved entirely by an automatic process that worked independently of the agent's intentional behaviour.

---

[10] For discussion of a large range of real cases, see Baumeister, 1996, ch. 2. Perpetrators, even of the most horrific crimes, typically see themselves as victims.

[11] Geoffrey Keynes talks of his experiences as a doctor in the trenches in the First World War, finding his legs reluctant to take him towards the falling shells, despite his intention to go and tend to the wounded (Keynes, 1981, p. 137). But that involves lack of action, not action. It would have been odder if his legs had started walking of their own accord. Odder still if his body had embarked on a complex series of actions that were truly contrary to his current intentions—walking to his horse, mounting it, riding back to his quarters, writing a letter to his commanding officer asking for compassionate leave or whatever.

[12] Indeed, the level of addiction to alcohol and tobacco seems to be somewhat sensitive to price in the way that one would expect with a normal commodity consumed by rational consumers—as the price goes up, levels of addiction go down—though it is controversial just how sensitive it is. For discussion, see Skog, 1999, pp 196–200.

This is important: it is the fact that addiction works through one's intentional system that makes resistance possible. If it were a process quite outside one's intentional control, then no one could intentionally overcome an addiction.[13] Yet we know that people do. Overcoming an addiction is not impossible; it is simply very hard.

What is it then that makes it so hard? To understand this we will need to understand more about the mechanism of addiction. Work by Robinson and Berridge has indicated that addiction involves, very roughly, a decoupling of wanting and liking. Standardly, once we like something, or once we believe that we will like it, we want it; and conversely, once we don't like it, or believe that we will not, we do not want it. Addicts are different. They need not like the substances to which they are addicted: they need take no pleasure in getting them, nor in the prospect of getting them.[14]

Underpinning this account is the idea that the liking system and the wanting system are quite distinct. Liking can be identified across a wide range of species—including rats, monkeys, and infant human beings—by the facial responses it provokes: tongue protrusion, lip sucking and smiles.[15] It appears to be realized in a number of brain systems, including opiod, denzodiazepine and perhaps serotin systems. Wanting something, in contrast, can be identified by its impact on being motivated to get the thing. It is realized in different brain systems, most centrally the mesolimbic dopamine system. Addiction thus involves the activity of the wanting system without the liking. Rats need show no pleasure in getting a substance to which they are addicted, though they are strongly driven to get it. The converse

---

[13] That is, in the sense of no longer letting one's behaviour be controlled by the addiction; as we shall see, it might not be possible to change some of the mechanisms underlying addiction.

[14] This provides some explanation of how addictions differ from natural appetites like those for food or sex, an issue that concerns both Watson, 1999, and Wallace, 1999.

[15] The responses appear to be suppressed in older human beings, but reappear, for instance, in those with Alzheimer's disease. For more details of the responses, and of why they should be understood as indicating pleasure, and not simply as responses to a certain sensory stimulus (pleasure is typically induced by giving sugar), see Berridge, 2000, and Berridge and Kringelbach, 2008. Although the tongue protrusions appear very fast for mice and rats, and very slow for gorillas and human beings, they appear to be constant in proportion to the animal's size, further evidence that there is a common mechanism here. See Berridge, 2000, p. 179.

is also possible: there can be liking without wanting. Rats whose dopamine levels are chemically lowered show pleasure when sugar is placed in their mouths, but are not motivated to get it.[16]

How does the dissociation of liking and wanting arise in cases of addiction? The basic idea is that addiction involves a sensitization of those parts of the mesolimbic dopamine system that govern wanting: what Robinson and Berridge call 'incentive-sensitization'.[17] This sensitization appears to involve structural changes in the brain, both in the neurotransmitter systems, and in the neurons themselves. The result is that certain stimuli have a far greater impact than they would otherwise have: the perception, or just contemplation, of the addictive substance provides a far stronger desire to get it than it would prior to the addiction.

Work on rats by Wyvell and Berridge provides striking evidence both for the existence of separate wanting and liking systems, and for the process of sensitization.[18] The basic idea is to get the rats to associate both a random stimulus (a noise), and an activity (lever-pressing) with each other by pairing each with a sugar reward. As a result, the noise will tend to trigger the lever-pressing. The experiment is then to see the effect of changes in dopamine level on this triggering, even when the sugar is not present.[19] Let me explain.

On some days the rats are trained to press a lever to gain sugar. On other days a conditioned stimulus is created: a sound heralds freely available sugar, and the rats come to associate the two things. They clearly like the sugar. It elicits the standard facial responses.

The rats are now operated upon: a cannula is inserted into their brains so that their mesolimbic dopamine systems can be affected directly. A control group receives an inert substance through this cannula. The other group receives amphetamines, which greatly increase dopamine release. The effects of the action of the mesolimbic

---

[16] Berridge and Robinson, 1998. Similar effects are found in rats that are genetically engineered to have low dopamine levels; see Robinson et al., 2005. I am grateful to Leonard Katz for bringing this latter literature to my attention.

[17] For a survey of a large body of work, see Robinson and Berridge, 2003; for comparison with some rival accounts of the role of dopamine, see Berridge, 2007a.

[18] Wyvell and Berridge, 2000, 2001; for summary, see Berridge, 2004, pp. 255–8.

[19] See Robinson and Berridge, 2003, pp. 41–3, for discussion of why this feature is important for ruling out explanations other than incentive salience.

dopamine system can now be determined by observing the differences between the two groups.

Both groups continue to like the sugar. Moreover, they appear to like it to the same degree: the rats in the amphetamine group do not show an increased facial pleasure response when given it. Nor does the amphetamine seem to increase anticipated pleasure from the sugar: when given the lever to press, the rats in the amphetamine group do not press it any more frequently than the controls. So the increased activity of the dopamine system does not increase pleasure, nor anticipated pleasure.

The difference comes when the rats hear the noise that they have been conditioned to associate with sugar. Now the results are dramatic. Rats in the amphetamine group press the lever more than four times as frequently as those in the control group. And, as Berridge says, this effect is switched on and off as the cue comes and goes:

One moment the dopamine-activated brain of the rat simply wants sugar in the ordinary sense. The next moment, when the cue comes, the dopamine-activated brain both wants sugar and 'wants' sugar to an exaggerated degree, according to the incentive salience hypothesis. A few moments later it has returned to its rational level of wanting appropriate to its expectation of reward. Moments later still the cue is reencountered, and excessive and irrational 'wanting' again takes control.[20]

What is happening here? It appears that the increased dopamine levels result in a massive amplification of the conditioned response that was already present. Hearing the cue signal causes the control rats to press the lever. But the presence of high levels of dopamine causes the group that is receiving the amphetamines to press it far more.

Whilst the results described so far provide excellent evidence that raised dopamine levels cause an increase in wanting (rather than an increase in liking, or in anticipated liking), they do not by

---

[20] Berridge, 2004, p. 257. Berridge keeps the term 'wants' in scare quotes since he thinks that it lacks two of the features that the normal concept of wanting requires: that it be conscious, and that we expect to like the thing wanted (ibid., p. 253). I doubt that ordinary usage is so restrictive as to insist on these features. Berridge does suggest, though, that the excessive wanting engendered in the rats, and in human addicts, may have a different physiological basis (ibid., pp. 253–4).

themselves give evidence of the long-term sensitization that Robinson and Berridge proposed. To see that we need to look to a parallel set of experiments run on rats who received earlier amphetamine injections, rather than infusions into their brains at the time of the stimulus. Despite being free of the drug for ten days, the conditioned stimulus of the sound still elicited twice the frequency of lever-pressing from these rats as from a control group who had not received the injections. This behaviour cannot result from the elevated dopamine levels caused directly by amphetamines, since the rats receive no amphetamines when they hear the sound; it looks instead to be caused by the structural changes produced by the earlier administration of amphetamines.

Assuming that much the same process takes place in human beings, we can now see what happens when a person becomes addicted. The drug has much the same effect on the brain as was produced in the rats by the amphetamine. Dopamine levels are raised, and structural changes are effected that sensitize the subject to certain cues. In this case, though, the cues are typically not arbitrary features (like the sound for the rats) that have been independently conditioned; rather they are the sight, or even the mere contemplation, of the drug itself, and of the circumstances surrounding its use. Just as the rats' cues provoked a very strong desire for—and then typically a burst of activity to get—the sugar, so the addict's cues provoke a very strong desire for—and then typically a burst of activity to get—the drug.[21] As against rational-choice accounts which understand addiction in terms of a desire to avoid the pains of withdrawal, this account explains how the desire for the addictive substance can start before withdrawal sets in, and can continue long after it has passed. Indeed there is some evidence that the sensitization might be permanent.

Now it might seem that the absence of liking would make it easier to resist an addiction: after all, it means that one just has to struggle against the urge to take the substance, and not also against the further motivation that would be provided if one liked it. But, as these

---

[21] There is some tendency for the increased wanting to spill over into other domains; for instance, there is some evidence that cocaine addicts experience increased sexual desire, something that is also true of rats addicted to amphetamines. See Berridge, 2007a, p. 413.

findings show, that is to misunderstand how human beings work. The urges and the liking do not provide two parallel motivational systems.[22] Instead, liking standardly has its effect *through* the same motivational system; increased liking gives one the urge to get more. Conversely, if one likes something less, one has less urge to pursue it. Once wanting and liking are decoupled that is no longer so: the motivational system goes on, despite changes that would normally act as a brake upon it.

As we have seen, Robinson and Berridge's work is largely based on animal research, where one can measure liking by facial expression. Things in human beings are more complex. Sometimes wanting is driven by simple liking or the expectation of liking—that is plausibly what happens in the Karniol and Miller experiment—and here facial expression will provide a good measure. But often it is driven by more complex cognitive states. Suppose I struggle to put in place something that will benefit my children after my death; I might know that the struggle will make me miserable, and that I will never know whether I have succeeded. It seems unlikely that my motivation can be ascribed to simple pleasure. Instead I am motivated by my judgement that this outcome, if I achieve it, is a good one.

It is one of the horrors of human addiction that it results in these sorts of judgements also having so little impact on behaviour. Addicts will routinely service their addiction in ways that preclude outcomes that they know to be good for themselves or for those they love. So, if Robinson and Berridge's account is to apply to human addiction, we must assume that the decoupling that holds between wanting and simple liking must also apply between wanting and the more cognitive attitude of judging a thing good. Standardly if someone wants something—a clever device for peeling garlic, say—and then discovers it does not work, the want will simply evaporate. It is, as we might say, *undermined*.[23] In contrast, if Robinson and Berridge are right, in cases of addiction there must be an almost complete

---

[22] For something like the picture that the different forces are addictive as this picture would suggest, see Velleman, 1992.

[23] In this case the desire is instrumental—the garlic peeler is wanted to peel garlic—so it may seem obvious that the desire will be undermined by the discovery that it cannot do the job. But the phenomenon occurs even if the desire is not instrumental. A conversation

disconnection between judging an outcome good and wanting it, or, conversely, between judging it bad and not wanting it.[24]

Despite this disconnection, the wanting involved in addictive temptation does not appear fundamentally different from the wanting involved in more ordinary circumstances. It is strong, but it works in much the same sort of way as that already discussed: by capturing the attention, focusing on what is desired, and narrowing horizons. In cases of addiction this is often extreme enough to count as craving: horizons are narrowed entirely to my desire for *this* thing, for *me, now*.[25] But this does not seem to be different in kind from what happens in cases of non-addicted desires, which can themselves involve a similar narrowing. And once the desires are in place agents act on them in much the same way that they do in normal cases. They can reason in the standard ways about *how* to satisfy such desires; their activity becomes fully intentional. Where then do the differences lie?

Comparing Standard Temptation and Addictive Temptation

Recall that the standard philosophical picture sees addictive temptation as compelling, whereas standard temptation is not. Can we endorse that conception on the basis of considerations raised so far? Since addictive desire is uncoupled from judgements about what is best, whereas non-addictive desire is not, it might seem that we have just the basis we need: ordinary temptation is potentially responsive to judgement, whereas addiction is not.

---

with a friend who has seen a certain new film can completely remove the non-instrumental desire to watch it.

[24] Again it might be argued ordinary usage would not count states disconnected in these ways as desires; Scanlon, for instance, writes that 'what is generally called having a desire involves having a tendency to see something as a reason' (Scanlon, 1998, pp. 39). Again, though, that strikes me as too strong. Addictive desires are surely desires. What is plausible is the thought that desire might be a cluster concept, and that there might be dissociable elements within the cluster. For a nice discussion of how this can lead to difficulties in deciding which desire is strongest, see Humberstone, 1990.

[25] See Loewenstein, 1999. A similar narrowing takes place when food consumption is restricted; I discuss this in Chapter 8.

But that is too quick. In the first place, as we have seen, in many standard cases of temptation we get judgement shift: where the options are judged as close, judgements are revised to bring them into accord with desires, rather than desires being revised to bring them into accord with judgements. So, whilst in the non-addicted subjects we don't have a disconnection between judgement and desire, the causal influence is going in the wrong direction. In both standard temptation and addicted temptation judgement is not in control.

Nevertheless there are some important contrasts with ordinary temptation here. As we saw, in ordinary cases in which there is a big disparity in the judgements of the worth of the options, there is no tendency for judgement to shift: the alternative option is not even tempting. So in these cases, where there is a big disparity, judgement is in control. In contrast, addictive behaviour can persist even when the person is convinced that the outcome will be horribly worse than an alternative, along any dimension that one may care to choose. Addictive behaviour can thus be really self-destructive, in ways that ordinary temptation rarely is. A second contrast concerns self-understanding. Perhaps surprisingly, this is to the favour of the addicted subject. Since the judgement of the disparity between the addictive option and the alternative is typically greater in addicts, judgement shift is less likely to occur. So it can be clearer to addicts than it is to normal subjects that it is their desire that is calling the tune.

The second reason that the traditional picture is wrong is that it sees the addict as unable to resist temptation. If there is a disconnection between judgements and desires, then it is true that addicts will not be able to *undermine* their desires by reflecting on their judgements. Moreover, if the sensitization that underlies addiction is permanent, then this cannot be avoided. But this does not show that they will be bound to act on their desires. For there may be a way of *resisting* desires that does not involve undermining them and that is compatible with ongoing sensitization. This is the idea that I will develop in the next chapter in discussing the idea of strength of will. And this is another place where standard temptation and addictive temptation come together. For if normal subjects are vulnerable to judgement shift, then they too will not be able to undermine temptation by reflecting on their judgements. I suggest that the mechanism that each uses is much the same.

Here, however, the advantage in self-knowledge is likely to go the other way: it is the addict who is likely to be the more self-deceived. Given that addicts are unlikely to undergo judgement shift, the natural way of avoiding dissonance when addicts succumb to temptation is to think that resistance is impossible. This is a topic to which we shall return in Chapter 8.

6

Strength of Will

I have argued that weakness of weakness of will is the over-ready revision of resolutions; and that its natural contrary is strength of will, which agents exhibit when they stick with their resolutions. If that is right, then the interesting question is no longer the traditional philosophical one of how weakness of will is possible. It is all too easy to see how an earlier resolution could be overcome by the growth of a subsequent desire. Rather, the interesting question is how strength of will is possible. How do agents succeed in persisting with their resolutions in the face of temptation, especially when they undergo judgement shift, or find that their judgements have become disconnected from their desires in the ways discussed in the last chapter?[1] My answer, in brief, is the common-sense one that we standardly achieve strength of will by exercising willpower. That can sound like a pleonasm, but I mean it as more than that. My claim is that willpower is substantial; it is at least a skill and perhaps a self-standing faculty, the exercise of which causally explains our ability to stick to a resolution.

To get some idea of what a substantial account of willpower might be, let us contrast this approach with the two alternatives that have been dominant in recent philosophical discussion (alternatives first):

I. The Humean account (belief/desire account)

All intentional action is explained just in terms of the agent's beliefs and desires. Agents act on whichever of their desires are strongest.[2] An explanation of how agents stick by their resolutions

---

[1] Kent Bach (1995) makes much the same point in his review of George Ainslie's *Picoeconomics*.

[2] More strictly we should factor in agents' beliefs about which of their desires can be realized: agents will be unlikely to act on their strongest desires in cases in which they think

must show how they thereby act on their strongest desires. (Insofar as resolutions are accepted as mental states at all, they must be thus reducible to beliefs and desires.)

In previous chapters I have argued against the Humean account, claiming, first, that intentions (including those special intentions that I identify as resolutions) are states that are distinct from beliefs and desires; and, second, that choices, and the intentions that result from them, are not determined by beliefs and desires. But we can accept this and hold on to much of the spirit of the Humean account by claiming that whilst the ontology must change, the mechanism can remain much as before:

II. The augmented Humean account (belief/desire/intention account)

All intentional action is explained just in terms of the agent's beliefs and desires and intentions. Agents act on whichever of their con- ative states—i.e., whichever of their desires and intentions—is the strongest. If a resolution is stronger than any contrary desires, the agent will stick to it; if the contrary desires are stronger, then the agent will act on them instead.

In this chapter I argue that this gets the mechanism wrong. In resisting temptation willpower plays a substantial independent role:

III. The willpower account

Action is not determined just by the agent's beliefs, desires and intentions. In addition willpower plays an independent contrib- utory role. Agents whose willpower is strong can stick by their resolutions even in the face of strong contrary desires; agents whose willpower is weak readily abandon their resolutions even when the contrary desires are relatively weak.

There is reason to develop an account of this third sort simply to show that there is the necessary conceptual space for it: the recent dominance of the other two accounts has tended to obscure the very

them probably unattainable, but think of other desires, nearly as strongly held, as readily attainable. To keep things manageable I ignore these complications here, though they are relevant to some of the motivational issues discussed below.

possibility of taking willpower seriously. But, of course, I want to go further than that. I want to argue that there are considerations, both philosophical and psychological, that show its advantages over the others. I start by outlining the most promising versions of the Humean account. Seeing what is wrong with them will also help us see what is wrong with the augmented Humean account, and that will pave the way for the willpower alternative.

Explaining Strength of Will in the Humean (Belief/Desire) Approach

Take a classic case of the need for strength of will. Suppose that you have a desire to give up smoking; that is, you prefer:

A. I give up smoking for good soon

to:

B. I don't give up smoking for good soon.[3]

However, you know that you will also strongly desire any particular cigarette that you are offered. 'And why not?', you might think: 'No single cigarette is going to do me much harm, yet the pleasure it will give will be great.' So you know that, for each cigarette at the moment before smoking it, you prefer:

C. I don't resist this cigarette

to:

D. I resist this cigarette.[4]

---

[3] For reasons outlined in the last chapter, I don't think that it makes much difference that I have chosen an example that is addictive. If that worries you, substitute an example that you take to be innocuous.

[4] I say that these are the preferences *at the moment just before smoking each cigarette*. If you were to think *at all times* that it was preferable to smoke each cigarette than not to, then these preferences would be simply inconsistent with your preference to give up: in wanting to give up you would simply have failed to sum your individual preferences properly. In the situation I have in mind, you avoid that kind of inconsistency since your preferences change in the proximity of a cigarette. George Ainslie famously understands this in terms of *hyperbolic* discount curves (see Ainslie, 1992, 2001); for a very clear presentation, see

It is easy to see where this reasoning will lead. It seems that if you act on your strongest desires, you will always put off giving up until after the next cigarette; and so you will never give up. This is true even if your desire to give up is greater than your desire for any particular cigarette (i.e., if you prefer A to C), since it seems that it is possible both to smoke any particular cigarette, and to give up in the near future.

It might appear then that the belief/desire account is in trouble right from the beginning. Given a pattern of desires that has this form—surely a very common one—it looks as though an agent who is motivated solely by desire will be unable to exercise strength of will. And that looks like a refutation of the belief/desire account, since surely agents with just this pattern of desires do sometimes display strength of will.

There are, however, two responses that the proponent of the belief/desire account can make. The first involves adding further desires; the second involves adding further beliefs. I take them in turn.

Adding a Further Desire

Although the belief/desire account makes do with just beliefs and desires, that does not mean that it can have no place for resolutions. They might be accepted as complex mental states, to be analysed as a form of belief, or a form of desire, or some combination of the two. Alternatively they might be seen, not as mental states at all, but as something like illocutionary acts. The obvious model here is promising. On this second approach, when a person makes a resolution she makes something like a promise to herself. This will typically give rise to a mental state: to the belief that she has made the resolution. But that belief isn't itself the resolution. The resolution is the illocutionary act that the belief is about.

Either of these ways of accommodating resolutions, the reductive or the illocutionary, now provides for a possible way out of the

---

Rachlin, 2000, ch. 2. For reasons outlined in the last chapter, I am unconvinced that we need understand this in terms of discounting at all: very often what happens is that the evaluation of the thing itself, quite independently of the evaluation of the wait, changes as a result of the proximity (temporal or spatial) of the object.

problem. For suppose that you do not simply *desire* to give up smoking; in addition you *resolve* to do so, forming a resolution that bears some particular date for its implementation. And suppose that you have *a strong desire to be resolute*: a strong desire to stick to your resolutions. Then, when the date for implementing the resolution comes, provided that your desire to be resolute is stronger than your desire to smoke, you have a desire-driven way to give up. Unlike the desire to give up sometime soon, the desire to be resolute cannot be satisfied compatibly with taking the next cigarette after the resolution is to be implemented. The date on which you resolve to give up can be completely arbitrary, but it becomes significant because you choose it.[5]

Adding Some Further Beliefs

An alternative approach works by adding further beliefs rather than further desires. Recall that the initial difficulty arose because at each point you thought that it was possible both to take the next cigarette and to give up smoking sometime soon. Suppose that you come to doubt that: suppose that at some point you come to believe that whether you give up smoking sometime soon is dependent on whether you smoke the next cigarette. Then you will be able to use your stronger desire to give up smoking soon (A) to overcome your desire to smoke the next cigarette (C). It is important to see what talk of 'dependent' here must mean. If the desire to give up smoking is to exert the requisite leverage, you must believe both:

Effective: If I resist this next cigarette, I'll give up smoking for good

and:

Necessary: If I don't resist this next cigarette, I won't give up smoking for good.

The names should make clear the functions of the beliefs, but let us spell them out nonetheless. If *Effective* is absent you will fail to think that resisting the next cigarette will have any effect in realizing

---

[5] For a discussion of an approach along these lines, see Sobel, 1994, pp. 249–50.

your desire to give up soon, and so you will have no reason to resist. If *Necessary* is absent you can consistently think that you will be able both to smoke the next cigarette and to give up, so again your desire to give up will provide no reason for resisting this cigarette.[6]

Why should you come to believe both *Necessary* and *Effective*? *Effective* might be justified on simple inductive grounds. If you feared that you would be simply unable ever to resist a cigarette, then resisting one now will show that your fear was ungrounded. Perhaps too it will be underpinned by some kind of sunk-cost reasoning. The more suffering you have endured to resist cigarettes, the more likely you will be to be motivated to resist them in the future: what a waste of effort otherwise! We can accept that people are in fact motivated in this way whether or not we think, with most economists, that there is something irrational about it.

Necessary is harder to justify. Presumably in forming a resolution to stop smoking you will have chosen some particular point as the point at which to give up.[7] Then your conviction in *Necessary* might be underpinned by some kind of *now-or-never* thinking. You can accept that the point which you chose is arbitrary. Nevertheless, you can think that, having chosen this point, you must stick to it: if you break your resolution to give up smoking now, you will never be in a position to stick to a similar resolution at any point in the future.

Moreover, we can see how this reason for believing in *Necessary* might interact with the phenomenon of wanting to be resolute that was discussed above. You might think that a failure to stick to this resolution to give up smoking would adversely affect your ability to stick to any other resolutions that you might form, resolutions about things quite unconnected with smoking. And so, insofar as that is an

---

[6] This approach, though cast in a game-theoretic context which views agents as collections of (potentially competing) time-slices, originates with George Ainslie in the works mentioned above. For criticism of the time-slice framework, see Bratman, 1996. For a reworking of the approach without time-slices, resulting in a position similar to that presented here, see Nozick, 1993, pp. 14–21, and Mele, 1996.

[7] If you didn't, your resolution is unlikely to succeed; as we saw in Chapter 1, there is good evidence that resolutions without 'implementation intentions' are far less effective.

ability that you strongly want to keep, you have a further motivation for sticking to this particular resolution.[8]

Problems

So we have two attempts to explain strength of will within the belief/desire framework. Both involve ideas that have some plausibility. Yet neither, I think, will work as a complete account. For a start, both are vulnerable to serious problems of detail.[9] These, however, won't be my concern here. More fundamentally, both completely misrepresent the phenomenology of the exercise of strength of will.

The central point is this. If these accounts were right, then sticking to a resolution would consist in the triumph of one desire (the stronger) over another. But that isn't what it feels like. It typically feels as though there is a *struggle*. One maintains one's resolution by dint of effort in the face of the contrary desire. Perhaps not every case of maintaining strength of will is like that (we shall mention some that are not). But, by and large, maintaining strength of will requires effort.[10]

Moreover the empirical evidence bears this out. We shall see more evidence shortly, but for now consider just the most straightforward,

---

[8] The parallel again is with promising, understood in a broadly Humean way: resolutions are devices that enable you to stake your general reputation on each individual case.

[9] The *further desire* approach seems to involve attributing to the strong-willed agent a desire for resoluteness that approaches a fetish. It is surely crazy to want to be resolute for its own sake, especially if, as a result of judgement shift, the agent comes to believe that the resolute course of action is the less desirable. The *further belief* approach faces at least two difficulties. First, as mentioned in the last chapter, there is empirical evidence that the effect of temptation is not just to shift the desire for the immediately available good. It also tends to shift the long-term desires (in this case the desire to give up for good soon), so that it is not available to perform the leverage. See Wang et al., forthcoming. Second, the account has problems in establishing that a reasonable agent would believe both *Necessary* and *Effective*. Why not think, for instance, that *Effective* would be undermined by the inductively sustained belief that, at least for the first few weeks, resolutions become harder to maintain as time goes on? It is easy enough to refuse the first cigarette; the difficult thing is to keep on refusing. Similarly, why wouldn't *Necessary* be undermined by the knowledge that many agents only give up smoking after several attempts to do so? In their cases the failure of one resolution didn't entail the failure of all subsequent ones.

[10] Traditionally, acknowledging that maintaining a resolution is effortful has been the preserve of libertarians. See, for instance, Campbell, 1939. As I argue in Chapter 8, they have no monopoly on the idea.

which comes from simple measures of the physical arousal to which the exercise of willpower gives rise. Ask agents to regulate themselves in ways which involve acting against contrary inclinations—to regulate their emotions, for instance, the expression of their emotions, their attention or their thoughts—and they will show the standard signs of physiological arousal that accompany effort: increased blood pressure and pulse, with changed skin conductance, etc.[11]

Intentions and Willpower

How can we make sense of this idea of struggle? A first move is to abandon the Humean account, and to sharply distinguish resolutions from desires, for only then can we make sense of the idea of struggle involved in sticking with a resolution rather than bending to a desire. Resolutions, I have suggested, can be seen as a particular kind of intention. Nevertheless, like desires, they are motivating states: an intention can move one to action. Intentions can thus work to preserve the motivational power of earlier desires: a desire can give rise to an intention, and this intention can result in subsequent action even when the desire is no longer present. Indeed an intention can result in subsequent action even when there are, by that time, contrary desires present. That, I suggested earlier, is precisely the role of resolutions. Resolutions are contrary inclination defeating intentions: intentions formed by the agent with the very role of defeating any contrary inclinations that might emerge.

Let us spell out some of the respects in which an approach that treats resolutions in this way departs from the Humean theory of motivation. It is not the case that to be motivated to act, an agent requires a belief and a desire. Nor is it true that agents will always act on their strongest desires. For an intention can serve as a motivation even when the desires that gave rise to it have been lost. Moreover, this intention can overcome the desires that are present at the time of action.

Once we introduce intentions in this way, how should we fill out the account? One possibility is to preserve something of the

---

[11] Muraven, Tice and Baumeister, 1998, include a survey of this at pp. 774–5.

spirit of the Humean account. We might simply increase the class of motivating attitudes to encompass intentions as well as desires. Then, rather than saying that agents will act to satisfy their strongest *desire*, we might say that they will act to satisfy whichever is the strongest of their *desires and intentions*. Thus agents' actions will be determined by their beliefs, desires and intentions. This takes us to the second of the accounts of strength of will that was mentioned at the outset: the augmented Humean account.

Alternatively we could move further still, to the account I shall defend: the willpower account that acknowledges the distinct roles of beliefs, desires and intentions but adds an independent contribution from willpower as well. How does this change things? One obvious difference is that here the strength of the agent's desires and intentions is not the only determinant of what she will do. We also need to add the strength of her willpower as a separate factor. Putting things in these terms can, however, be misleading, for it suggests a picture in which willpower is simply a third input in the process that determines the agent's actions, a process on which the agent will seem like a spectator. I want rather to defend a picture in which willpower is something that the agent actively employs. The extent to which this can be achieved, will emerge, I hope, in what follows.

What, then, are the grounds for preferring the willpower account over the apparently simpler augmented Humean alternative? My main contention is simply that it is better supported by the empirical evidence, both from ordinary common-sense observation, and from psychology. Indeed, the psychological literature does not just provide evidence for the *existence* of willpower as a force that works to block reconsideration of past resolutions; it also provides some quite detailed evidence about the *nature* of that force. Roughly, it seems that willpower works very much like a muscle, something that it takes effort to employ, that tires in the short run, but that can be built up in the long run.

I shall present some of the psychological evidence shortly. But to see its relevance, first let us return to the commonplace observation that we used in rejecting the simple belief/desire approach: the observation that exercising willpower takes effort. Sticking by one's resolutions is hard work. This seems to count against the augmented Humean account too. It certainly doesn't feel as though in employing willpower one is simply letting whichever is the stronger of one's desires or intentions have its way. It rather feels as though one is actively doing something, something that requires effort.

My suggestion is that effort is needed because one is actively employing one's willpower. What exactly does the effort consist in? It cannot be straightforward physical effort, since it is present whether the resolution is to perform an action—like starting on an exercise regime—or to refrain from performing an action—like giving up smoking. However much the desire might seem to drag one towards it, we cannot think that the effort of resisting literally consists in pulling back muscles that are straining for the cigarette. Rather, the effort involved has to be a kind of mental effort. It is the mental effort of maintaining one's resolutions; that is, of refusing to revise them. And my suggestion here is that one achieves this primarily by refusing to *reconsider* one's resolutions. On this picture, then, the effort involved in employing willpower is the effort involved in refusing to reconsider one's resolutions.

Before discussing the relevant empirical literature, we need to get a little clearer on the distinction between revision and reconsideration that is invoked here. We will also need to get clear on a further distinction between reconsideration and the simple rehearsal or reminder of the reasons for which one is acting.

Revision, Reconsideration and Rehearsal

To revise one's intentions is to change them; that much is clear. Obviously reconsiderations differ in that they do not have to result in change. But I suggest that the full-blown reconsideration of a resolution does involve *suspension* of that resolution. To fully reconsider a resolution is to open oneself to the possibility of revising it if the considerations come out a certain way; and that is to withdraw one's current commitment to it. Someone might say that the resolution remains in place pending the outcome of the revision. But such a claim is not very plausible. For much of the point of a resolution, as with any intention, is that it is a fixed point around which other actions—one's own and those of others—can be coordinated. To reconsider an intention is exactly to remove that status from it.

Although to reconsider a resolution is not, *ipso facto,* to revise it, it can be hard to keep the two separate. For, when temptation is great, its force will quickly turn a reconsideration into a revision. Suspending a resolution can be like removing the bolts on a sluice gate: although one only meant to feel the force of the water, once the bolts are gone there is no way of holding it back.

At the other extreme from full-blown reconsideration is the state of not thinking about one's resolutions at all: form them and then act on them, without so much as contemplating them or the possibility of acting otherwise. Perhaps this is the idea that we have the very strong-willed individual who, as we might say, is never really tempted by the alternatives. It might seem then that this is what we should aim for with our resolutions. In fact in typical cases it would not work.

This kind of unthinking pattern best describes those actions that are automatic. Force yourself to get up at six every morning to go for a run, and after a while it will probably become automatic. The alarm clock will go, you will get out of bed, put on your running kit, and get outside without really giving thought to what you are doing. Much recent work in social psychology has shown just how widespread automatic behaviour is; there is even evidence to suggest that it involves quite different parts of the brain to those that are involved in volitional behaviour.[12] But the point at which an action becomes automatic is really the point at which willpower is no longer needed. There is good reason for this. At least to begin with, a resolution is typically a resolution to reform one's behaviour into paths that are not automatic. Indeed, standardly, the automatic behaviour is exactly the behaviour that one has resolved to stop—lighting up a cigarette, for

---

[12] On the former point, see, for instance, Bargh and Chartrand, 1999. On the latter, see Jahanshahi and Frith, 1998; my thanks to Michael Scott for alerting me to the relevant neuropsychological literature.

instance. If one is to be successful in resisting having a cigarette, and if cigarettes are around, one must constantly monitor whether or not one has picked one up; and one can hardly do that without thinking about cigarettes, and the possibility of smoking them. Successful resolutions cannot work unthinkingly.[13]

So to maintain a resolution like giving up smoking we need something in between full-blown reconsideration and unthinking action. Most resolutions are, I suspect, like this. What we need is a state that involves awareness of the resolution, and perhaps of the considerations for which it is held, but which does not involve reconsideration. The crucial factor here is that the resolution is not suspended. To remind oneself of one's resolutions is not, by itself, to bring them into question. (One can inspect the bolts on the sluice gate without removing them.) We thus need a state of awareness that falls short of suspension: what I shall call *rehearsal*.

I speak as though the contrast between reconsideration and rehearsal is a sharp one. In fact, of course, there will be many states in between: what I have marked out are the extremes of a continuum. Moreover, very often mere rehearsal will lead one into reconsideration, and hence into revision. This is unsurprising when one's rehearsal leads one to dwell on the benefits to be gained by yielding to temptation; but empirical work shows that resolve is undermined even when one's focus is on the benefits to be gained by holding out.[14]

Can we resist the slide from rehearsal to reconsideration by dint of mental effort? It might seem that this would require an ability to repress thought. The difficulty with such advice is that it is very hard to control one's thoughts directly. Indeed, the effort is typically

---

[13] The need for self-monitoring is central to Carver and Scheier's (1998) feedback account.

[14] As we saw from Karniol and Miller's (1983) work, discussed in the last chapter. Recall that this effect only occurs when the rewards of holding out are broadly comparable to the rewards of yielding. When the rewards of holding out are judged to be much larger, focusing on them seems to strengthen resolve. Similar findings appear in the work of Walter Mischel discussed below, although here things are complicated by the fact that the reward for resisting temptation was just more of what one would have got had one succumbed. Hence it is hard to distinguish thought about the reward for wanting from thoughts about the reward for succumbing.

counterproductive: attempting to repress a thought leads one to dwell on it all the more.[15] But need it be that mental control involves such direct repression?

In seeing the possibilities it is useful to look to the advice given by those professionally concerned with the business of resisting temptation. Here is a representative passage from the *Spiritual Exercises* of Ignatius of Loyola, founder of the Jesuits:

There are two ways of gaining merit when an evil thought comes from outside: the first . . . I resist it promptly and it is overcome; the second I resist it, it recurs again and again and I keep on resisting until the thought goes away defeated . . . One sins venially when the same thought of committing a mortal sin comes and one gives ear to it, dwelling on it a little or taking some sensual enjoyment from it, or when there is some negligence in rejecting this thought.[16]

Quite what does 'resisting' a thought amount to? It does not seem that Ignatius is calling for outright thought suppression. Rather he talks of the risks of dwelling on a thought, or of taking some sensual enjoyment from it. The idea seems to be not that we can keep certain thoughts out entirely, but that we can avoid focusing on them and developing them. Here it does seem far more plausible that we have some control.

I know of no studies on this, but some light might be shed by considering some parallel cases, even if the parallel is far from perfect. Suppose I ask you not to think of the number two. That is almost impossible, and the very effort of monitoring what you are doing makes your failure all the more certain. But suppose I ask you not to multiply 345 by 27. Unless you are extraordinarily good at mental arithmetic, so that the answer simply jumps out at you, you will not find my request hard to comply with at all. Nor will your monitoring of what you are doing undermine your compliance. Similarly, suppose I ask you not to think through, in detail, the route that you take from

[15] Wegner, 1989; Uleman and Bargh, 1989. Again, it has been suggested that this is connected with the idea of self-monitoring: in order to be sure that one is not thinking about something one needs to monitor that one is not (Wegner, 1994).

[16] Ignatius of Loyola, 1548, ¶¶33–5, p. 291. My thanks to Annamaria Schiaparelli for the recommendation to look at Ignatius.

home to work. You might not be able to resist imagining the starting point; but I suspect, unless you live very close to work, that you will be able to stop yourself somewhere down the track. The point seems to be that there are quite a few steps needed to perform a long multiplication or to imaginatively trace one's route, steps that have to be taken in a particular order, and one is able to exercise some control over such a process.

I suggest that things are typically similar with the thoughts involved in the revision of resolutions. It might be impossible to control whether we entertain the thought of having a cigarette. But it might be possible to control whether or not we go through the procedure that is involved in revising one's resolution not to. This also seems to be the kind of thing that Ignatius has in mind. The sin does not consist in having the evil thought that 'comes from outside'; Ignatius accepted that that is inevitable. The sin comes with what I do with it.

Evidence for Willpower

My suggestion, then, is that whilst rehearsal is needed for maintaining a resolution, reconsideration should be avoided. Let us turn to the empirical evidence for this. I start with a discussion of the developmental evidence that suggests that resolutions really do work to block reconsideration in the way I have said. I then turn to the other considerations that show that abiding by a resolution does involve the active employment of willpower.

Developmental evidence

Walter Mischel and his colleagues tested children on their ability to delay gratification to achieve greater reward.[17] For instance, they are told that they will receive one cookie if they ring a bell, which they are free to do at any time; but that they will get two if they refrain from ringing the bell until an adult comes in. They found that ability to wait comes in around the age of four or five. By the age of six

---

[17] For a summary of a large body of work, see Mischel, 1996. The work of Karniol and Miller that we examined in the last chapter was inspired by Mischel.

almost all children have it, though to markedly different degrees. Strong self-control is a very good predictor of later success in a wide range of academic and social skills.

What are the strategies that children used? Mischel initially expected them to do better by being reminded of the rewards of waiting. In fact, however, those who could see the reward for waiting did far worse than those who could not. Those who could see the reward for not waiting did equally badly. Mischel's account is illuminating and entertaining enough to be worth quoting at length:

Some of the most effective strategies that the children used were surprisingly simple. From time to time they reaffirmed their intentions quietly ('I'm waiting for the two cookies') and occasionally they reiterated the choice contingency aloud ('if I ring the bell I'll get this one, but if I wait I'll get those'). But mostly these 4-year-olds seemed able to wait for long periods by converting the frustrating waiting situation into a more tolerable non-waiting one, thus making the difficult task easier for themselves. They appeared to achieve this by purposely creating elaborate self-distraction. Instead of fixing their attention and thoughts on the rewards, as initially theorizing had predicted, they seemed to avoid thinking about them entirely. Some put their hands over their eyes, rested their heads on their arms, and invented other similar techniques for averting their gaze most of the time, occasionally seeming to remind themselves with a quick glance. Some talked quietly to themselves or even sang ('This is such a pretty day, hooray'); others made faces, picked their noses, made up games with their hands and feet, and even tried to doze off while continuing to wait. One of the most successful 'delayers' actually managed to nap during the delay time.[18]

Here the children do seem to conform to the model I have proposed. They sometimes rehearse their resolution, and the reasons for having it (though in this case there is little benefit from so doing, since there is little need for self-monitoring). Seeing the cookies—whether the one to be gained by ringing the bell, or the two to be gained by waiting—radically undermined the children's ability to wait. It seems that this undermines resolve because it provokes reconsideration.[19] In a further series of experiments Mischel found that being able to

---

[18] Ibid. p. 202.
[19] Ibid. pp. 201–2. This finding is corroborated by the Karniol and Miller study.

see the rewards did not undermine the resolution if the children were encouraged to see them as in some way unreal. A plausible explanation is that thinking of the rewards in this way does not encourage reconsideration since they are not being thought of as the objects (or, at least, not as the objects with the salient 'hot' properties) about which the resolution was made.[20]

Mischel's findings do, however, raise one question. Consider the children who had very effective strategies for distracting themselves. Considered in a behaviouristic way these might be thought of as those exercising the greatest willpower, since they are the ones who are most successful at resisting temptation. This is how Mischel describes them. But in another sense we might think of them as the children who have least need for willpower; after all, these are the ones who are putting in little effort since their strategies are so effective (think of the child who took a nap). I suspect that our ordinary talk of willpower is ambiguous here. In this it is no different from our talk of many other virtues. Do we count as brave those who distract themselves in the face of danger? Or do they need to fight to overcome their fear? I doubt that our ordinary usage provides an answer. Similarly, I doubt that our ordinary usage dictates whether to be exercising willpower an agent has to be involved in an effortful struggle. However, to avoid confusion, I will legislate. I will limit talk of willpower to situations of effortful refusal to reconsider a resolution. In some cases then—such as the case of the automatic early-morning runner considered earlier—agents achieve strength of will without recourse to willpower at all. It is unlikely that any of the children in Mischel's experiments were in quite that situation. They all had to employ willpower initially. But some had no need to go on employing willpower, exactly because their initial employment had been so effective.

Evidence for Willpower as a Faculty

The considerations marshalled so far support the idea that one exercises willpower by refusing to reconsider an intention. This in turn suggests that the augmented Humean account is going to be inadequate, for

[20] Ibid., pp. 203–7.

one's ability to refuse to reconsider is not going to be determined just by the strength of one's desires and intentions. One does not acquire a practical ability just by wanting it. But we might wonder whether this does much to show that willpower is a separate faculty. Here we need to turn to some evidence from social psychology.[21]

Consider first the fact that the ability to abide by a resolution is affected by features that do not themselves seem to be desires or resolutions. Reformed alcoholics are far more likely to relapse if they are depressed, or anxious or tired.[22] Moreover states such as these affect one's ability to abide by *all* of one's resolutions: resolutions not to drink, not to smoke, to eat well, to exercise, to work hard, not to watch daytime television or whatever. Now of course it is possible to explain this by saying that these states (depression, anxiety, fatigue, etc.) systematically strengthen all of one's desires to drink, smoke, eat, etc., or weaken all of one's resolutions not to; but it is surely a more economical explanation to say that they affect one's ability to act in line with one's resolutions.[23] For why else would there be such systematic effects?

Consider next the remarkable empirical literature on what is known as 'ego depletion'. It appears that willpower comes in limited amounts that can be used up: controlling oneself to eat radishes rather than the available chocolates in one experiment makes one less likely to persist in trying to solve puzzles in the next;[24] suppressing one's emotional responses to a film makes one less likely to persist, later on, in maintaining a squeezed hold on a handgrip exerciser.[25] And this

---

[21] For an excellent general survey of the relevant literature here, see Muraven and Baumeister, 2000. Talk of *self-control* here, and elsewhere in the psychological literature, is, I think, roughly equivalent to my talk of *strength of will*. I would rather use *self-control* to describe the related but distinct phenomenon which is the contrary of akrasia: on this usage one lacks self-control if one does other than that which one judges best, even if one does not thereby violate one's resolve (and hence is not weak-willed).

[22] Baumeister, Heatherton and Tice, 1994, pp. 151ff. The same is true of those who are dieting (ibid., pp. 184ff.), or trying to give up smoking (ibid., pp. 212ff.) or taking drugs (Muraven and Baumeister, 2000, p. 250).

[23] Moreover, whilst bad moods tend to make dieters eat more, they have the opposite effect on those who are not on a diet, which suggests that it is the dieters' resolution being affected, not their desire. See Muraven and Baumeister, 2000, p. 251.

[24] Baumeister, Bratslavsky, Muraven and Tice, 1998. The puzzles were in fact insoluble.

[25] Muraven, Tice and Baumeister, 1998.

has effect on resolutions: dieters eat more when they have been asked to suppress their emotional responses.[26] Again it is possible to think that what happens here is that the strength of people's resolutions are affected: that maintaining one's resolution to suppress one's emotional responses weakens one's resolution to persist with handgrip exercises. But why should there be effects on such disparate resolutions? And why do some activities (those that involve willpower to act in the face of inclinations to the contrary) bring about these effects, whilst others do not?[27] A much better explanation is that one's action is determined not simply by the strength of one's desires and one's resolutions, but also by one's willpower; and that it is this component that is being affected by repeated exercise.

A final piece of evidence is that one can apparently develop one's faculty of willpower by repeated exercise. Again, the idea that one becomes virtuous by behaving virtuously is a commonplace one, stressed by Aristotle and by many who have followed him: 'From holding back from pleasures we become moderate, and also when we become moderate we are most capable of holding back from them.'[28] Some research suggests that this might be right: subjects who undergo a regime of self-regulatory exercises—working on improving their posture for instance—show markedly less tendency to suffer ego-depletion.[29]

---

[26] Vohs and Heatherton, 2000. This finding parallels the finding of the effect on dieters of bad moods mentioned above. Further research shows that making choices also has a depleting effect on dieters. See Kahan, Polivy and Herman, 2003, pp. 165–71.

[27] Muravin, Tice and Baumeister, pp. 781–2.

[28] *Nichomachean Ethics*, 1104a34. Aristotle is here talking about how we develop the excellences. He does not explicitly say the same about the development of self-control though. He does say that lack of self-control can be cured, but he doesn't say how.

[29] Muraven, Baumeister and Tice, 1999. Note that there was no effect shown on the *power* of the subjects' wills; only on their *stamina*, i.e., the degree to which they became fatigued. One thing that this research doesn't establish is whether the effect really comes from strengthening the faculty of willpower or from increasing the subjects' confidence that their resolutions will be effective. Indeed, the further finding that attempts to implement resolutions in which it is hard to succeed (control of mood) don't have the same effect on willpower might be explained by the hypothesis that we are observing a self-efficacy effect. (In general, *self-efficacy*—one's confidence in one's degree of control—is extremely important in explaining one's behaviour; we shall meet it again in Chapter 8. For a general overview, see Bandura, 1992.) As the authors accept, we need more research here before any firm conclusions can be drawn.

Once we think this way, a host more explanations become available. We have looked so far at intra-personal differences: why do we sometimes stick by our resolutions, and sometimes not? But parallel explanations apply in inter-personal explanations: why do some people stick by their resolutions when others do not? It could be because their resolutions are stronger, or because the desires that they must overcome are weaker. Alternatively, it could be that their willpower is stronger: that having formed a resolution not to be moved by certain desires, they are better at acting in accordance with it, and at turning the corresponding intentions into action.

The approach employed here is a very general one. It has been a central feature of the cognitivist revolution that mental explanations, like explanations elsewhere, can be improved by positing further internal processes. Of course it is always possible to insist that wherever there is an intentional action, it is determined solely by strength of our pro-attitudes, whether these are understood just as desires, or as desires or intentions; and then to read off strength of those attitudes accordingly. But such an approach is not only untrue to our experience of sticking to a resolution; it also gives us, as the experiments I have cited show, inferior explanations of the behaviour that agents exhibit.

Motivation and Willpower

I have argued that there is faculty of willpower—something like a muscle—and that, when desires and resolutions clash, we can succeed in sticking to our resolutions by employing this faculty. Moreover, employing the faculty is hard work: it requires effort on the part of the agent. What implications does this have for our explanations of why people do and do not stick to their intentions?

Obviously one class of explanations becomes immediately available. If agents lack willpower, then they will not be able to stick to their intentions in the face of contrary desires. This might happen as a result of never having acquired a faculty of willpower (as in the case of a young child) or from having lost it temporarily (from stress or fatigue or whatever) or perhaps even permanently (from damage to the pre-frontal cortex).

So some cases of failure to stick by a resolution will be explained by the absence of sufficient willpower. Will all explanations be of this form? That would require that agents always stick by their resolutions when they possess the willpower to do so: that the presence or absence of sufficient willpower is the only factor. Yet that is most implausible. If willpower is a faculty which agents actively employ, then it should be something that they can fail to employ. Surely sometimes people have the willpower to stick by a resolution and yet decide not to do so. I have resolved not to have wine with my dinner, and I know full well that I could resist, but I decide to have it anyway: the wine appeals very strongly, and I am not much moved by the need to keep a clear head afterwards. Such cases are very common. Indeed, even in cases where willpower is depleted by stress or prior demand or whatever, it seems likely that I will typically abandon the effort to stick by the resolution before my willpower gives way completely. It is not that I could no longer resist; it is that the effort becomes too great and I give up the fight.

Here again the analogy of the muscle, and of muscular fatigue, is helpful. Recall the subjects in the ego-depletion experiments who were asked to hold squeezed a handgrip exerciser. We can easily imagine what it was like for them. The first few seconds were easy. Then, as the muscles got tired, they got more difficult. The hand started to ache, and the ache became more and more pressing, until the subject let go. We can imagine someone going on until the muscles literally could work no more. That is the kind of behaviour one sometimes sees in sporting competitions: grimacing, the competitor keeps on with the pull-ups, arms quivering uncontrollably, until, finally, the muscles give way. In such cases there is, quite literally, nothing more that the person could have done. In contrast, I doubt that any of the subjects with the handgrip exerciser pushed themselves so far. They got to a point where they said, perhaps even to themselves, they could go no further; but, offered a large financial incentive, I suspect that they would have managed a few more seconds.

It is the ordinary handgrip subject rather than the competitive athlete who provides the better model for the typical defeat of willpower. Normally one does not find oneself literally powerless to resist a desire; rather, one *decides* to give in to it, since resistance is so hard (often, at the same time, convincing oneself that there is no good reason to resist). A subject whose will is weakened by fatigue or prior demand simply finds the effort of resistance greater, and so typically gives up earlier. It is as though the handgrip subject started with an already tired hand. Of course, in this case, fatigue of the hand muscles accompanied exhaustion of willpower (though the two processes didn't quite walk in step: those whose wills had been earlier depleted presumably didn't start with fatigued hand muscles). In other cases there will be no concomitant muscular fatigue. The effort of resisting a cigarette is not literally a muscular effort; but it is no less real for that.

In determining whether agents will stick with their resolutions we need then to factor in not just their immediately relevant beliefs, desires and intentions, and the strength of their faculty of willpower, but also their motivation to employ that faculty. And this motivation will in turn be cashed out in terms of further beliefs, desires and intentions. Does this mean that we are back with a Humean model, or at least with an augmented Humean model, in which actions are determined by the strength of the beliefs, desires and intentions? It does not. An analogy might be helpful. If you want to know how fast I can run a mile on a given occasion, you'll certainly need to know about my beliefs and desires. Have I been offered some reward for running it fast? Will an embarrassingly poor time be publicized? But you will also need to know about the state of my body: is it any good for middle-distance running? It is the same for sticking to resolutions. If you want to know whether someone will stick to a given resolution you'll need to know about their beliefs and desires, including their desires with respect to the content of that resolution and with respect to maintaining resolutions in general. But you'll also need to know about their willpower: how strong it is, how much it has been depleted and so on.

At this point, however, proponents of the Humean model might object. Isn't saying that one must be motivated to use one's willpower tantamount to saying that one must desire to use it above all? And isn't that just introducing once again the *further desire* account within the belief/desire model? I think not. What this challenge fails to recognize is the radical difference between intentions and desires. Intentions motivate directly: to act on an intention one doesn't need a further desire to act on that intention. Similarly, in the special case of resolutions, to act on a resolution one doesn't need a desire to act on that resolution, or on resolutions in general. For many agents in many cases, a resolution will simply work on its own; the agent's desires will be irrelevant. However, agents will be tempted to revise resolutions when acting upon them requires a large amount of effort. Whether or not they will do so will depend on, amongst other things, the strength of their desire to maintain those resolutions in particular, and the strength of their desire to maintain their resoluteness in general. But even here, to be effective, these desires need not be the strongest. If the agent's willpower is sufficiently strong, a weak desire to be resolute might be all that is needed to keep it in place when it wavers in the face of a strong contrary desire.

It is here, I think, that the true importance of the considerations raised in attempting to defend the belief/desire account come in; and this explains their plausibility. A desire to be resolute does indeed help an agent to be resolute, but it needn't be the overwhelming desire that the further-desire account held it to be. Similarly, belief in *Necessary* and *Effective* is highly relevant to whether agents will persist in their resolutions. An agent who has no confidence at all in *Effective*—an agent who fails to believe that if she refuses this cigarette then she will refuse others—will have little motivation to persist in her resolution. So even if she has the necessary willpower, it will not be used. Of course, an agent who knows that she has the necessary willpower will be far more likely to believe *Effective*, and so an absence of belief in *Effective* is likely to mark those who lack it. But it need not: willpower and self-knowledge need not go together.

The situation for *Necessary* is more plausibly the other way round. It is not that to be motivated one needs to believe *Necessary*: one can doubt it and still be resolute. It is rather that those who do believe *Necessary*—who believe that if they don't give up smoking now, they never will—are likely to be strongly motivated to maintain the resolution.

A Distinct Faculty?

Exerting willpower results in ego depletion. But so do a number of other things. As we saw in the last chapter, subjects experience ego depletion from making choices. Furthermore, the effect of ego depletion is not just on the ability to stick to resolutions. It has also been shown to lower IQ,[30] and to make subjects more prone to be taken in by bad arguments.[31]

So we cannot use the ego-depletion arguments by themselves to show that there is anything like a distinct faculty of willpower. Ego depletion looks like a much more general phenomenon. One plausible account sees it as the depletion of the central, conscious, slow, rule-governed cognitive system (System II in the terminology discussed in Chapter 3), leaving the agent with the modular, unconscious, fast, but inflexible System I. Research by Hamilton, Hong and Chernev lends support to this: priming System I has the same effect on preferences as ego depletion.[32]

Neil Levy concludes from this that talk of a distinct faculty of willpower is misleading. We would do better to think that willpower is simply a skill that agents implement by means of System II.[33] To make my main point I need not disagree. Talk of faculties is vague in the first place. My aim was to refute the Humean and augmented Humean accounts by showing willpower to be something that agents have to actively employ, and something that they can be more or less good at. I have characterized it as a form of thought control, and that is plausibly seen as a kind of skill. Talk of a faculty should not be read as involving more than that.

Nevertheless, I think it remains an open question just how specific that skill is, and how much its employment requires the development of a distinct part of System II. Certainly an ability to use other System II resources well is not the same as an ability to employ willpower. Mischel showed that IQ is not the same as ability to delay gratification, yet both employ System II. And it is unlikely that the arousal that is triggered by employing willpower is triggered by all other activities using System II: that solving logic puzzles would result in the same sorts of change in heart rate, skin response, etc., that are triggered by resisting temptation. So there is surely something special going on in

---

[30] Schmeichel, Vohs and Baumeister, 2003.
[31] Wheeler, Briñol and Hermann, 2007.
[32] Hamilton, Hong and Chernev, 2007.   [33] Levy, forthcoming.

the employment of willpower. Quite what it is, is not yet clear. These are empirical issues that have still to be resolved.

Resisting Temptation

Let us return to temptation. Here is my picture of what happens. The agent arrives at the tempting scene with a set of beliefs and desires and intentions. Amongst the latter might be a resolution against the very temptation at issue. If so, then what happens next will depend on the agent's motivation to abide by the resolution, on how well drafted the resolution is (how realistic, how specific and well-tied to cues) and on the strength of the agent's willpower. Whether the temptation is ordinary or addictive, the process will be much the same. If the agent can succeed in monitoring what they are doing, whilst at the same time resisting reconsidering the resolution, then they will resist. If not, they will succumb.

We can generalize this account in two dimensions. First, not all resolutions will be explicit resolutions. Some will be more like general policies not to be moved in certain ways. Many moral commitments have this form. Agents commit themselves to follow through on promises, to behave considerately, not to take advantage and so on. None of these need have been formed as explicit resolutions. They may have been arrived at through a slow process of education; some could even be innate. Nonetheless, they have much the same structure as resolutions, and are implemented in the same way. Temptations to violate them will arise; and the agents who resist this temptation will standardly be those who do not reconsider their prior commitments.

Second, not all temptations will be what we would normally think of as temptations. Fear can knock one from a resolution; so can disgust. Again the process is much as before. Successful resistance requires a prior commitment, and the ability to stick to it achieved via non-reconsideration.

Once we have this picture in place—of the initial beliefs, desires, intentions and resolutions, and then of a distinct level of control over them—various otherwise baffling features of our practices become explicable. For instance, the English common-law defence of provocation, which reduces a murder charge to one of manslaughter, requires not simply that the defendant be provoked to kill, but that they be provoked so as to lose their self-control, and as a result of that to kill. Theorists have tended not to take this two-stage requirement seriously. But once we do we can make much better sense of when the defence has been seen as applicable, and when it has not.[34] Similarly, the idea that our self-control can be undermined by the belief that it will be inefficacious can explain some of our reactions to determinism. I shall turn to that in the final chapter. First I shall say something about whether the exercise of self-control, given that it so often flies in the face of our current judgements about what is best, can be rational.

[34] Stephen Shute and I discuss this in Holton and Shute, 2007.

7

Rationality

My topic now is the normative one left over from the last chapter. Granted that resolutions do work, can they be rational? At first sight it seems that the answer must be yes. After all, they enable us to hold to our considered judgements against the desires that temptation engenders. Yet things are not so simple. In the first place, on desire-based accounts of rationality it is rational to act to maximize satisfaction of one's desires, whether or not they correspond with one's judgements about what is best; and, when tempted, one's desire is exactly to succumb.

So much the worse, we might think, for desire-based accounts. Surely things will be better if we move to a reason-based account on which rational agents are understood as those who act as they judge they have best reason to act.[1] Yet the problem remains. As we saw in Chapter 5 it appears that temptation typically threatens to take judgement with it, so that those who succumb not only desire to succumb, but judge that they are following the best path after all: what I there called *judgement shift*. Those who suffer from it might be weak-willed when they abandon their resolutions, but, having revised their judgements, they are not akratic.

Judgement shift is easily explained on broadly Humean accounts, where the judgement of what is best is nothing more than the projection of the strongest desire. But even accounts that hold to a more independent picture of practical judgement need to acknowledge that, as a matter of fact, it is very common. The reasons one can give to oneself for abandoning a resolution are many: the good for which one was holding out is not so good as was originally envisaged; or the

---

[1] See, for instance, Scanlon, 1998, ch. 1.

reward of the temptation is greater; or succumbing just this once will do no real damage to the cause for which the resolution was formed. As Gary Watson puts it, typically when we succumb to temptation, 'we are not so much over-powered by brute force as seduced';[2] and the mark of this seduction is that our judgements are affected. As we saw, empirical work in social psychology bears out this idea: when subjects yield to temptation they tend to lower their evaluation of the good they stood to gain by holding out.[3] Of course, not every case of yielding to temptation will bring judgement shift: sometimes we judge that we are doing wrong even as we do it. But many will; and among these are certainly many cases in which we take resolution to be rational. So whether we take a Humean or a more cognitive approach to practical judgement (an issue that I leave open here) it will raise a problem.

Take a concrete case. Homer has not been getting much exercise, and it is starting to show. He judges, and desires, that he should do something more active. He resolves to go for a daily run, starting next Saturday morning. But as his alarm goes off early on Saturday, his thoughts start to change. He is feeling particularly comfortable in bed, and the previous week had been very draining. He could start his running next weekend. And does he really want to be an early-morning runner at all? That was a decision made in the abstract, without the realization, which now presents itself so vividly, of what such a commitment would really involve.

The case raises two challenges to the idea that it would be rational for Homer to persist in his resolution. The first is that, if he were to open the question of whether it would be best to go for the run, he would undoubtedly now conclude that it would not. Succumbing to temptation would thus be in line with the judgement that he would make of what would be best. Conversely, maintaining his resolution would, it seems, be contrary to his best judgement. And, since many have thought that acting contrary to best judgement must be irrational, it seems that maintaining a resolution in a case of judgement shift will be irrational. Call this the *problem of akratic resolution*. Of course, it might be contended that the judgements made under the sway of

² Watson, 1999, p.10.   ³ See Karniol and Miller, 1983.

temptation are themselves irrational, and so should be discounted. Sometimes that may be right. But in many cases, Homer's included, that would be too hasty. Homer's judgements are not crazy. The bed *is* very comfortable; he *has* had a hard week. Indeed it is far from obvious that someone in Homer's situation should go for a run every morning; physical fitness is surely not a prerequisite of the good life.

This brings us to the second challenge: if it is rational for Homer to stick with his resolution, this is at least partly because he has formed it. Suppose he had decided, reasonably enough, that early-morning runs were not for him: that, all things considered, he would rather go on as before and live with the consequences. It is hard to think that such a decision would be irrational. But, relative to that decision, getting up early on Saturday morning to go for a run would look irrational. At the very least, there is no sense in which Homer would be rationally *required* to get up, in the way that he is after having made the resolution. It seems then that it is the existence of the resolution that makes all the difference. But that, in turn, seems to imply that agents can give themselves reasons for an action just as a result of resolving on that action; and that doesn't seem right. Following Bratman, call this *the bootstrapping problem*.[4]

My aim in this chapter is to answer these two problems; and it is here that the idea of how it can be rational to think less comes in. To get an intuitive sense of my solution, suppose that Homer, despite his recent inactivity, is a super-resolute type. Suppose that he springs out of bed on Saturday morning, brushing aside his desire to stay in bed, and any nagging doubts about the worth of exercise, with the simple thought that he has resolved to run, and so that is what he is going to do. This changes things radically. In the first place, whilst it remains true that *if* he were to reconsider his resolution he would decide to stay in bed, and so would be enkratically irresolute, that is beside the point. For, since he doesn't reconsider, he doesn't form the judgement that the best thing would be to stay in bed. His judgement shift is potential rather than actual. In sticking with his resolution he

---

[4] Bratman, 1987, pp. 24 ff. For further discussion, see Broome, 2001.

thus doesn't act contrary to his best judgement. He acts resolutely, but not akratically.

This provides the bones of the answer to the problem of akratic resolution: in the absence of actual reconsideration the resolution is not akratic after all. This solution will not extend to all cases. Sometimes agents will go on to reconsider their resolutions, and will form temptation-induced judgements that they should abandon them. In such cases sticking to the resolution will be akratic, and I shall have nothing to say to defend its rationality. But as I hope to show, to form such a judgement is to move a long way beyond simply feeling the pull of temptation. Homer, early on Saturday morning, feels a desire to stay in bed, and perhaps has beliefs that this would cause him less harm than he once thought. However, to think this is not in itself to think that he would do better to stay in bed. Such a judgement will typically only come when he reconsiders his resolution; and it is this that he refuses to do.

Now consider the bootstrapping problem. Since Homer does not reconsider, he does not have to think that his having resolved to go for a run provides an extra reason for going for a run. Rather, it provides a reason for *not reconsidering* whether to go for a run. Insofar as he thinks there are reasons for going for a run, these are simply the reasons that led him to form the resolution in the first place. The resolution serves to entrench these reasons; it does not provide an extra one.

The key idea here is that of *rational non-reconsideration*. Homer has rational tendencies not to reconsider his resolutions and these tendencies can confer rationality on his persistence. I am not suggesting that all resolute agents are super-resolute in the way that Homer is. But the empirical literature indicates that the approach is not far-fetched. It is exactly by developing habits of non-reconsideration that agents manage to resist temptation. Moreover, even if we do not always exemplify it, the super-resolute agent provides a model that shows how sticking with a resolution can be rational, even in the face of potential judgement shift. It is rational to have a tendency not to reconsider resolutions, even in cases where, if one were to reconsider, it would be rational to change one's mind.

In proposing this account I side with those authors who have argued for the rationality of resolute choice.[5] In the details, I follow a model that has been developed by Michael Bratman for intentions more generally.[6] Bratman calls it the *two-tier model* since it involves the assessment of the rationality of an action (the lower tier) by considering the rationality of the habit of non-reconsideration from which it follows (the higher tier); an obvious analogy is with rule utilitarianism, whereby the rightness of an act is judged by means of the rightness of the rule from which it follows. However, surprisingly to my mind, Bratman does not endorse the extension of the two-tier model to cover the case of resolutions, i.e., to those intentions that function to block temptation. On the contrary, he thinks that resolutions have a very different structure from ordinary intentions, with the result that a wholly different account of their rationality is needed.[7] That, I aim to show, is a mistake.

Of course, it is one thing to argue that it *can* be rational to stick to one's resolutions; it is quite another to argue that it will *always* be so. The Russian nobleman forms commitments in his radical youth to philanthropic projects that he later comes to believe are worthless.[8] Is it rational for the nobleman to maintain his earlier resolution? It seems implausible that it is, however much we might find it morally praiseworthy. Or consider the pre-adolescent boy who resolves never to be susceptible to the charms of girls.[9] Surely maintaining that resolution in the face of his later attraction will not be rational. We thus need some account of *when* it is rational to maintain a resolution. I suspect that nothing like a rigorous formal theory will be forthcoming. Nevertheless, the approach advocated here gives us some purchase on the circumstances in which the non-reconsideration of a resolution, and hence its maintenance, will be rational.

---

[5] McClennen, 1990; DeHelian and McClennen, 1993; Gauthier, 1994, 1996, 1997. I have disagreements with Gauthier's final position that will be mentioned later. In contrast, I think that my position is broadly consistent with McClennen's; indeed, it might be thought of as developing philosophical underpinnings for his more formal work. One point of difference: McClennen structures his discussion in terms of the satisfaction of the agent's current and future *preferences*. I want to talk more broadly in terms of benefit, leaving it open whether this must correspond to the agent's preferences.

[6] Bratman, 1987. [7] Bratman, 1998. [8] Parfit, 1973, p. 145.

[9] Gauthier, 1997.

The Nature of Practical Rationality

We are concerned with practical rationality rather than theoretical rationality: with the rationality that governs what we do rather than what we believe. I will think of this primarily as a set of rules for action that can provide guidance for an agent, rather than as a set of standards to enable third-party evaluation.[10] It would be rather nice to start with a characterization of what practical rationality, understood in this way, is. I cannot offer that, but I will make a few remarks.

One approach characterizes the practical rationality of a rule in terms of the *outcome* that it enables one to achieve: if the outcome is beneficial then the rule is practically rational. We can leave open entirely the nature of the benefit; we need not even assume that it must be benefit to the agent. Then we might say that adopting the defeasible rule 'stick to your resolutions' is practically rational if it enables us to achieve outcomes that are beneficial, even if we don't desire them, or judge them to be good, at the time.

Leaving aside the difficult issue about how to characterize the beneficial outcomes, it strikes me that there is something fundamentally right about this approach. Yet there is an obvious worry that accompanies it. Couldn't it be the case that the world is so arranged that the practically irrational flourish? To put the point picturesquely: couldn't there be a perverse god who rewarded the practically irrational by making sure that they received benefits, and penalized the practically rational by making sure that they didn't? Then receiving benefits would be no indication of practical rationality.

Someone might object that such arguments are only effective in showing that pragmatic advantage is no guide to *theoretical* rationality: false beliefs can be more advantageous than true. But perhaps pragmatic advantage is a good guide to *practical* rationality. Perhaps the practically reasonable thing to do in the world of the perverse god is that

---

[10] For a discussion of the difference here, see Arpaly, 2000. In saying that the rules provide guidance for agents, I do not mean that they need to explicitly formulate them, or even realize that their behaviour is being regulated by them. Perhaps, though, if they are really to count as agents, there must be some level on which they are endorsed. On this last point, see Jones, 2003.

which brings his reward, that is, that which would *otherwise* be unreasonable.

Such a response would surely be too glib. We have an independent grip on certain principles of practical rationality, just as we have a grip on principles of theoretical rationality, and sometimes it can benefit us to violate these principles. So, for instance, people who are prepared to pursue vendettas with no regard for the cost involved might do very well in certain kinds of negotiation.[11] They are prepared to violate a certain principle of practical rationality—do not perform acts that you believe will cost you more than they benefit you—and thereby reap the benefits of a fearsome reputation. Does that make their attitude to vendettas practically rational? No; all it shows is that it can be rational to make oneself irrational.

So discovering that following a rule is beneficial gives only prima facie grounds for saying that it is practically rational. We need to be sure that there are no principles of rationality infringed. And it is here that we confront the two problems mentioned at the outset: the problem of akratic resolution and the bootstrapping problem. They seem to show that maintaining a resolution in the face of judgement shift will typically involve one in irrationality, notwithstanding any benefit that it might bring. The time has come to consider them in a little more detail, and in particular to see if they extend to cases of mere potential judgement shift. I start with the second, the bootstrapping problem. The solution to it will bring a natural solution to the problem of akratic resolution.

The Bootstrapping Problem

Recall the worry here as it applies to intentions in general: forming an intention to do something surely cannot give one a reason to do it that one wouldn't otherwise have. If it did, we could give ourselves a reason to do something just by intending to do it; and that cannot be right. Resolutions are just special kinds of intentions, so a parallel argument should apply. They too cannot give us a reason to act

---

[11] See Schelling, 1960, pp. 16–20, for an early discussion of this.

that we would not otherwise have. It seems then that sticking with a resolution, where one would otherwise rationally act differently, cannot be rational.

Two different responses might be made. The first looks for some special feature of resolutions, a feature that distinguishes them from ordinary intentions and that does enable them to provide extra reasons for action. I think that there is something right about this approach, but I doubt that it can provide a full answer to the bootstrapping problem. The second response, which I find far more promising, is the two-tier strategy. I take these two responses in turn.

First Strategy: Resolutions Furnish Extra Reasons

The first response holds that whilst bootstrapping is unacceptable for intentions in general, it is acceptable for the special case of resolutions. The idea is that once we have resolved to do something, that does give us an extra reason to do it, a reason that we can factor into any reconsideration of the resolution, and that will make it rational to persist. What extra reason? One possibility is that we might simply have an overwhelming desire to persist in our resolutions, a desire that outweighs any desire to succumb to the temptation.[12] Alternatively, the reason might come from the need to maintain and develop the faculty of willpower, a need that does not apply to the case of intention more generally. We know that if we fail to persist in our resolutions our faculty of willpower will be diminished, and that gives us a new reason to stick with any resolution that we might have made. This might be because, like a muscle, the faculty will atrophy without use.[13] Or it might be because, if we fail in our attempts to exercise it, our confidence in the faculty will decline, which in turn will reduce its effectiveness.

I think that there are some important considerations here: resolutions are indeed special. But this is not enough to give us a completely general defence of the reasonableness of willpower. For a start, the picture that is required for such a defence just isn't descriptively accurate.

---

[12] Since I'm not endorsing this possibility, I leave aside the vexed question of whether desires can provide reasons.

[13] We saw some evidence for this in the last chapter. Whether ordinary agents are aware of it is, of course, another matter.

Whilst most of us would doubtless prefer to be resolute than weak, it is not true that this preference is strong enough to outweigh temptation in all cases in which persistence would be rational.[14] Nor do we always believe that by defaulting on a resolution we will massively diminish our chances of maintaining other resolutions in the future; we all know that most smokers only manage to give up after several attempts. Further, the need to preserve the faculty of willpower is only present if the faculty will be needed in the future. So, paradoxically, if I know that the rewards of one single exercise of willpower will be so great that I will not need it in the future, that will be the very time that I will be unable to exercise it. Finally, it appears that the whole approach of adding further reasons into our reconsiderations is misguided. We do not in fact manage to stick by resolutions by reconsidering them and deciding that the balance of reasons favours their maintenance. Once we get to that point it is too late. If I reconsider when the temptation has substantially skewed my judgement, it will seem to me that the resolution should be rationally revised, and thus that persistence will not display strength of will, but rather obstinacy. Obstinacy is not a faculty whose power I will want to maintain.

Could it be, however, that even if we do not go through a process of reconsideration, the factors cited here can explain why it is rational to persist? In other words: could resolutions provide extra reasons for persisting in them, even though these are not reasons that the agent will consider? This seems more plausible, but it takes us to the second, two-tier approach. For, if agents do not consider the reasons, the way in which they can influence their actions will be through unreflective dispositions. It is to this that I now turn.

Second Strategy: The Two-tier Account of Resolutions

The second strategy is to embrace a two-tier account, which we have seen is what Bratman does for the case of intentions in general. Let

---

[14] Perhaps for a few it is. Consider the case of Gordon Liddy, who, by his own account, went in for a programme of intentionally burning himself in order to build up his willpower (Liddy, 1997). His resulting reputation certainly strengthened his bargaining power; though here we seem to be entering the territory in which it is rational to make oneself irrational. Thanks to Andrew Woodfield for the reference.

us follow his reasoning there. The central idea there is that it can be rational to have a general policy of not reconsidering intentions in certain circumstances. This policy can confer rationality on one's action when one acts on a particular intention, rationality that that action might not otherwise have. In order to confer this rationality, Bratman convincingly argues, it must have been rational to form the intention in the first place, and it must have been rational not to revise it at each point between its formation and the time of action.[15]

Unlike the first strategy, the thought here isn't that forming an intention gives an extra reason to follow through with that intention. However, whilst intentions don't create new reasons for the action, they do entrench the decisions that are arrived at on the initial consideration, since they give *reasons for not reconsidering*. If the agent had not earlier considered what to do, they would now have reason to consider; but their earlier consideration provides a reason for not considering again.

The entrenchment that intentions provide is defeasible: sometimes things will change so radically from what was expected that it will be rational to reconsider the intention. However, provided things do not change radically, it will be rational to go ahead with the intention without reconsidering. This gives the possibility of Nietzsche's 'occasional will to stupidity', mentioned in Chapter 4: sometimes one will follow courses of action that would seem stupid if one were to have reconsidered.[16] But by and large not reconsidering is beneficial. It enables economy of effort (I consider once, and then do not waste scarce time and effort in further consideration); and it provides coordination advantages (having fixed an intention, my other actions, and the actions of others, can be coordinated around it).

It might be thought that to embrace the two-tier strategy is to accept that it is rational to make oneself irrational. That, I think, is a mistake. I would be irrational if I reconsidered an intention, and decided to stick with it even though the reasons I then had went against it. But the whole point is that there is no reconsideration; to reconsider would defeat the point of having intentions. Indeed, very often I do not even consider whether to reconsider. I simply

---

[15] Bratman, 1987, p. 80.   [16] Nietzsche, 1886, §107.

have unreflective habits that determine when to reconsider, and when not.

A more plausible line of objection is that the two-tier strategy makes our actions *arational*: since we do not reconsider, rational assessment simply does not come into it. Certainly there are ways of sticking with intentions that do involve making oneself arational. If I intend to stay in the same place for the next six hours, a powerful sleeping drug will do the job at the price of making me arational for that period. However, that is not the model that we are proposing. There are good reasons for thinking that agents who employ a strategy of non-reflective non-reconsideration do not thereby make themselves arational. First, rationality concerns what we have the *capacity* to do. In employing a habit of non-reflective non-reconsideration we do not make ourselves unable to reconsider. We still *could* open the question up again, even if circumstances do not change. It is just that we do not. (In developing the skill of catching a ball I do not make myself unable to drop it.) Second, employing a habit of non-reconsideration does not involve completely closing down one's faculties. We still engage in lower-level thought about how the intention is to be implemented; and we still need to monitor to ensure that things have not changed so radically that the intention requires reconsideration after all. Although this monitoring will often be non-reflective, it is still a rational process.

Can we apply the two-tier account to resolutions? My main contention here is that we can. The idea, of course, is that resolute agents acquire the disposition not to reconsider resolutions, even though, were they to reconsider, they would revise them. In many cases such revisions would be rational, by the lights of the agent at the time: their judgement about what it would be best to do would have changed. Yet despite this potential judgement shift, the failure to revise would not be irrational since it would result from a policy of non-reconsideration that was itself rationally justified on pragmatic grounds. The earlier consideration, and the resolution that came from it, provide a reason for not now reconsidering.

Again it might be objected that, in training oneself not to reconsider resolutions, one makes oneself arational. The issues here are exactly parallel to those for intentions in general. Certainly there are strategies for resisting temptation that involve making oneself arational; again, sleeping through the temptation is one.[17] But having the disposition not to reconsider resolutions need not be among them. It need not involve losing the capacity to reconsider; indeed, keeping oneself from reconsidering will often involve effort. Furthermore, pursing a policy of non-reconsideration doesn't involve switching one's mental faculties off. Normal intentions, as we have seen, come with thresholds beyond which reconsideration will take place. Certainly for resolutions any such thresholds should be set very high: otherwise the corrupting effects of temptation on judgement will make the resolutions all too easily broken. Nevertheless, some such thresholds are surely needed; there is no point in persisting with one's resolution to exercise if one discovers that exercise is actually damaging one's health.[18] Equally importantly, we need to survey our resolutions to ensure that they are being implemented. This is especially so where we are trying to overcome habits—like smoking or sleeping in—that are so deeply ingrained that the actions become automatic.[19]

The Problem of Akratic Resolution

Having seen how the bootstrapping problem can be answered, we now return to the problem of akratic resolution. The problem here, recall, is that in cases of judgement shift it seems that to act resolutely will be to act akratically; and that appears irrational.

The problem of akratic resolution is an instance of a general problem about whether it can be rational to be akratic. There is little doubt that acting akratically can sometimes be the most rational course of those available: the judgements against which one acts might be crazy. The question is rather whether it nonetheless necessarily involves a degree of irrationality. Recently a number of authors have

---

[17] As we saw in the last chapter, this is the strategy used by one of the children in Mischel's delayed gratification experiments. See Mischel, 1996, p. 202.

[18] We might here distinguish pressure for revision coming from the very inclinations that the resolutions were designed to overcome, from pressure coming from other sources: genuinely new information, for instance. Perhaps the thresholds should be sensitive only to the latter sort of pressure.

[19] For discussion of the importance of such self-monitoring, see Carver and Scheier, 1998.

argued that it need not. To take one example: it is clear that our emotional responses can track reasons that we fail to notice in our judgements; and hence some have concluded that it can be rational to be moved by these emotions even when they run contrary to our judgements. We might, for instance, have an emotional sense that we should not trust a person, and this sense might be reliable, even though our explicit judgement is that the person is quite trustworthy.[20]

Perhaps this is right; but it is far from obvious that it is. It certainly seems as though if one makes a serious and considered judgement that a certain action is, all things considered, the best, it will involve a degree of practical irrationality to act against that.[21] It seems that this is the practical analogue of believing something when one thinks the evidence is against it; and that seems to involve irrationality, even if one's belief is true. We saw in the discussion of vendettas that it can be beneficial to be irrational. Why isn't this just another instance of the same thing? At most it seems that we have distinguished a new sense of rationality: an externalist, reliabilist sense, in which acting against one's best judgement is not irrational, to set against the internalist sense in which it is.

I cannot resolve the general issue between internalist and externalist conceptions of rationality here. What is important for us is that the two-tier account simply sidesteps the problem. For, if agents do not reconsider, they do not ever form the judgement against which their resolution requires them to act. In the face of temptation they have the disposition to form those judgements, but the disposition is not realized. The judgement shift is merely potential. So they are not akratic. Moreover, this is no ad hoc solution; it is independently motivated by the need to solve the bootstrapping problem.[22]

In saying that agents do not reconsider, I do not mean that they do not think about the issue at all; as we have seen, some thought will typically be necessary for effective monitoring. Non-reconsideration

---

[20] McIntyre, 1990; Anthony, 1993, 2000; Arpaly, 2000. For a criticism of some features of the approach of these writers (though not of the overall conclusion), see Jones, 2003.

[21] For a presentation of the internal ('narrow') conception of irrationality, see Scanlon, 1998, pp. 25 ff.

[22] There is an interesting question, but one that I shan't address, of how many other cases of apparent akrasia can be understood in this way.

only requires that they do not seriously reopen the issue of what to do, and seriously arrive at a new judgement. Nonetheless, it might seem that this makes rationality far too fragile. I am arguing that rationality can be preserved provided that the agent does not form the all-things-considered judgement that it would be best to abandon the resolution. Yet mightn't the agent form that judgement without reconsidering what to do? A little too much thought in the wrong direction, and the agent will fall over the abyss into irrationality. This in turn will mean that irrationality will be very frequent. For surely it is part of the nature of temptation that judgement shift is frequently not merely potential, but actual.

But this is to misunderstand the nature of temptation. It is certainly true that, prior to any reconsideration, temptation brings new, or newly strengthened, desires. It is also true that it will bring new judgements: the judgements, for instance that abandoning the resolution will not have some of the bad consequences previously envisaged, or that it will bring unforeseen benefits. Yet such judgements fall far short of the judgement that it would be best, all things considered, to abandon the resolution. That judgement involves not just an evaluative judgement, but a comparison: a *ranking* of one option as better than the others. And that ranking is not an abstract, impersonal one; it is ranking of options as options for the agent. Such a ranking is not easily arrived at. It requires real mental activity from the agent. It is not the kind of thing that simply arrives unbidden.[23]

I think that this is enough to rebut the fragility worry. But I want to go further, and suggest that there is an even stronger reason for thinking that we will not arrive at new all-things-considered judgements in the absence of reconsideration of what to do. How do we form all-things-considered judgements? I suggest that, standardly,

---

[23] I speak of judgements, rather than of beliefs, because of a strong tendency in philosophy to think of beliefs dispositionally: what one believes is what one would judge if one were to consider the matter. But that is exactly to obscure what is at issue here. These are cases in which agents would arrive at different judgements if they were to consider the matter at different times; and the question is whether they should go in for such consideration. I suspect that, in a desire to avoid a certain crude reified picture of both beliefs and desires, philosophers have in general moved too far towards dispositional accounts. Our dispositions are simply not stable enough to support beliefs and desires understood in this way: they are far too sensitive to framing effects.

we form them by deciding what to do. That is, rather than thinking that we first arrive at a judgement about what is best, and then decide what to do on the basis of that judgement, things are the other way around. We start by deciding what to do, and then form our judgement of what is best on the basis of that decision. This is not to say that the judgement about what is best is identical to the decision about what to do; we know that we might have made a mistake in our decision so that it does not correspond to what is best, a possibility made all the more vivid by reflecting on our own past decisions, or those of others. It is simply that one's best way of deciding which action is best is via serious consideration about what to do.[24]

I do not claim that it is impossible to reach a judgement about what is best except via a judgement about what to do. In psychology few things are impossible. There are, for instance, reckless agents who know that their decisions about what to do are no guide to what is best; and there are depressed agents whose will is paralysed, so that they judge what is best without being able to bring themselves to decide to do it. It is enough for my purposes if the typical, non-pathological, route to best judgement is via decision about what to do. For that will guarantee that, in the typical case, the only route to a new judgement about what is best is via a reconsideration of what to do. So if agents do not reconsider, they will not arrive at new judgements, and will not be akratic. Rationality is even less fragile than was feared.

What of those cases in which the agent does arrive at the judgement that it would be best to succumb? This might happen, unusually, without the agent reconsidering what to do: perhaps the immediate judgement shift is so enormous that the agent can see no benefit whatsoever in persisting with the resolution. (I take it that such cases are very unusual: whilst temptation often leads us to believe in the advantages of succumbing, we normally retain a belief that there is

---

[24] There is a parallel here with the much discussed phenomenon that one's best way of determining whether one believes that p is simply by doing one's best to determine whether or not it is the case that p. Here, again, although one provides a route to the other, we recognize that the two states are different, since one's beliefs can be false. See Moran, 2001, pp. 60 ff., for a nice discussion. The parallel, however, can be taken too far: in some sense the belief case is the opposite to the case of practical deliberation. In the former, one looks to the world to discover a truth about oneself; in the latter, one looks to oneself to discover a truth about the world.

something to be said for holding out.) Alternatively the agent will reconsider what to do, and will make a judgement that it is best to succumb as a result of that reconsideration. In such circumstances, would persisting in the resolution involve irrationality? Addressing this takes us straight back to the general problem of the irrationality of akrasia. I suspect that it will: that even if persisting in the resolution is the most rational course, some local irrationality will be required if they are to get themselves out of the problem into which their revised judgement of what is best has led them.

The two—tier account thus does not ascribe rationality in every case; but it does provide a promising explanation of how maintaining a resolution will typically be rational. It is particularly attractive since it chimes so well with the empirical work on how we in fact stick by our resolutions: the primary mechanism, it seems, is exactly that of avoiding reconsideration. Even thinking about the benefits to be gained by remaining resolute makes an agent more likely to succumb. Once we have resolved the best plan is to put things as far out of mind as possible.

Bratman's Objections to the Two-tier Account

Bratman himself declines to extend the two-tier account to the case of resolutions. He argues that the cases of ordinary intentions, and of resolutions, are not parallel. In some ways this is obviously right. Typically my reason for forming a resolution is not to avoid wasting time thinking further about it; nor is it to gain coordination advantages.[25] The resolution might issue in advantages of this kind, but that is incidental. What is distinctive about resolutions, what distinguishes them from standard intentions, is that they are meant to overcome temptation. So the distinctive advantage to be gained from sticking to them is that which comes when temptation is indeed resisted. However, granting this difference does not show that the

---

[25] DeHelian and McClennen argue that sticking to resolutions can be seen as a coordination problem, once we treat the individual as a population of time-slices. See DeHelian and McClennen, 1993; also Gauthier, 1994. Very often the time-slice asked to make the sacrifice will gain no advantage from it; these will only be gained by subsequent slices.

rationality of resolutions cannot be defended in the same way as the rationality of intentions. The structure is still the same: one gains benefit by developing habits of non-reconsideration.

If the two-tier defence is not to stretch to resolutions, there must be more substantial differences. Bratman gives two. First:

(i) We need to acknowledge that we are 'temporally and causally located' agents: resolutions cannot work to overcome temptation by locking us in to a strategy, since we are always free to revise them; to pretend otherwise would be to engage in an irrational plan-worship.[26]

Now it is surely true that resolutions do not work as a kind of mental binding. They cannot *force* us along a certain course of action; nor, if we are to maintain our rationality, should they be able to. However, this is a point that I have already argued the two-tier account can accommodate. We remain free agents, able to evaluate and revise our actions in the light of how things appear at the moment of action. Moreover, as we have also seen, this is not a way in which resolutions differ from ordinary intentions. For sticking with an intention also involves us in not reconsidering, whilst keeping the ability to do so. It seems then that the issue about our ability to reconsider a resolution will only be pertinent if there is reason to do so; and this brings us to Bratman's second point:

(ii) Standardly when we need strength of will to stick to a resolution, nothing unanticipated happens: resolutions are exactly meant to overcome *anticipated* temptation. In contrast, the standard two-tier account explains how it can be rational to maintain an intention in the face of *unanticipated* changes.[27]

This second point is initially puzzling. Why doesn't the fact that there is typically no unanticipated information make it all the more reasonable to stick by one's resolution? Bratman's thought, presumably, is that in the standard cases in which it is rational to maintain an intention, one doesn't know whether one would rationally revise if one reconsidered. One would only know that if one did reconsider, and the point of the intention is to avoid such reconsideration. In contrast, in the standard cases of resolutions, one believes that if one were to reconsider at the

---

[26] Bratman, 1998, pp. 72–3, 1999, p. 4.   [27] Bratman, 1999, pp. 4, 8.

time of the temptation, one *would* rationally revise (more precisely: the revision would be rational from the perspective of the state of mind at the time of reconsideration). This is the crux of the matter. Bratman thinks that it cannot be rational to form an intention that one believes one should later rationally revise. He endorses:

> The Linking Principle: *I should not form an intention that I now believe I should, at the time of action, rationally revise.*[28]

There is clearly something plausible about this principle. But, once we distinguish between the rationality of revision and the rationality of reconsideration, it is ambiguous between:

> Weak Link: *I should not form an intention that I now believe I should, at the time of action, rationally reconsider and revise*

and:

> Strong Link: *I should not form an intention that I now believe that if I were, at the time of action, to reconsider, I should rationally revise.*

The two-tier account of resolutions is quite compatible with Weak Link; when I form a resolution I do think that I should not reconsider it in the face of temptation. The incompatibility is between the two-tier account and Strong Link. For, in cases in which I expect reasonable judgement shift, I will think that were I to reconsider I would rationally revise. To get from Weak Link to Strong Link one needs to add a principle about when it is rational to revise; something along the lines of:

> Rational Reconsideration Principle: *If I now believe that if I were to reconsider at the time of action I would reasonably revise, then I should reconsider at that time.*[29]

---

[28] More precisely, his formulation is: 'If, on the basis of deliberation, an agent rationally settles at t_1 on an intention to A at t_2 if (given that) C, and if she expects that under C at t_2 she will have rational control of whether or not she A's, then she will *not* suppose at t_1 that if C at t_2 she should, rationally, abandon her intention in favor of an intention to perform an alternative to A' (Bratman, 1998,p. 64). Bratman puts as a constraint on rational intention formation what I am putting as an explicit injunction. For readability, I am suppressing the reference to the availability of rational control; I assume that that is available.

[29] A rather different principle arises if we substitute 'If I believe *at the time of action* that if I were to reconsider . . .'; it is vulnerable to the same counterexamples.

Once we have distinguished the two readings, we can ask where the plausibility resides. It is Weak Link that strikes me as plausible: if I think that I should reconsider and revise an intention at a later time, what reason can I have for forming it now? In contrast Strong Link, the principle that is incompatible with the two-tier account, is far less plausible. Indeed, I think that it is false. It is true that Strong Link is not normally violated in standard two-tier intention cases, since, in those cases, given that I do not reconsider, I do not have a belief about whether or not I would reasonably revise. But in some fairly standard intention cases it is violated. The cases I have in mind are those in which people form an intention on the basis of imprecise information, knowing that more precise information will be available later. A *Boy's Own* example: You are defending your ship. Your instruments tell you that you are being attacked from somewhere in a $30°$ arc to the North East. If you waited and calculated you could find out the exact position of the attacker. But you are anticipating further attacks that will need your attention. Rather than waiting, finding the exact position of the attacker, and responding with a single missile, you form the intention of launching, when the optimum time comes, a barrage of missiles to cover the whole arc. In effect you trade missiles for time to attend elsewhere.

Here it is rational not to reconsider your intention, even though your expectations about what will happen are not wrong (the attacker does come from within the arc you expect), and you believe that if you were to reconsider you would revise. Strong Link is violated. Yet this is a case of a straightforward intention that functions to economize on the time and effort that would be expended in reconsideration: exactly the kind of function that intentions should serve.

It is all the more plausible then to think that Strong Link will be violated in cases of resolutions, when the point is exactly to block reconsideration. Indeed, we can easily turn the ship-defence example into an example of a resolution by adding a few more features. Suppose that I know that I have a tendency to reopen questions that I should leave closed, thereby wasting time and decreasing my effectiveness. So I do not simply intend to fire the barrage of missiles; I *resolve* to do so, steeling myself against the temptation to reopen it that I know I will feel. When it was a simple intention, it was surely rational not to reconsider. Turning the intention into a resolution in this way cannot now make it rational to reconsider; on the contrary, if anything it makes it even more rational not to do so.[30]

I conclude then that Strong Link is false, both as applied to ordinary intentions and to resolutions; and hence that Bratman has given us no reason for rejecting the two-tier approach to resolutions as well as to ordinary intentions. I want to try to strengthen its appeal by examining Bratman's own positive account of when following through with a resolution is rational. I want to suggest that, despite his explicit rejection of the two-tier account for resolutions, his own is best understood as a restricted version of it. This goes to show just how compelling the two-tier account is. However, once we understand Bratman's account of resolutions in this way, we will see that the restriction it imposes is not well founded. We need a much more general two-tier approach which I shall outline in the following section.

Bratman's Positive Account and the No-Regret Condition

Central to Bratman's positive account of resolutions is the *no-regret condition,* a condition on when it is rational to persist with a resolution. I meet the condition iff:

(i) were I to stick with the resolution, then at plan's end I would be glad about it; *and*

(ii) were I to fail to stick with it, then at plan's end I would regret it.

---

[30] Does it make a difference that, at the time of forming the intention, although I know that I would revise it in the light of later evidence, I do not know *how* I would do so? It is true that it is this feature that makes it rational to form the intention to fire the barrage of missiles. The proponent of Strong Link might try rewriting the principle so that such cases do not fall within its scope, by requiring that the agent have a belief about how to revise:

> Strong Link*: *I should not form an intention to f if I now believe that if I were, at the time of action, to reconsider that intention, I should rationally intend to perform a different action y.*

The problem with this approach is that then very many resolutions will fall outside the scope of the principle, since we will not know quite how we would respond to temptation; indeed, the resolution version of our missile example provides a case in point. The approach would thus classify some resolutions as rational, and others as not, on the basis of a distinction that looks utterly unimportant.

There are two different ways of understanding the role of the no-regret condition, corresponding to the two strategies that we have examined so far. We could understand it as providing an extra reason to be factored into any reconsideration. Alternatively we could understand it as working within a two-tier account, providing a constraint on the kinds of tendencies it would be rational to have.

Bratman's rejection of the two-tier account of resolutions suggests that he must mean the former. The condition will then work to describe rational reconsideration: as a rational agent, in reconsidering my resolutions I will decide to persist with them if they meet the condition, and to abandon them if they do not. If the condition is to be factored into reconsideration in this way, then it must be one's *expectation* of regret that does the work; we cannot factor in what we do not anticipate. So the condition will have to be prefaced with a belief operator: I meet the condition iff *I believe* that were I to stick with the resolution I would be glad, and so on.

But why should we think that expecting that you will later regret abandoning a resolution will in general be what provides you with the additional grounds for rationally maintaining it? The problem is that if there is judgement shift, then at the moment of temptation you might not believe that you will later regret succumbing. And, even if you do, you might well not care about the later regret. You'll believe that it is unimportant, or misguided, or corrupt, and so should not influence you. Bratman acknowledges that the no-regret condition is rightly defeasible as a result of these sorts of factors: corrupt or misguided regret should not matter. What I am arguing is that, if reconsideration is allowed, the belief that regret will not be felt, or that it will be misguided, will mean that agents will abandon resolutions even when they should not. Of course, we could just stipulate that a person will only be rational if they have true beliefs about what and when they will regret, and if they care about avoiding it. But that is a quite unwarranted stipulation.[31]

---

[31] There is much in common here with Bratman's own arguments against a similar suggestion in the case of ordinary intentions: if we just think of them as providing a further reason to add alongside the others, there is no guarantee that the reason is strong enough; Bratman, 1987, p. 24.

I see no alternative but to understand Bratman's account within the context of a two-tier theory. Here it makes much better sense. The claim now is that it is rational to have a tendency not to reconsider those resolutions that meet the no-regret condition, even if, for whatever reason, this fact would not move you at the time.[32] With the condition operating in this way we no longer need to insert the belief operator; rational tendencies are those that operate to protect you from regret, whether or not you recognize that this is what they do. If this construal is right, then Bratman's own positive account seems to entail the falsity of Strong Link and of the Rational Reconsideration Principle. The no-regret condition will often countenance maintenance of a resolution, even though I know that if I were to reconsider it I would revise it on grounds that would strike me as rational at the time.

However, once we think of it in this way, we should question how helpful the no-regret condition is. Indeed, what exactly is its role supposed to be? Bratman does not think that meeting the condition is *always* sufficient for the rational maintenance of a resolution, since we might view the regret as misplaced or corrupt. He only claims that it is *sometimes* sufficient.[33] Bratman also concedes that it is not necessary.[34] I agree. Some resolutions simply don't have an in-built end point at which the regret might be evaluated: I resolve to exercise in an ongoing way, rather than just to the end of the year. Other cases, which do have an end point, seem to call out for the maintenance of resolutions even though they do not meet the no-regret condition.

Thus consider, and pity, Yuri. He has managed to fall in love with both Tonia and Lara. When he is with Tonia he is convinced that she is the one, and vows his undying commitment; unfortunately

---

[32] That is how I understand Bratman's own response to a similar objection raised by Tim Schroeder (Bratman, 1998, p. 87).

[33] Bratman, 1998, p. 87.

[34] Bratman, 1998, p. 98, n.53. However, at places his argument seems to require that meeting the condition is a necessary condition for rational persistence: he holds that various cases of persistence will be irrational since they do not meet it (his main example concerns the toxin case, to which we shall attend shortly). Perhaps we should say, more cautiously, that he takes the no-regret condition to be the only sufficient condition yet identified; so that a failure to meet it gives prima facie grounds for a charge of irrationality.

things are just the same when he is with Lara. Worse still, his life is so structured that he keeps spending time with each of them. As one commitment is superseded by another, and that by another, trust is lost all round. Clearly it would be rational for Yuri to persist in his commitment to one of the women, and to restructure his life accordingly; all of them recognize that. However, the no-regret condition is not met. We can imagine him as a naturally contented type, who will not feel regret whomever he ends up with; in which case the second clause of the condition would not be met. Or we can imagine him as a naturally discontented type, who will feel regretful either way; in which case the first clause will not be met. Or we can imagine him as ambivalent, fluctuating between regret and happiness however he ends up; in which case neither clause will be stably met. Meeting the no-regret condition is not necessary for the rationality of persisting in a resolution, even for those resolutions that have an end point.[35]

If the no-regret condition is neither necessary nor sufficient, what role can we see it performing? From the perspective of the two-tier model, there is an obvious answer. The condition does not place a formal constraint on the *rationality* of persisting with an intention at all. After all, on the two-tier model it is quite possible that one will sometimes rationally perfom actions that one will subsequently regret having performed: global benefit can give rise to local cost. Rather, it provides one consideration (amongst many) that is relevant to an assessment of the *benefit* of forming, and persisting in, a resolution. That is, its role is in diagnosing substantial rather than formal failures. Regret is a blunt tool: I can regret doing something I could never have known would be damaging; and I can regret doing what I know to be best if it still involves some harm. Nonetheless, anticipated regret is a defeasible indicator that I could do better, and as such an *indirect* indicator of the irrationality of persistence. Let us

---

[35] The example is modelled *very* roughly on Dr Zhivago; the situation there is rather less symmetrical (Pasternak, 1957). There are general reasons for thinking that the presence or absence of regret cannot be criterial for the rightness of an action. For example: I decide to bet $20 on a horse. Whatever happens, I shall regret. If the horse wins I shall regret that I did not stake more. If it loses, I shall regret having staked anything (Humberstone, 1980).

now turn to address the question of the rationality of persistence directly.[36]

When is Resolution Rational?

When, in general, is it rational to persist in a resolution? Since typically the decision on whether or not to reconsider will not stem from a deliberate judgement, but will follow from the operation of unconscious tendencies, this question will resolve into a question of which such tendencies are rational. So what can we say about them?

I doubt that we can say anything precise, but we can adapt some of the rules of thumb given for intentions generally in Chapter 4 to the specific case of resolutions:

It is rational to have a tendency not to reconsider a resolution:

- if one is faced with the very temptations that the resolution was designed to overcome;
- if one's judgement will be worse than it was when the resolution was formed.

It is rational to have a tendency to reconsider a resolution:

- if the reasons for forming the resolution no longer obtain;
- if circumstances turn out to be importantly different from those anticipated;
- if one made an important mistake in the reasoning that led to the resolution.

The obvious difficulty comes in the tension between the two sets of conditions. Cases of judgement shift will be cases where the first two rules will recommend non-reconsideration, but where the agent will believe, if he reflects on the matter, that one or more of the final three rules will recommend reconsideration. Moreover, in many cases such

---

[36] I say much the same about the proposal in Gauthier, 1997, as I have said about Bratman's proposal: the conditions proposed there on when it is rational to persist with an intention are best understood on the two-tier account; but under that understanding they only tell part of the story.

beliefs would be warranted. Circumstances do change; acquaintance with temptation provides new information; mistaken reasoning does come to light.

When I say that this is a difficulty, I do not mean that it is a difficulty in the account I am offering. Rather I think that the account reflects a difficulty that we have in deciding when reconsideration is in fact rational. Agents will have to learn when to put weight on the principles that favour non-reconsideration, and when to put weight on those favouring reconsideration. This will be driven by knowledge of what works best; knowledge that will be different for different sorts of resolution. Resolutions concerning when to stop drinking might, for instance, need to be more insulated from reconsideration than resolutions concerning how to spend one's free time. Moreover, things will be different for different people. Those prone to self-deception will have reason to put more weight on the principles governing non-reconsideration than those who are not.

Spelling out these weightings is an exercise in practical psychology. Sometimes certain conditions will clearly not be met: the elderly Russian nobleman will, quite reasonably, be unlikely to think that he was in a better position to deliberate at the time that he made his resolution than he is at the time he comes to act on it. The same is true of the adolescent boy recalling his childish resolution to resist girls. We might say that they lack trust in their earlier selves.[37] This will lend strong support to the idea that reconsideration here is rational.[38] But in other cases it will be hard to say. Should a new study on the dangerous side effects of exercise lead me to revise my resolution to go for a daily swim? Should I postpone my resolution

[37] This idea has been interestingly explored in Hinchman, 2003. Whilst I agree with much of what is said there, I don't take self-trust as *criterial* for rationality. Note that trusting one's earlier self exactly does not require that, if one deliberated, one would come to the same beliefs, not even when the trust is explicitly factored in.

[38] Gauthier (1997), introducing the adolescent example, claims that it tells against a two-tier account, on the grounds that the boy's current and future desires will be better satisfied by sticking to the resolution. But the comparison that he seems to be making is between the desires satisfied by sticking with the resolution, and the desires satisfied by embarking on some other strategy that renders the resolution unnecessary, such as joining a military academy that will keep him away from girls. The relevant comparison, on the account I am suggesting, is between the benefits (including desire satisfaction) to be gained by sticking with the resolution, and those to be gained by reconsidering, and hence revising, it.

to give up smoking when my personal life takes an unexpected turn for the worse? Such questions will be hard to answer in the abstract, and even when all of the relevant facts are available, might still resist a clear-cut answer.

Toxin Cases and Reciprocity

Much of the recent philosophical literature on intention has been concerned with the difficulties raised by Kavka's toxin puzzle.[39] It is a gloriously unrealistic puzzle; not, I think, the place to start when thinking about how intentions work in real human beings in actual situations. Now, however, I think it is safe to see how it will be handled by the account I have been proposing and to examine the associated issue of reciprocity. At the very least this will provide more opportunity to show how the account is supposed to work. I hope, in addition, that the plausible treatment it affords to these cases will make it all the more convincing.

Here is Kavka's puzzle. You are offered an enormous sum of money if you will form the intention to drink a toxin that will cause very unpleasant symptoms for a day, but will not otherwise harm you. Let us suppose that you judge that the benefit of the money hugely outweighs the cost of the toxin's unpleasant effects, and so judge it rational to form the intention to drink it. However, there is a catch. You will be rewarded simply for *forming* the intention (as indicated by a reliable brain scanner) and your reward will come before the moment to drink the toxin arrives. Can you rationally form the intention to drink the toxin? There is an argument that you cannot. Suppose, for *reductio*, that you could. Then, once you have received the money, it will be rational to revise your intention, since you now stand only to lose by drinking the toxin. But knowing that you will rationally revise it, it will not be possible for you to rationally form the intention in the first place.

Let us focus on whether or not it is rational to revise the intention once you have the money. Some have argued that, given the pragmatic

---

[39] Kavka, 1983.

advantages that forming the intention brings, it is rational to do anything that is needed in order to form it. So if in order to form it one needs to avoid revising it, it is rational to avoid revising it.[40] Others counter that, pragmatic advantages notwithstanding, it must be rational to revise a resolution whose realization will bring only costs: the best that can be said is that it is rational to make oneself irrational.[41]

On the approach suggested here, we can do justice to both of these thoughts. For there are now two questions: whether it is rational to reconsider the intention; and whether, once it is reconsidered, it is rational to revise it.[42] On the second of these questions, I side with those who argue that revision must be the rational course. Once you reconsider, knowing that the money is in your account and that drinking the toxin will bring no further benefit, it must be rational to revise. The question of the rationality of reconsideration is harder. It seems that two of the five rules of practical rationality mentioned above are engaged, and that they pull in opposite directions. You now believe that circumstances have changed in such a way that the reasons for forming the intention no longer obtain (you have the money), so you have grounds for reconsideration. On the other hand, this intention will be a resolution (a resolution not to be tempted to refrain from drinking the toxin once you have the money), and there is, as we have seen, a rational requirement to have a tendency not to reconsider resolutions in the face of the temptations that they were designed to overcome.

How might we resolve the uncertainty? We might argue that the justification for the rules of practical reason is pragmatic; that it would be beneficial not to reconsider since that would enable us to form the intention in the first place; and hence that the rule urging non-reconsideration should dominate. This would mean developing a

---

[40] For instance, Gauthier, 1994, pp. 707–9.

[41] See, for instance, the discussion in Bratman, 1987, pp. 101–6, and then in Bratman, 1998. Indeed, I suspect that the conviction that drinking the toxin must be irrational, together with the thought that the two-tier account will lead to the opposite conclusion, is one of the factors that led him to abandon the two-tier account of resolutions.

[42] McClennen phrases his discussion in terms of the rationality of reconsideration rather than the rationality of revision (McClennen, 1990, pp. 227–31).

specific tendency not to reconsider in toxin-style cases. The difficulty here is that the toxin case is a one-off. You were not brought up with similar cases; you are unlikely to meet with another. Non-reconsideration has to be a non-reflective business, resulting from habits and tendencies that have been deeply ingrained. We cannot simply decide to have a disposition not to reconsider toxin-style resolutions in order to get the money in this case. And knowing that we do not have this disposition, it seems likely that we will not be able to form the resolution to drink the toxin at all, let alone do so rationally.[43]

Nevertheless we can bring out the pragmatic rationale for non-reconsideration in cases like these by considering situations in which there would be reason and opportunity for the relevant habits and tendencies to be laid down. Suppose that we lived in an environment in which almost every decision had the form of the toxin case. Suppose that, for his own mysterious ends, a perverse god arranged things so that the necessities of life were distributed to those who intended to endure subsequent (and by then pointless) suffering. Imagine how we would bring up our children. If resolute commitment to such intentions were really the only way to form them, that is just what we would encourage. We would inculcate habits of non-reconsideration of resolutions even when their benefit had already been gained, and there was only avoidable cost to come. Such habits would, I suggest, be perfectly rational, since we would go on benefiting from them.

A more realistic instance of this comes with another set of cases that have been much discussed, those involving reciprocity.[44] Suppose that I agree to do some onerous thing for you if you agree to do

---

[43] The same response applies to the idea that the ideal strategy in the toxin case would be to develop an unreflective tendency which involves: (i) up to the delivery of the money, thinking that one is going to persist with drinking the toxin; and (ii) once the money is delivered, reconsidering. Again, one couldn't just develop such a dispositions in response to a one-off case, no matter how desirable it would be. Moreover, this idea involves further complications. First, as a matter of fact it seems unlikely that we could ever form such a complex disposition. And, even if we could, such a disposition would be bound to involve self-ignorance that would border on self-deception: one would have to believe that one was not going to reconsider when one was. In contrast, the simple habit of sticking with toxin-style resolutions could be totally transparent.

[44] See, for instance, Gauthier, 1994; Bratman, 1998; Broome, 2001.

some onerous thing for me. Both of us would benefit from the exchange. Suppose that, by the nature of the case, you need to act first, and do so. I have got what I want. Why should I now bother reciprocating? There are, of course, moral reasons for acting. Let us suppose, however, that we are two entirely amoral creatures, moved only by considerations of our own benefit. Then we have a parallel worry to that which arose in the toxin case. For once you realize that I would have no reason to reciprocate, and so come to believe that I would not do so, you will not act either. So neither of us will benefit. It seems that we cannot get rational reciprocators; or, more accurately, that rational agents driven entirely by their self-interest cannot come to reciprocate in circumstances like these.

Once again I suggest that the rational agents need to develop, and get others to recognize, a defeasible tendency not to reconsider their resolutions to reciprocate. And once again I suggest that this involves no irrationality: the tendencies bring benefit to the agents concerned, but do not involve them in akratic action, or commit them to any kind of bootstrapping fallacy. Note, moreover, that this argument is not the reputation argument that is often advanced. It is not that it is rational for an agent to persist in reciprocation because it will give others reason to trust them next time round. That argument doesn't work if there will be no next time. Rather, it is that it is rational to develop a habit of reciprocating. Whilst it is true that that habit loses its utility if there is to be no next time, that does not entail that we will cease to have it, nor that its employment will cease to be rational.

Summing Up

I hope that I have shown how it can be rational to stick to a resolution in the face of contrary inclination and contrary beliefs. The mechanism involved—that of developing unreflecting tendencies not to reconsider—is the same as that involved in the effective management of intentions more generally. Avoiding temptation makes use of the same mechanisms that enable us to allocate our cognitive energies wisely and to coordinate our activities over time and with others. Of course it is open to someone to say that a truly rational creature would have no use of such mechanisms; that what I have been proposing are fixes for the constitutionally irrational. Yet when we come to see what such 'truly rational' creatures would have to be, we realize that they cannot provide models for us. They would not simply be immune from temptation; they would also, as Bratman has shown, be unlimited in their cognitive powers. Even then, they would lose many of the coordination benefits that we can gain. Rationality for creatures like us has to fit with the capacities and concerns that we have. It is here that rational resolve finds its place. The surprising upshot is that rationality can require us to learn when not to think.

8

Freedom

Doubtless the most quoted sentence in the English free-will literature comes from Samuel Johnson: 'Sir we *know* our will is free, and *there's* an end on't.'[1] Later, in Boswell's *Life*, the point is developed in what we now think of as a distinctively Moorean way: 'You are surer that you can lift up your finger or not as you please than you are of any conclusion from a deduction of reasoning.'[2] Our knowledge of our own free will is more certain than any thesis of philosophy; so if it comes to a clash between the two, it is philosophy that should give way.

Despite the frequency with which Johnson's passage is quoted, I think that its true importance has been missed. For what is it of which we are so certain? I take it that the certainty of which Johnson speaks comes from an *experience* of free will. He says as much: 'All theory is against the freedom of the will; all experience for it.'[3]

Once we start to contemplate the experience of free will, much of the literature on it seems beside the point.[4] Libertarians insist

[1] Boswell, 1790, AD 1769, Ætat. 60 (Everyman Edition, p. 366). Compare Locke's comment that 'I cannot have a clearer perception of any thing than that I am free,' (Locke, 1693, p. 625).

[2] Boswell, 1790, AD 1778, Ætat. 69 (Everyman Edition, p. 833).   [3] Ibid.

[4] Though not all; in particular, there is a growing literature on the experience of free will. See, for instance, Nahmias et al., 2004, which also contains a very useful review of some of the twentieth-century psychological literature. For some earlier philosophical treatments of the experience of free will, see Strawson, 1986, and Velleman, 1989b. There is also an interesting recent literature trying to elucidate ordinary intuitions empirically; but the questions asked so far do not enable one to distinguish what is believed on the basis of experience, and what is believed for other reasons. See, for instance, Nahmias et al., 2005, and Nichols and Knobe, 2007.

that a truly free will is one that is fundamentally uncaused; it is the true originator of action. But this is not to describe an experience; it is hard to think what an experience of that would feel like. It is too theoretically loaded. The libertarian thesis looks like a bit of speculative philosophy, rather than the fundamental knowledge to which Johnson thinks speculative philosophy should defer.

The complaint here has been made before: Anthony Collins objects to those who appeal to vulgar experience to support libertarian views, 'yet, inconsistently therewith, contradict the vulgar experience, by owning it to be an *intricate matter*, and treating it after an intricate matter'.[5] By 'intricate' I take it that Collins doesn't mean simply complicated; there is nothing to stop the vulgar having complicated experiences. The real objection is to an account that invests vulgar experience with philosophical properties that are not the kind of thing that are, or perhaps even could be, experienced.

This leaves us with something of a mystery. Johnson is surely right to insist that we have an experience of freedom; and surely right to insist that we would need very good grounds before rejecting it as illusory. But what is the nature of that experience? My aim here is to understand where it comes from. What we need, I think, is to identify ways in which action is experienced as something that agents instigate, rather than something that just happens to them as they look passively on. And it will be all the better if we can have some explanation of how that experience could be somehow mistaken for an experience of being an uncaused cause.

It is here, I suggest, that we can gain some understanding from the account of intention and the will that I have been developing. I suggest that there are two sources of our experience of freedom, corresponding to the two discretionary points in the account that I have proposed. First, there is the experience of choosing, that is, of forming an intention. Second, there is the experience of sticking to an intention once chosen. Both are points at which agents act, rather than simply letting themselves be moved by their

---

[5] Collins, 1717, p. 30.

prior mental states. Both are points where that action makes a difference.

Let us start with choice.

First Experience of Freedom: Choice

A quick and effective way to generate a conviction in undergraduates that they have free will is to get them to choose. Tell them to make an arbitrary choice and act on it—to raise their left hand or their right, for instance—and they are, by and large, left with an unshakeable conviction that their choice was a free one. Likewise, ask students to remember a time when they have exercised their free will, and they will almost always remember a case in which they made a choice.

What is happening here? The undergraduates have in the first instance an experience: an experience of doing something, namely, making a choice. Quick on its heels comes a judgement, or a clutch of judgements: most modestly, that they could have chosen any of a number of options; or, more theoretically committed, that *given their beliefs, desires and intentions prior to the choice*, they could have chosen any of a number of options; or, more committed still, that *given their entire mental and physical state prior to the choice*, they could have chosen any of a number of options; or, maximally committed, that *given the entire state of the world prior to the choice*, they could have chosen any of a number of options and hence that they are, in that respect, unmoved movers.

Clearly the experience and the judgements are related; but equally clearly judgements like the last go well beyond the contents of the experience. How could one have experience of the rest of the world in a way that revealed that one's action was itself uncaused by it? Nonetheless the experience itself is an experience of something. It is the experience of the act of choosing. So, to see which of the judgements is justified, we need to understand the nature of that experience.

In Chapter 3 I argued that choice has three core features. First, it is an action. Second, it is efficacious, by which I mean that, in cases where the question of what to do arises, choice is both necessary and sufficient for action—choose to raise your right hand, and you'll raise it, likewise with your left; fail to make either choice and you won't raise either.[6] Third, different choices are compatible with a given set of prior beliefs, desires and intentions. Believing, desiring and intending as one does, one could either choose to raise one's left hand or one's right hand.

I suggest that we have evidence for the latter two features—for the efficacy of choice, and for its non-determination by beliefs, desires and intentions—from our experience. It is the same kind of evidence that we have from our experience for causal claims in general.[7] Just as we come to form beliefs about what causes what by intervening in the world around us and observing what happens, so we get evidence about the causal power of choice from making our own choices and observing the outcomes. Try not making a choice, and you find that you don't act; make the choice, and you do. Try choosing differently in situations in which your beliefs, desires and intentions appear much the same—raising your right hand once, your left another—and you will find that your different choices are both efficacious.

If this is right, then the experience of choice does provide evidence for the more modest judgements that agents might make: that they could have acted differently given their prior beliefs, desires and intentions. But it provides no support for the more radical judgements that the choices are not determined by anything, and so, despite what various philosophers have claimed, provides no support for libertarianism.[8] Certainly the picture that I have proposed is very different to that of classical compatibilists, those in Hobbes' mould, who, as we saw in Chapter 3, leave little space for the agent to *do* anything. Nevertheless choice as I understand it is clearly quite compatible with determinism. All that is denied is that agents' choices are determined by their explicit psychological states: their beliefs, desires, and intentions. It is quite compatible with that that they

---

[6] Recall that the qualification 'when choice arises' is an important one. As we have seen, much contemporary social psychology holds that most actions are performed automatically, with no need for choice.

[7] I leave aside the contentious question of whether we have a direct experience of causation, or whether we infer causation on the basis of non-causal experience.

[8] See, for instance, Donagan, 1987, esp. Chs 9 and 10; Kane, 1996.

are determined in other ways. It is easy to see, though, how the experience of choice could be mistaken for the experience of one's actions being undetermined: one is mistaking a local claim of non-determination (one's action is not determined by one's prior beliefs, desires and intentions) for a global one (one's action is not determined by anything).

I suspect that this is the primary route by which the experience of choice gives rise to libertarian beliefs. Alternatively, but not incompatibly, it could be that libertarian beliefs are sometimes generated by an overly mechanistic understanding of what determinism would be like. There is a common way of thinking about determinism—amounting to a form of fatalism—according to which it leaves agents completely passive: nothing agents can do will have any effect on how they act. Thought of in this way, determinism would undermine the effectiveness of choice as I have characterized it. No matter how we choose, we will end up doing the same thing.

But, before saying more about this, let me introduce what I take to be the second source of our experience of our freedom. For the mental activity needed to form an intention is not the only source of activity needed prior to action: as we saw in discussing strength of will, there is also sometimes activity needed to turn an intention—typically a resolution—into action. What is needed is a certain kind of mental control that takes effort. This too gives rise to an experience of freedom. To see how this might work, let me start somewhere else: with some studies linking deterministic beliefs to a lack of moral motivation.

Determinism and Moral Motivation

Some recent work in social psychology has apparently showed that getting subjects to reject the existence of free will, or to believe in the truth of determinism, makes them less likely to behave morally. In a pair of studies, Vohs and Schooler found that getting subjects to read some passages arguing that free will is an illusion subsequently made them more likely to cheat in a test.[9] In further

[9] Vohs and Schooler, 2008.

studies, Baumeister, Masicampo and DeWall found that reading passages propounding determinism increased subjects' tendency to behave aggressively, or, at least, carelessly, towards others (for example, by serving hot salsa to those who had said they hated it), and decreased their tendency to say that they would behave helpfully in various situations.[10]

Assuming that these results are real, how are we to explain them? One obvious explanation will occur to philosophers: if the subjects believe that free will is necessary for moral responsibility, then, given minimal rationality, undermining their belief in free will should be enough to undermine their belief that they are morally responsible. And, if they no longer think that they are morally responsible, immoral behaviour will follow.

Supporters of this interpretation might then point to a set of recent studies that seem to show that most people do think that moral responsibility is absent in a deterministic world, at least so long as they think sufficiently abstractly, and so long as they think that it is not ours.[11] If determinism is in fact true, the conclusion is a rather depressing one: we should either cultivate a belief in free will as a necessary illusion for moral behaviour; or else we need to embark on a probably fruitless attempt to convince the masses of the truth of compatibilism.

I want to suggest an alternative interpretation. Although it is true that some studies do suggest that most people believe that there is no moral responsibility in a deterministic world, it appears that this finding is highly sensitive to how the deterministic world is described. A study by Eddy Nahmias and colleagues has found that what subjects really find inimical to moral responsibility is mechanism: the idea that we are being pushed along by happenings at the molecular level.[12]

---

[10] Baumeister, Masicampo and DeWall, forthcoming.

[11] See, for instance, Nichols and Knobe, 2007. For the caveat about the need for abstract thinking, see Nahmias et al., 2005; for differential impact of thinking that it is our own world that is being talked about, or some other, see Nichols and Roskies, forthcoming.

[12] Nahmias, Coates and Kvaran, 2007. The study found that people think that neurological determinism (everything we do is determined by the prior arrangement of our neurons) poses more of a threat to free will and to moral responsibility than does psychological determinism (everything we do is determined by our prior beliefs, desires and intentions). The authors interpret this as driven by different reactions to more or less mechanistic

And this finding is even more marked when they are asked, not about moral responsibility, but about freedom. This opens the door to the possibility that the apparent commitment to incompatibilism stems from a misunderstanding of the true nature of determinism, one that sees it as more mechanistic than it need be. And on the basis of this we might try for an alternative explanation of the Vohs and Baumeister results: perhaps the deterministic texts are encouraging a mechanistic view of the way the world works, and the moral demotivation stems from the subject's belief that that is incompatible with moral responsibility.

I think that this interpretation is a step in the right direction. But it still involves a highly theoretical bit of reasoning from the subjects: they have to think about the nature of morality and of the conditions that it requires. Mightn't the explanation be rather more primitive than that? Sticking with the thought that stories of determinism encourage an overly mechanistic view of the world, mightn't it be the case that this view is itself morally demotivating? Perhaps reading the deterministic texts tends to make agents think of themselves as powerless. This can pick up on a very normal distinction that people ordinarily make, between the things we can change, and the things we cannot. So let us start by looking to the nature of that distinction.

What You Can Change and What You Can't

Luckily, there is an obvious place to begin, with Martin Seligman's admirably straightforward book *What You Can Change and What You Can't*.[13] Seligman's focus is on the things that people typically want to change about themselves and on the extent to which, by committing themselves to change and by employing the right approach, they can succeed in changing. It turns out that some things are relatively easy to change. If you suffer from panic attacks, then with application and the right kind of cognitive therapy, you should be able to get

conceptions of determinism. I think that is very plausible, but the data could be interpreted rather differently. It could be seen as indicating an implicit belief in dualism.

[13] Seligman, 1993.

over them. Around 95 per cent of sufferers do. Other conditions are more rarely shaken: if you are an alcoholic then there is around a 33 per cent chance that you will succeed in giving up. For others the success rate is even lower. If you are overweight and want to slim by reducing the number of calories you eat, there is very little chance—around 5 per cent—that you will much reduce your weight in the long run.

A number of things are interesting about this. Obviously, one is that the relative likelihood of change is not what one would expect: we know that losing weight by dieting is hard, but it is shocking that success is so uncommon. A second, more philosophically interesting, point is that Seligman is working with a notion of what can and can't be changed that is statistical or probabilistic. It is not that it is impossible to permanently lose weight by dieting, in the sense that no one ever does it: 5 per cent do. It is rather that it is unusual to do so. Moreover, and here is a further philosophically interesting point, if we look in more detail at why that is, we find that it is because such change is difficult: it requires a tremendous amount of effort. We know from a range of data that starvation leads to an obsession with food. It dominates all thought and conversation. A starving Arctic explorer commented, on finding a food depot: 'It is long since we have been able to talk of anything but food, and now that our hunger is for the moment appeased, it is quite a relief to talk of something else.'[14] The Minnesota experiment of the late 1940s, in which thirty-six subjects were kept on a diet of half their normal calories, found a similar effect:

Food in all its ramification became the principal topic of conversation, reading, and daydreams for almost all Minnesota subjects. When they read books or attended movies, they were much impressed by the frequency with which food and eating were mentioned. Cookbooks, menus, and information bulletins on food production became intensely interesting to many of the men who previously had had little or no interest in dietetics or agriculture.[15]

[14] Mikkelsen, quoted in Keys et al., 1950, p. 817.
[15] Keys et al., 1950, pp. 833–4.

Those who try to reduce their weight by reducing their calories typically become hungry; and then they become obsessed by food much as the Minnesota subjects did. And in the end this incessant intrusion wears them down. That is why so few succeed.[16]

So we are left with a graded notion of what agents are able to do, which in turn is a function of the degree of difficulty. Philosophers have historically been little concerned with such graded measures. In looking at what an agent can or cannot do, the philosophical conception is typically absolute. Either one can lose weight or one cannot. And this is all the more marked when we look to discussions of freedom of the will. Typically this is thought to be a property of agents, rather than of particular actions. Beings either have free will, or lack it: the classic question is whether human beings fall into the first or the second class. Even when freedom is relativized to actions—when philosophers talk of an agent being free *to do a certain thing*—the conception is still typically absolute, not graded: the thought is that the agent either is, or is not, free to do this thing. In contrast, Seligman implicitly takes a graded approach to freedom itself: an agent is more or less free to perform a certain action depending on how difficult that will be.[17] At the limits perhaps there are things that no one will do, however hard they try; and others where no one who puts their mind to it will fail. But the interesting cases fall in between.

It is not just philosophers who think in absolute terms; it is very widespread. Indeed it is reflected even in the title of Seligman's book: *What You Can Change and What You Can't*, not the more accurate (though admittedly rather less punchy) *What Is Easy To Change, and What Isn't*. But I suspect that philosophers' worries go deeper than this; I suspect that many doubt that there is any good sense to be made

---

[16] For an accessible survey of some of the empirical data on how hard it is to lose weight by dieting, see Kolata, 2007, ch. 5. Of course this is a controversial issue, upon which I don't want to rest too much (and it could be diets are more effective if they control the kinds of food that are eaten, rather than just the number of calories: see Taubes, 2006, for a wealth of discussion). If you are sceptical, substitute something else that is very hard to change: an example from Seligman is sexual orientation (for 'pure' homosexuals, not for bisexuals).

[17] I say 'implicitly', since the explicit discussion of free will is in all-or-nothing terms (Seligman, 1993, pp. 22ff.).

of the idea of degree of effort, the idea that is needed in accounts like Seligman's.[18] In contrast, I think that findings like those summarized by Seligman, and other findings that I will discuss later, show that we have to make sense of it: it is the best explanation of why some things are harder to change that others.

Of course, other factors are relevant to the likelihood of success. Motivation plays a role too: one is much more likely to succeed in a task that takes a lot of effort if one is well motivated to do so. But we have no reason to think that differences in motivation are major explanations of the differences in success in the areas that Seligman treats, so I won't discuss that further. It also matters which techniques one uses to try to effect a change. Panic attacks are relatively easily cured using cognitive behavioural therapy, but do not respond well to psychoanalysis. Clearly this is something that we do need to factor in.

So let us give a rough characterization of a graded constraint on freedom as follows:

> Given the techniques they have at their disposal, an agent is less free to F the harder it is to follow though on a decision to F.[19]

This is not a definition of freedom; for a start, there may be other ways in which freedom could be lost or diminished. It rather provides the basis of a necessary condition: one is not very free if following through is very difficult. Clearly even in specifying a necessary condition the account it offers is far from reductive. It leaves open quite what the relevant kind of difficulty is (it is the kind of thing that is more present in sticking to a diet than in the regulation of breathing needed to avoid panic attacks), and what it is to follow through (we are talking about success in achieving the actions immediately under the control of an agent, not their more distant consequences). But it should be clear enough to be going on with.

There are a lot of philosophers to whom this will not be of much interest. For them the interesting question will be: are you free to

---

[18] Gary Watson (1977), for instance, endorses an account based around the idea of degree of difficulty of resistance, but denies that there is any place for a notion of effort.

[19] Don't put the definition in classic conditional form: 'if one were to decide to F one would...'. We know from Frankfurt cases that that will fall foul of the conditional fallacy; moreover, it is quite unclear how to convert it to a graded form.

make the decision to F in the first place? And the worry is that determinism shows that you are not. I do not want to deny that this is an interesting question; it is an instance of a radical scepticism which philosophy has always been good at pursuing. But just as Cartesian scepticism is not the only interesting question in epistemology, so this radical scepticism is not the only interesting issue surrounding freedom. I want to suggest that thinking about freedom in the way that Seligman does helps us understand more about where our experiences of freedom come from; and that whilst this in turn does not answer all of the questions about moral responsibility—it does not help with those that stem from radical scepticism—it does help to explain the issues about our moral motivation. So let us return to the issue of the experience of freedom.

Second Experience of Freedom: Maintaining Resolutions

Could it be then that we have an experience of a graded notion of freedom along the lines that Seligman proposes? Earlier I discussed one source of our experience of freedom: choice. But choice doesn't seem to be of much help here. For whilst making a choice can be hard work—we saw in Chapter 3 that it can lead to ego depletion—finding oneself unable to make a choice is pretty unusual. It happens perhaps in cases of Parkinson's, and depression, and with certain forms of pre-frontal damage, but not in normal subjects. And, whilst it might be that agents find it difficult to commit themselves to the kinds of self-improvement regimes that Seligman discusses, this is surely primarily because they envision that sticking to the regimes will itself be difficult.

So it is not making the choice that is difficult; it is sticking with it. The regimes that Seligman is discussing require one to form resolutions: resolutions not to over-eat, not to drink too much, not, in the case of panic attacks, to respond to an elevated pulse with panic. As we saw in earlier chapters, sticking with a resolution requires us to *do* something: we are not passive spectators. This it has in common with choice. But, unlike choice, sticking with a resolution does require ongoing effort. It requires a difficult form of mental control. And the degree of difficulty is something that will vary from case to case.

How does this help explain the experience of freedom? As with making a choice, one's prior psychological states—desires, beliefs, intentions—do not suffice for determining what one will do. Here, though, it is because they do not determine how much effort one will put in. How does this explain a tendency to embrace incompatibilism? Again, one possibility is that people misrepresent this local non-determinism as global. They think that, because their action is not determined by their beliefs, desires and intentions, it is not determined at all. Alternatively, and this is the interpretation I favour, it could be that they tend to misunderstand what determinism would be like, as something that is incompatible with effecting change by employing effort. That is a kind of fatalism. Let us consider it in more detail.

Muddling Fatalism and Determinism

Fatalism is a common theme in fiction. An excellent, and much quoted, example comes in the speech that Somerset Maugham gives to Death:

There was a merchant in Baghdad who sent his servant to market to buy provisions and in a little while the servant came back, white and trembling, and said, Master, just now when I was in the market-place, I was jostled by a woman in the crowd and when I turned I saw it was Death that jostled me. She looked at me and made a threatening gesture; now, lend me your horse, and I will ride away from this city and avoid my fate. I will go to Samarra and there Death will not find me. The merchant lent him the horse and the servant mounted it, and he dug his spurs in its flanks and as fast as the horse could gallop he went. Then the merchant went down to the market-place and he saw me standing in the crowd and he came to me and said, Why did you make a threatening gesture to my servant when you saw him this morning? That was not a threatening gesture, I said, it was only a start of surprise. I was astonished to see him in Baghdad, for I had an appointment with him tonight in Samarra.[20]

---

[20] Maugham, 1933, Act III. It is quoted by many authors from John O'Hara on. The origin of the story appears to be from the ninth-century author Fudail ibn Ayad; see Shah, 1967, p. 191. I am indebted here to Sobel, 2004.

The servant's effort and enterprise will make a difference to the *immediate* outcome: he will get on the horse and ride to Samarra. But whatever he does he will not be able to escape the *ultimate* outcome which fate has assigned to him. The theme is a familiar one in classical mythology, and more recently in those time-travel stories in which an agent is involved in a project in which we know they must fail—trying to kill their own younger self, for example. In terms of Seligman's continuum, one's fate belongs at the extreme end of what one cannot change, beyond even the fruitless attempt to lose weight.

My suggestion is that it is commonly held that if determinism were true, everything would be like that: determinism would bring a global fatalism. In particular, on this view, determinism would bring a kind of internal fatalism, in the sense that there would be nothing one could do—no choice that one could make, no effort that one could expend—to influence any of one's actions. This brings a difference with the classic fatalism. As I mentioned, classic fatalism involves frustration at a distance. One performs one's immediate action, only to find that it does not help: the servant gets to Samarra, only to find that death is there waiting for him. If determinism is seen as a global form of fatalism, it will also bring a more direct frustration: if one is fated to do otherwise, then one will not even perform the immediate action that one is aiming to perform, no matter how much effort one puts in. But this just makes the fatalism all the more pressing. Now it begins at home. No exercise of effort will change anything. Everything is crowded at one end of Seligman's spectrum.

I hope it is clear how this fatalism involves something like a mechanistic picture. It is certainly one in which it is reasonable to think of us as pawns in the hands of impersonal forces of fate. I hope too that, with a bit of thought, it is equally clear that as an interpretation of determinism, or at least of *causal* determinism, which is the only kind that is in the running, it is a mistake. This fatalism is saying that if an outcome is determined to obtain, nothing can have causal impact upon it. But causal determinism holds that outcomes obtain exactly because things have causal impact upon them. Far from saying that our actions or our choices are causally inefficacious, causal determinism holds that they have the impact they have through their causal consequences.

This fatalism is reminiscent of the Lazy argument used against the Stoics: if one is fated either to recover or to die, what use is there in calling the doctor? Chryssipus's response, whether or not it answers all the worries, is certainly apposite to our concerns here. To hold that it is determined that Oedipus will be born to Laius is not, says Chryssipus to hold that this will be so 'whether or not Laius has intercourse with a woman'.[21] Having intercourse is a necessary condition for having a son. If it is determined that Oedipus will be born to Laius, then it is determined that Laius will have intercourse; the two are 'co-fated', to use Chryssipus's term. But that is in no way inconsistent with admitting the causal efficacy of intercourse; on the contrary, it presupposes it.[22]

Similarly, if we got conclusive proof of the truth of determinism, we should not throw Seligman's book away, on the grounds that we now know that one cannot change anything, and so trying to distinguish what can be changed, and what can't, is a waste of time. Seligman is talking about how much effort is needed to effect different kinds of change. In a deterministic model it is still true that different changes require people to put in different amounts of effort, and, crucially, that the effort they put in makes a difference. If there hadn't been the effort, the outcome would have been different. So it is still true that in that sense people act: their efforts are not thwarted by forces that ensure an inevitable outcome.

Despite being a mistake, my suggestion is that this is the view that reading much deterministic literature tends to induce in people, at least implicitly. I doubt that they would spell out the argument quite as I have done. But they understand the impact of determinism in terms of a distinction that they already have—Seligman's distinction between what you can change and what you can't. Determinism is then understood as entailing that every attempt to influence things by putting in effort falls on one side of that distinction. Then we know,

---

[21] As quoted by Cicero, *On Fate* 30, translation in Long and Sedley, 1987, p. 339.

[22] For discussion of Chryssipus's argument, see Bobzien, 1998, ch. 5. As she points out (pp. 231–3), Chryssipus is not really concerned to answer the question of how something that is determined can still be up to us: what I earlier called the more global scepticism.

from a large body of research, what the effects will be. Once people come to think that they will fail at something, or even that failure is likely, they stop trying. To use the psychological terminology, their self-efficacy is undermined.[23]

Determinism and Moral Motivation Again

Inducing belief about the futility of struggle is a classic seduction strategy. If proof be needed, witness Rodolphe's seduction of Emma Bovary. Rodolphe attempts to overcome any remaining resistance from Emma by describing how fate works to draw lovers together:

Come what may, sooner or later, in six months, ten years, they will be together, will be lovers, because Fate ordains it, because they were born for each other.

And now applying the lesson to the two of them:

Look at us ... why did we meet? By what decree of Fate? It must be because, across the void, like two rivers irresistibly converging, our unique inclinations have been pushing us towards one another.[24]

In short: resistance is futile. Where Emma would normally think that she could resist the inclination to be unfaithful to her husband, a belief in fate will make her more sceptical. The outcome is not that she will fail to act at all. It is that she will relax her self-control. She will no longer try to resist her attraction to Rodolphe, or will give up more readily if she does.[25] This is a form of passivity, but of an interesting kind: it is passivity in the face of one's desires, a relinquishing of self-control.

With Emma we have clearly reached the moral sphere. She has a desire to do something, and a belief that to do it would be morally wrong. Will she act on her desire, or do what she believes morally

---

[23] For a general overview of the evidence, see Bandura, 1992.

[24] Flaubert, 1857, ch. 8. The second line is not merely fictional: Flaubert had written something very similar in a letter to Louise Colet (15 November 1846).

[25] Rodolphe's approach is actually subtler still, since he suggests that it is merely the pressure of conventional morality that will be overcome by fate; he does not want to acknowledge to Emma that she is struggling against her conscience.

right? That depends on a lot of things, but one of them is whether she thinks that she can resist the desire. If her belief in that is shaken—if she comes to believe that she is going to succumb anyway—then she is much less likely to resist. The belief that she is likely to succumb serves to undermine the self-control that she might otherwise have exercised.

This is how I suggest we interpret the experiments that show that a belief in determinism is morally demotivating. It is not that the subjects stop acting altogether. On the contrary, it is their acts that cause the trouble: they cheat; they give chilli to those who loathe it. What is happening, I suggest, is that, like Emma Bovary, they stop exercising self-control. They have desires that would normally be held in check by various moral commitments; but, as they come to believe that determinism is true, they come to doubt that this self-control will be effective. As a result they relax their control. They no longer resist the desire to get themselves a better score. They no longer resist the desire to have some malicious fun with the chilli; or, at least, they no longer make the effort to be careful about who gets it.

On this account the effect of the belief in determinism is relatively direct. Subjects need not think about the nature of morality, nor of whether the existence of moral responsibility requires the falsity of determinism. Indeed the considerations that move them are not directly about morality at all. Rather they are just about whether putting in effort will make any difference. Moral commitments are one instance of the more general phenomenon of resisting contrary inclinations. And this fact provides a way of evaluating whether my conjectures are true. For, if they are, the effect should be just as marked on cases that do not involve morality at all. Dieters who read deterministic passages should be more ready to break their diets.

The effect here stems from something that has been one of the main themes of this book. Motivation is a multi-stage affair. People are moved by certain desires, but also by certain resolutions and commitments; and they have some ability to control which of these they act on. I am suggesting that a belief in determinism, and a belief that there is no such thing as free will, acts differentially on the elements of this system. It diminishes self-control, without diminishing the desires that self-control is normally used to manage.

If this is right, then it in turn is evidence that our experience of free will stems, at least partly, from the experience of exercising self-control. For the belief that there is no such thing as free will leads people to stop exercising it. Can similar support be given to the claim made in the first part of this chapter, that the experience of freedom comes also from the making of choices? We would need to show that belief in determinism also tends to undermine the making of choices. It would be interesting to find out whether it does, but any experiments would be difficult to perform. We would need situations in which the question of what to do arises, and yet where it is still possible for agents not to choose; moreover, we would need to show that any failure to choose did not stem entirely from a scepticism about whether the chosen course will be maintained.[26]

Remaining Questions

Let me conclude by stressing what I said at the beginning. Free will is a complex notion. It embraces moral, religious, mental and metaphysical themes, and tries to answer to concerns from all of them. Correspondingly there are many sources of our belief in free will. I have here addressed only one such source, that of direct experience. And even here, I do not claim that I have exhausted the source. I have simply tried to indicate two important ways in which it might work, and to show that the beliefs that derive from it need not be thought of as illusory.

So there remain many questions about free will. In particular, there remains what I earlier called global scepticism—whether there can

[26] Are my claims that choosing and resisting are sources of the experience of free will challenged by the experiments in Nahmias et al., 2007, discussed above, n.12. They found that subjects thought that psychological determinism—actions are determined by a subject's prior beliefs, desires and plans—*is* compatible with free will. Yet I have been arguing that the experience of free will consists partly in the experience that this is not so. I have two responses: (i) the subjects might not have thought through quite what this entails—it would be interesting to know whether they would agree that someone whose effort had no effect on whether they stuck to resolutions would nevertheless have free will; (ii) there is a difference between subjects' explicit beliefs, and the sources of those beliefs. My claim is that beliefs in free will partly stem from the experiences of making choices and sticking by those choices. It is compatible with this that people don't believe that this is so.

be free will, and moral responsibility, if everything—including what we choose, and whether we stick to our resolutions—is understood as being determined. My own view is that this question is badly formed, since it assumes that we have a clear and determinate notion of free will, clear and determinate enough that we can ask whether it is compatible with determinism. Whereas, as we might expect given its diverse sources, our notion of free will is far from determinate. When we are questioned we work fast to make it determinate; so fast that we do not notice that it was not. Why do I say this? As we saw at the outset, the concept that we come up with is highly sensitive to the exact question that we were asked. For instance, we are more likely to ascribe freedom and moral responsibility to agents in a deterministic world if: (i) we think that world is our own rather than a merely possible world; or (ii) the case is described in a concrete rather than an abstract way.[27] The best explanation of this, I think, is not that our concept of free will is highly complex, sensitive to very subtle factors. It is rather that we are constructing the concept as we try to answer; and since it is bound to so many different features, we construct answers that fit those that the question makes most salient.

But this is business for another place. My concern here has been with the experience of freedom. I hope that I have at least made a start on showing what it might be an experience of: an experience of choosing, and of maintaining the resolutions chosen. In this it involves no mistake.

---

[27] See the studies cited in n.11 above.

Bibliography

Ainslie, George, 1992, *Picoeconomics* (Cambridge: Cambridge University Press).

——, 2001, *Breakdown of Will* (Cambridge: Cambridge University Press).

Alloy, Lauren and Lyn Abramson 1979: 'Judgment of Contingency in Depressed and Nondepressed Students: Sadder but Wiser?', *Journal of Experimental Psychology: General* 108: 441–85.

Amis, Kingsley, 1956, *Lucky Jim* (London: Gollancz).

Anscombe, G. E. M., 1963, *Intention*, 2nd edn (Oxford: Blackwell).

Anthony, Louise, 1993, 'Quine as Feminist: The Radical Import of Naturalized Epistemology', in Louise Anthony and Charlotte Witt (eds), *A Mind of One's Own* (Boulder, CO: Westview Press), pp. 185–225.

——, 2000, 'Naturalized Epistemology, Morality and the Real World', *Canadian Journal of Philosophy* Supp. 26: 103–37.

Arpaly, Nomy, 2000, 'On Acting Rationally Against One's Best Judgement', *Ethics* 110: 488–513.

Austin, J. L., 1956, 'A Plea for Excuses', *Proceedings of the Aristotelian Society*; reprinted in his *Philosophical Papers* (Oxford: Clarendon Press, 1961), pp. 123–52.

Bach, Kent, 1995, 'Review of George Ainslie's *Picoeconomics*', *Philosophy and Phenomenological Research* 55: 981–3.

Bandura, Albert, 1992, 'Exercise of Personal Agency Through the Self-Efficacy Mechanism', in Ralf Schwarzer (ed.), *Self-Efficacy* (Washington, DC: Hemisphere), pp. 3–38.

Bargh, John, 2002, 'Losing Consciousness', *Journal of Consumer Research* 29: 280–5.

——and Tanya Chartrand, 1999, 'The Unbearable Automaticity of Being', *American Psychologist* 54: 462–79.

Baumeister, Roy, 1996, *Evil* (New York: W. H. Freeman).

——, Ellen Bratslavsky, Mark Muraven and Diane Tice. 1998, 'Ego-depletion: Is the Active Self a Limited Resource?', *Journal of Personality and Social Psychology* 74: 1252–65.

——, Todd Heatherton and Dianne Tice, 1994, *Losing Control* (San Diego: Academic Press).

——, E. Masicampo and C. Nathan DeWall, forthcoming, 'Prosocial Benefits of Feeling Free: Manipulating Disbelief in Free Will Increases

Aggression and Reduces Helpfulness', *Personality and Social Psychology Bulletin*.

Bayne, Tim, 2006, 'Phenomenology and the Feeling of Doing', in Susan Pockett, William Banks and Shaun Gallagher (eds), *Does Consciousness Cause Behavior?* (Cambridge: MIT Press), pp. 169–85.

Bechara, Antoine, Antonio Damasio, Hanna Damasio and Steven Anderson, 1994, 'Insensitivity to Future Consequences Following Damage to Human Prefrontal Cortex', *Cognition* 50: 7–15.

——, Hanna Damasio, Daniel Tranel and Antonio Damasio, 1997, 'Deciding Advantageously Before Knowing the Advantageous Strategy', *Science* 275: 1293–5.

——, Daniel Tranel, Hanna Damasio and Antonio Damasio, 1996, 'Failure to Respond Autonomically to Anticipated Future Outcomes Following Damage to Prefrontal Cortex', *Cerebral Cortex* 6: 215–25.

Bem, Daryl, 1972, 'Self-Perception Theory', *Advances in Experimental Social Psychology* 6: 1–62.

Berridge, Kent, 2000, 'Taste Reactivity: Measuring Hedonic Impact in Infants and Animals', *Neuroscience and Biobehavioral Reviews* 24: 173–98.

——, 2004, 'Pleasure, Unfelt Affect and Irrational Desire', in A. Manstead, N. Frijda and A. Fischer (eds), *Feelings and Emotions: The Amsterdam Symposium* (Cambridge: Cambridge University Press), pp. 243–62.

——, 2007a, 'The Debate over Dopamine's Role in Reward: The Case for Incentive Salience', *Psychopharmacology* 191: 391–431.

——, 2007b, 'Brain Reward Systems for Food Incentives and Hedonics in Normal Appetite and Eating Disorders', in T.C Kirkham and S. Cooper (eds), *Progress in Brain Research: Appetite and Body Weight* (New York: Academic Press), pp. 191–216.

—— and Morten Kringelbach, 2008, 'Affective Neuroscience of Pleasure: Reward in Humans and Animals', *Psychopharmacology* 199: 457–80.

—— and Terry Robinson, 1998, 'What is the Role of Dopamine in Reward: Hedonics, Learning, or Incentive Salience?', *Brain Research Reviews* 28: 308–67.

Bigelow, John, Susan Dodds and Robert Pargetter, 1990, 'Temptation and the Will', *American Philosophical Quarterly* 27: 39–49.

Bobzien, Susanne, 1998, *Determinism and Freedom in Stoic Philosophy* (Oxford: Clarendon Press).

Boswell, James, 1790, *The Life of Samuel Johnson* (London: Weidenfeld and Nicolson (Everyman's Library), 1992).

Bratman, Michael, 1985, 'Davidson's Theory of Intention', in Bruce Ver-mazen and Merrill Hintikka (eds), *Essays on Davidson: Actions and Events*, (Oxford: Clarendon Press), pp. 13–26.

———, 1987, *Intention, Plans, and Practical Reason* (Cambridge, MA: Harvard University Press).

———, 1992, 'Practical Reason and Acceptance in a Context', *Mind* 101: 1–15; reprinted in Bratman 1999, pp. 15–34.

———, 1996, 'Planning and Temptation', in Larry May, Marilyn Friedman and Andy Clark (eds), *Minds and Morals* (Cambridge, MA: MIT Press), pp. 293–310; reprinted in Bratman, 1999, pp. 35–57.

———, 1998, 'Toxin, Temptation and the Stability of Intention', in Jules Coleman and Christopher Morris (eds), *Rational Commitment and Social Justice* (Cambridge: Cambridge University Press), pp. 59–83; reprinted in Bratman, 1999, pp. 58–90.

———, 1999, *Faces of Intention* (Cambridge: Cambridge University Press).

———, 2006, 'Temptation Revisited', in *Structures of Agency* (New York: Oxford University Press), pp. 257–82.

———, forthcoming, 'Intention, Belief, Practical, Theoretical', in Jens Tim-merman, John Skorupski and Simon Robertson (eds), *Spheres of Reason* (Oxford: Oxford University Press).

Brehm, Jack, 1956, 'Postdecisional Changes in the Desirability of Alternatives', *Journal of Abnormal Psychology* 52: 384–9.

Broome, John, 2001, 'Are Intentions Reasons? And How Should We Cope with Incommensurable Values?', in Christopher Morris and Arthur Rip-stein (eds), *Practical Rationality and Preference: Essays for David Gauthier* (Cambridge: Cambridge University Press), pp. 98–120.

Budescu, David and Thomas Wallsten, 1995, 'Processing Linguistic Probab-ilities: General Principles and Empirical Evidence', in Jerome Busmeyer, Douglas Meldin and Reid Hastie (eds), *Decision Making from a Cognitive Perspective* (San Diego: Academic Press), pp. 275–318.

Byatt, A. S., 1989, *Possession: A Romance* (London: Chatto and Windus).

Campbell, C. A., 1939, 'The Psychology of Effort of Will', *Proceedings of the Aristotelian Society* 40: 49–74.

Carver, Charles and Michael Scheier, 1998, *On the Self-Regulation of Behavior* (Cambridge: Cambridge University Press).

Chang, Ruth (ed.), 1997, *Incommensurability, Incomparability and Practical Reason* (Cambridge, MA: Harvard University Press).

Charniak, Eugene, 1991, 'Bayesian Networks without Tears', *AI Magazine* 12: 50–63.

Chater, Nick, Joshua Tenenbaum and Alan Yuille, 2006, 'Probabilistic Models of Cognition: Conceptual Foundations', *Trends in Cognitive Sciences* 10: 287–91.

Chichester, Francis, 1964, *The Lonely Sea and the Sky* (London: Hodder and Stoughton).

Christensen, David, 1996, 'Dutch Books Depragmatized: Epistemic Consistency for Partial Believers', *Journal of Philosophy* 93: 450–79.

Collins, Anthony, 1717, *A Philosophical Inquiry Concerning Human Liberty*, 2nd edn, ed. J. O'Higgins (The Hague: Martinus Nijoff, 1976).

Cook Wilson, John, 1879, *Aristotelian Studies* I (Oxford: Clarendon Press).

Cooper, Joel, 2007, *Cognitive Dissonance: Fifty Years of a Classic Theory* (London: Sage).

Cordner, Christopher, 1985, 'Jackson on Weakness of Will', *Mind* 94: 273–80.

Damasio, Antonio, 1994, *Descartes' Error* (New York: Putnam).

Davidson, Donald, 1963, 'Actions, Reasons and Causes' *The Journal of Philosophy* 60: 685–700; reprinted in Davidson 1980, pp. 3–20.

——, 1969, 'How is Weakness of the Will Possible?', in J. Feinberg (ed.), *Moral Concepts* (Oxford: Oxford University Press), pp. 93–113; reprinted in Davidson 1980, pp. 21–42.

——, 1978, 'Intending', in Yirmahu Yovel (ed.), *Philosophy of History and Action* (Dordrecht: Reidel); reprinted in Davidson, 1980, pp. 83–102.

——, 1980, *Essays on Actions and Events* (Oxford: Clarendon Press).

DeHelian, Laura and Edward McClennen, 1993, 'Planning and the Stability of Intention: A Comment', *Minds and Machines* 3: 319–33.

Dijksterhuis, Ap, Maarten Bos, Loran Nordgren and Rick van Baaren, 2006, 'On Making the Right Choice: The Deliberation-Without-Attention Effect', *Science* 311: 1005–7.

Donagan, Alan, 1987, *Choice: The Essential Element in Human Action* (London: Routledge and Kegan Paul).

Elster, Jon, 1979, *Ulysses and the Sirens* (Cambridge: Cambridge University Press).

Fairbrother, W. A., 1897, 'Aristotle's Theory of Incontinence—A Contribution to Practical Ethics', *Mind* 6: 359–70.

Fischer, John Martin, 1994, *The Metaphysics of Free Will* (Oxford: Blackwell).

Flaubert, Gustave, 1857, *Madame Bovary*, trans. Geoffrey Wall (Harmondsworth: Penguin, 1992).

Fodor, Jerry, 1983, *Modularity of Mind* (Cambridge MA: MIT Press).

Frankish, Keith, 2009, 'Partial Belief and Flat-out Belief', in Franz Huber and Christoph Schmidt-Petri (eds), *Degrees of Belief* (Dordrecht: Springer): 75–93.

Gauthier, David, 1994, 'Assure and Threaten', *Ethics* 104: 690–721.

——, 1996, 'Commitment and Choice: An Essay on the Rationality of Plans', in Francesco Frain, Frank Hahn and Stefano Vannucci (eds), *Ethics, Rationality and Economic Behaviour,* (Oxford: Clarendon Press), pp. 217–43.

——, 1997, 'Resolute Choice and Rational Deliberation: A Critique and a Defense', *Noûs* 31: 1–25.

Godden, Rumer, 1975, *The Peacock Spring* (London: Macmillan).

Gollwitzer, Peter, 1993, 'Goal achievement: The Role of Intentions', in Wolfgang Stroebe and Miles Hewstone (eds), *European Review of Social Psychology* 4: 141–85.

——, 1996, 'The Volitional Benefits of Planning', in Peter Gollwitzer and John Bargh (eds), *The Psychology of Action* (New York: Guilford Press), pp. 287–312.

——, 1999, 'Implementation Intentions: The Strong Effect of Simple Goals', *American Psychologist* 54: 493–503.

——, 2003, 'Why We Thought the Action Mindsets Affect Illusions of Control', *Psychological Inquiry* 14: 259–67.

—— and Ute Bayer, 1999, 'Deliberative versus Implemental Mindsets in the Control of Action', in Shelly Chaiken and Yaacov Trope (eds), *Dual-process Theories in Social Psychology* (New York: Guilford Press), pp. 403–22.

—— and Ronald Kinney, 1989, 'Effects of Deliberative and Implemental Mindsets on Illusions of Control', *Journal of Personality and Social Psychology* 56: 531–42.

——, Ute Bayer and W. Wasel, 1998, 'Deliberative versus Implementational Mindsets: The Issue of Openmindedness' ms.

——, Kentaro Fujita and Gabriele Oettingen, 2004, 'Planning and the Implementation of Goals', in Roy Baumeister and Kathleen Vohs (eds), *Handbook of Self-Regulation* (New York: Guilford Press), pp. 211–28.

Grant, Alexander, 1857, *The Ethics of Aristotle* (London: J. W. Parker).

Grice, Paul, 1971, 'Intention and Uncertainty', *Proceedings of the British Academy* 57: 263–79.

Haggard, Patrick and H. Johnson, 2003, 'Experiences of Voluntary Action', *Journal of Consciousness Studies* 10: 2–84.

Hamilton, Ryan, Jiewen Hong and Alexander Chernev, 2007, 'Perceptual Focus Effects in Choice', *Journal of Consumer Research* 34: 187–99.

Hampshire, Stuart and H. L. A. Hart, 1958, 'Decision, Intention and Certainty', *Mind* 67: 1–12.

Hare, R. M., 1952, *Language of Morals* (Oxford: Clarendon Press).

——, 1963, *Freedom and Reason* (Oxford: Clarendon Press).

Harman, Gilbert, 1976, 'Practical Reasoning', *Review of Metaphysics* 29: 431–63.

——, 1988, *Change in View* (Cambridge, MA: MIT Press).

Heckhausen, Heinz and Peter Gollwitzer, 1987, 'Thoughts, Contents and Cognitive Functioning in Motivational versus Volitional States of Mind', *Motivation and Emotion* 11: 101–20.

Hill, Thomas, 1986, 'Weakness of Will and Character', *Philosophical Topics* 14; reprinted in *Autonomy and Self-Respect* (Cambridge: Cambridge University Press 1991), pp. 118–37.

Hinchman, Edward, 2003, 'Trust and Diachronic Agency', *Noûs* 37: 25–51.

Hobbes, Thomas, 1656, *The Questions Concerning Liberty, Necessity and Chance* in *Collected English Works*, Vol. V, ed. William Molesworth (London: John Bohn, 1841).

Holton, Richard, 2004, 'Review of Daniel Wegner's *The Illusion of Conscious Will*', *Mind* 113: 218–21.

Holton, Richard and Stephen Shute, 2007, 'Self–Control in the Modern Provocation Defence', *The Oxford Journal of Legal Studies* 27: 49–73.

Humberstone, I. L., 1980, 'You'll Regret It', *Analysis* 40: 175–6.

——, 1990, 'Wanting, Getting, Having', *Philosophical Papers* 19: 99–118.

Ignatius of Loyola, 1548, *Spiritual Exercises*, in Joseph Munitiz and Philip Endean (eds), *Personal Writings* (Harmondsworth: Penguin, 1996).

Iyengar, Sheena and Mark Lepper, 2000, 'When Choice is Demotivating: Can One Desire Too Much of a Good Thing?', *Journal of Personality and Social Psychology* 79: 995–1006.

Jackson, Frank, 1984, 'Weakness of Will', *Mind* 93: 1–18.

Jahanshahi, Marjan and Christopher Frith, 1998, 'Willed Action and its Impairments', *Cognitive Neuropsychology* 15: 483–533.

Jones, Karen, 2003, 'Emotion, Weakness of Will, and the Normative Conception of Agency', in Anthony Hatzimoysis (ed.), *Philosophy and the Emotions* (Cambridge: Cambridge University Press), pp. 181–200.

Kahan, Dana, Janet Polivy and C. Peter Herman, 2003, 'Conformity and Dietary Disinhibition: A Test of the Ego Strength Model of Self-Regulation', *International Journal of Eating Disorders* 33: 165–71.

Kahneman, Daniel and Amos Tversky 1973 'On the Psychology of Prediction', *Psychological Review* 180: 237–57.

——, 2000, *Choices, Values and Frames* (Cambridge: Cambridge University Press).

Kane, Robert, 1996, *The Significance of Free Will* (New York: Oxford University Press).

Kaplan, Mark 1996, *Decision Theory as Philosophy* (Cambridge: Cambridge University Press).

Karniol, Rachel and Dale Miller, 1983, 'Why Not Wait? A Cognitive Model of Self-imposed Delay Termination', *Journal of Personality and Social Psychology* 45: 935–42.

Kavka, Gregory, 1983, 'The Toxin Puzzle', *Analysis* 43: 33–6.

Kennett, Jeanette and Michael Smith, 1994, 'Philosophy and Commonsense: The Case of Weakness of Will,' in Michaelis Michael and John O'Leary-Hawthorn (eds), *Philosophy in Mind* (Dordrecht: Kluwer), pp. 141–57.

Keynes, Geoffrey, 1981, *The Gates of Memory* (Oxford: Clarendon Press).

Keys, Ancel, Josef Brozek, Austin Henschel, Olaf Mickelsen and Henry Taylor, 1950, *The Biology of Human Starvation* (Minneapolis: University of Minnesota Press).

Klein, Gary, 1998, *Sources of Power* (Cambridge, MA: MIT Press).

Knobe, Joshua, 2003, 'Intentional Action and Side Effects in Ordinary Language', *Analysis* 63: 190–3.

——, 2006, 'The Concept of Intentional Action', *Philosophical Studies* 130: 203–31.

——, 2007, 'Reason Explanation in Folk Psychology', *Midwest Studies* 31: 90–107.

—— and Arundra Burra, 2006, 'Intention and Intentional Action: A Cross-Cultural Study', *Journal of Culture and Cognition* 6: 113–32.

Kolata, Gina, 2007, *Rethinking Thin* (New York: Farrar, Straus and Giroux).

Langton, Rae 2004, 'Intention as Faith', in John Hyman and Helen Steward (eds), *Action and Agency* (Cambridge: Cambridge University Press), pp. 243–58.

Levy, Neil, forthcoming, 'Weakness of the Will: An Entirely Naturalistic Approach', ms.

Lewicki, Pawel, Thomas Hill and E. Bizot, 1988, 'Acquisition of Procedural Knowledge About a Pattern of Stimuli that Cannot Be Articulated', *Cognitive Psychology* 20: 24–37.

Lewis, David, 1996, 'Elusive Knowledge', *Australasian Journal of Philosophy* 74: 549–67.

Liddy, Gordon, 1997, *Will* (New York: St Martin's Press).

Locke, John, 1690, *An Essay Concerning Human Understanding*, ed. Peter Nidditch (Oxford: Clarendon Press, 1975).

——, 1693, Letter to Molyneux, 20 January 1693, in E. S. de Beer (ed), *The Correspondence of John Locke*, Vol. IV (Oxford: Clarendon Press, 1979).

Loewenstein, George, 1999, 'A Visceral Account of Addiction', in Jon Elster and Ole-Jørgen Skog (eds), *Getting Hooked* (Cambridge: Cambridge University Press), pp. 235–64.

Long, Anthony and David Sedley, 1987, *The Hellenistic Philosophers*, Vol. I (Cambridge: Cambridge University Press).

Luria, Aleksandr, 1966, *Higher Cortical Functions in Man*, trans. Basil Haigh (New York: Basic Books).

McClennen, Edward, 1990, *Rationality and Dynamic Choice* (Cambridge: Cambridge University Press).

McGuire, M., 1961, 'Decisions, Resolutions and Moral Conduct', *The Philosophical Quarterly* 11: 61–7.

McIntyre, Alison, 1990, 'Is Akratic Action Always Irrational?', in Owen Flanagan and Amelie Rorty (eds), *Identity, Character, and Morality* (Cambridge, MA: MIT Press), pp. 379–400.

——, 2006, 'What is Wrong with Weakness of Will', *Journal of Philosophy* 103: 284–311.

Malle, Bertram and Joshua Knobe 2001 'The Distinction Between Desire and Intention: A Folk-Conceptual Analysis', in Bertram Malle, Louis Moses and Dare Baldwin (eds), *Intentions and Intentionality: Foundations of Social Cognition* (Cambridge, MA: MIT Press), pp. 45–67.

Matthews, Gwynneth, 1966, 'Weakness of Will', *Mind* 75: 405–19.

Maugham, W. Somerset, 1915, *Of Human Bondage* (London: Heinemann).

——, 1933, *Sheppey: A Play in Three Acts* (London: Heinemann).

Mele, Alfred, 1987, *Irrationality* (New York: Oxford University Press).

——, 1992, *Springs of Action* (New York: Oxford University Press).

——, 1996, 'Addiction and Self-Control', *Behavior and Philosophy* 24: 99–117.

——, 1997, 'Introduction', A. Mele (ed.), *The Philosophy of Action* (Oxford: Oxford University Press), pp. 1–26.

Mischel, Walter, 1996, 'From Good Intentions to Willpower', in Peter Gollwitzer and John Bargh (eds), *The Psychology of Action* (New York: Guilford Press), pp. 197–218.

Monsell, Stephen, 1996, 'Control of Mental Processes', in Vicki Bruce (ed.), *Unsolved Mysteries of the Mind* (Hove: Psychology Press), pp. 93–148.

Moran, Richard, 2001, *Authority and Estrangement* (Princeton: Princeton University Press).

Muraven, Mark and Roy Baumeister, 2000, 'Self-Regulation and Depletion of Limited Resources: Does Self-Control Resemble a Muscle?', *Psychological Bulletin* 126: 247–59.

——, —— and Dianne Tice, 1999, 'Longitudinal Improvement of Self-Regulation Through Practice: Building Self-Control Strength Through Repeated Exercise', *The Journal of Social Psychology* 139: 446–57.

——, —— and ——, 1998 'Self-Control as a Limited Resource: Regulatory Depletion Patterns', *Journal, of Personality and Social Psychology* 74: 774–89.

Nahmias, Eddy, 2002, 'When Consciousness Matters', *Philosophical Psychology* 15: 527–42.

——, 2006, 'Close Calls and the Confident Agent', *Philosophical Studies* 131: 627–67.

——, Stephen Morris, Thomas Nadelhoffer and Jason Turner, 2004, 'The Phenomenology of Free Will', *Journal of Consciousness Studies* 11: 162–79.

——, ——, —— and ——, 2005, 'Surveying Freedom: Folk Intuitions about Free Will and Moral Responsibility', *Philosophical Psychology* 18: 561–84.

——, D. Justin Coates and Trevor Kvaran, 2007, 'Free Will, Moral Responsibility, and Mechanism: Experiments on Folk Intuitions', *Midwest Studies in Philosophy* 31: 214–42.

Nichols, Shaun and Joshua Knobe, 2007, 'Moral Responsibility and Determinism: The Cognitive Science of Folk Intuitions', *Noûs* 41: 663–85.

—— and Adina Roskies Forthcoming 'Bringing Moral Responsibility Down to Earth', *Journal of Philosophy*.

Nietzsche, Friedrich, 1886, *Beyond Good and Evil*, trans. Richard Hollingdale (Harmondsworth: Penguin, 1973).

Nisbett, Richard and Timothy Wilson, 1977, 'Telling More than We Can Know: Verbal Reports on Mental Processes', *Psychological Review* 84: 231–59.

Nozick, Robert, 1993, *The Nature of Rationality* (Princeton: Princeton University Press).

O'Shaughnessy, Brian, 1980, *The Will* (Cambridge: Cambridge University Press).

Owens, David, forthcoming, 'Freedom and Practical Judgement', in Lucy O'Brien and Matthew Soteriou (eds), *Mental Action* (Oxford: Oxford University Press).

Parfit, Derek, 1973, 'Later Selves and Moral Principles', in Alan Montefiore (ed.), *Philosophy and Personal Relations* (London: Routledge and Kegan Paul), pp. 137–69.

Pasternak, Boris, 1957, *Dr Zhivago*, trans. Max Hayward and Manya Harari (London: Collins and Harvill, 1958).

Pink, Thomas, 1996, *The Psychology of Freedom* (Cambridge: Cambridge University Press).

——, 2004, *Free Will* (Oxford: Oxford University Press).

—— and Martin Stone (eds), 2004, *The Will and Human Action: From Antiquity to the Present Day* (London: Routledge).

Rachlin, Howard, 2000, *The Science of Self-Control* (Cambridge, MA: Harvard University Press).

Raz, Joseph, 1997, 'Incommensurability and Agency', in Ruth Chang (ed.), *Incommensurability, Incomparability and Practical Reason* (Cambridge, MA: Harvard University Press), pp. 110–28.

Ridge, Michael, 1998, 'Humean Intentions', *American Philosophical Quarterly* 35: 157–78.

Robinson, Siobhan, Suzanne Sandstrom, Vistor Denenberg and Richard Palmiter, 2005, 'Distinguishing Whether Dopamine Regulates Liking, Wanting, and/or Learning About Rewards', *Behavioral Neuroscience* 119: 5–15.

Robinson, Terry and Kent Berridge, 2003, 'Addiction', *Annual Review of Psychology* 54: 25–53.

Rorty, Amelie, 1980, 'Where Does the Akratic Break Take Place?', *Australasian Journal of Philosophy* 58: 333–46.

Ross, David, 1923, *Aristotle* (London: Methuen).

Ryle, Gilbert, 1949, *The Concept of Mind* (London: Hutchinson).

Sartre, Jean Paul, 1945, *Existentialism and Humanism*, trans. P. Mairet (London: Methuen, 1948).

Scanlon, Thomas, 1998, *What we Owe to Each Other* (Cambridge, MA: Harvard University Press).

Schelling, Thomas, 1960, *The Strategy of Conflict,* (Cambridge, MA: Harvard University Press).

——, 1980, 'The Intimate Contest for Self-Command', *The Public Interest* 60: 94–118; reprinted in *Choice and Consequence* (Cambridge, MA: Harvard University Press, 1984), pp. 57–82.

Schmeichel, Brandon, Kathleen Vohs and Roy Baumeister, 2003, 'Intellectual Performance and Ego Depletion: Role of the Self in Logical Reasoning and Other Information Processing', *Journal of Personality and Social Psychology* 85: 33–46.

Schult, Carolyn, 2002, 'Children's Understanding of the Distinction between Intentions and Desires', *Child Development* 73: 1727–47.

Schwartz, Barry, 2004, *The Paradox of Choice* (New York: HarperCollins).

Seligman, Martin, 1993, *What You Can Change and What You Can't* (New York: Alfred Knopf).

Setiya, Kieran, 2007, 'Cognitivism about Instrumental Reasons', *Ethics* 117: 649–67.

Shafir, Eldar and Amos Tversky, 1990, 'Decision Making', in Daniel Osherson and Edward Smith (eds), *Thinking: An Introduction to Cognitive Science* (Cambridge, MA: MIT Press), pp. 77–99.

Shah, Idreis, 1967, *Tales of the Dervishes* (London: Jonathan Cape).

Shaw, George Bernard, 1914, *Pygmalion* (London: Constable).

Sidgwick, Henry, 1893, 'Unreasonable Action', *Mind* 2: 174–87.

Skog, Ole-Jørgen, 1999, 'Rationality, Irrationality and Addiction—Notes on Becker's and Murphy's Theory of Addiction', in Jon Elster and Ole-Jørgen Skog (eds), *Getting Hooked* (Cambridge: Cambridge University Press), pp. 173–207.

Sobel, Jordan Howard, 1994, *Taking Chances: Essays on Rational Choice* (Cambridge: Cambridge University Press).

——, 2004, 'Notes on "Death Speaks" ', at <http://www.scar.utoronto.ca/∼sobel/PuzzlesDEATHSPEAKS.pdf>.

Sorabji, Richard, 1988, *Matter, Space and Motion* (London: Duckworth).

Spenser, Edmund, 1590, *The Faerie Queen*, ed. Thomas Roche (Harmondsworth: Penguin 1978).

Stalnaker, Robert, 1984, *Inquiry* (Cambridge, MA: MIT Press).

Stanovich, Keith, 2004, *The Robot's Rebellion* (Chicago, IL: University of Chicago Press).

Stewart, John Alexander, 1892, *Notes on the Nichomachean Ethics of Aristotle* (Oxford: Clarendon Press).

Stocker, Michael, 1979, 'Desiring the Bad: An Essay in Moral Psychology', *Journal of Philosophy* 76: 738–53.

Stone, Jeff and Joel Cooper, 2001, 'A Self-Standards View of Cognitive Dissonance', *Journal of Experimental Social Psychology* 37: 228–43.

Strawson, Galen, 1986, *Freedom and Belief* (Oxford: Clarendon Press).

Stump, Eleonore, 2003, *Aquinas* (London: Routledge).

Swann, Jamie, unpublished, '*Akrasia* and Weakness of Will: Reply to Holton', University of Sheffield 2001.

Taubes, Gary, 2006, *Good Calories, Bad Calories* (New York: Knopf).

Taylor, Shelley and Jonathon Brown, 1988, 'Illusion and Well-Being: A Social Psychological Perspective on Mental Health', *Psychological Bulletin* 103: 193–210.

——, 1994, 'Positive Illusions and Well-Being Revisited: Separating Fact from Fiction', *Psychological Bulletin* 116: 21–7.

——and Peter Gollwitzer, 1995, 'The Effects of Mindsets on Positive Illusions', *Journal of Personality and Social Psychology* 96: 213–26.

Uleman, James and John Bargh (eds), 1989, *Unintended Thought* (New York: Guilford Press).

Ullman-Margalit, Edna and Sidney Morgenbesser, 1977, 'Picking and Choosing', *Social Research* 44: 757–85.

Vallacher, Robin, and Daniel Wegner, 1987, 'What Do People Think They Are Doing? Action Identification and Human Behavior', *Psychological Review* 94: 3–15.

Velleman, David, 1985, 'Practical Reflection', *Philosophical Review* 94: 33–61.

——, 1989a, *Practical Reflection* (Princeton: Princeton University Press).

——, 1989b, 'Epistemic Freedom', *Pacific Philosophical Quarterly* 70: 73–97; reprinted in Velleman, 2000, pp. 32–55.

——, 1991, 'Review of Michael Bratman's *Intention, Plans and Practical Reason*', *The Philosophical Review* 100,: 277–84.

——, 1992, 'What Happens When Someone Acts', *Mind* 101: 461–81; reprinted in Velleman, 2000, pp. 123–43.

——, 2000, *The Possibility of Practical Reason* (Oxford: Clarendon Press).

——, 2007, 'What Good is a Will?', in Anton Leist and Holger Baumann (eds), *Action in Context* (Berlin: de Gruyter; and New York: Mouton), pp. 193–215.

Vohs, Kathleen, Roy Baumeister, Brandon Schmeichel, Jean Twengy, Noelle Nelson and Dianne Tice, forthcoming, 'Making Choices Impairs Subsequent Self-Control', *Journal of Personality and Social Psychology*.

——and Todd Heatherton, 2000, 'Self-Regulatory Failure: A Resource-Depletion Approach', *Psychological Science* 11: 249–54.

——and Jonathan Schooler, 2008, 'The Value of Believing in Free Will', *Psychological Science* 19: 49–54.

Wallace, Jay, 1999, 'Addiction as Defect of the Will', *Law and Philosophy* 18: 621–54.

Wang, Jing, Nathan Novemsky, Ravi Dhar and Roy Baumeister, forthcoming, 'Effects of Depletion in Sequential Choices', ms.

Watson, Gary, 1977, 'Skepticism about Weakness of Will', *Philosophical Review* 86: 316–39.

——, 1999, 'Disordered Appetites', in Jon Elster (ed.), *Addiction: Entries and Exits* (New York: Russell Sage Foundation), pp. 3–28.

——, 2003, 'The Work of the Will', in Sarah Stroud and Christine Tappolet (eds), *Weakness of Will and Practical Irrationality* (Oxford: Oxford University Press), pp. 172–200.

Weatherson, Brian, 2005, 'Can We Do Without Pragmatic Encroachment?', *Philosophical Perspectives* 19: 417–43.

Wegner, Daniel, 1989, *White Bears and Other Unwanted Thoughts* (New York: Viking Press).

——, 1994, 'Ironic Processes of Mental Control', *Psychological Review* 101: 34–52.

——, 2002, *The Illusion of Conscious Will* (Cambridge, MA: Harvard University Press).

Westcott, Malcolm, 1988, *Psychology of Human Freedom* (New York: Springer).

Wheeler, S. Christian, Pablo Briñol and Anthony Hermann, 2007, 'Resistance to Persuasion as Self-regulation: Ego Depletion and its Effects on Attitude Change Processes', *Journal Of Experimental Social Psychology* 43: 150–6.

Wiggins, David, 1978, 'Weakness of Will, Commensurability, and the Objects of Deliberation and Desire', *Proceedings of the Aristotelian Society* 79: 251–77; reprinted in his *Needs, Values, Truth* (Oxford: Blackwell, 1987), pp. 239–67.

Williamson, Timothy, 2000, *Knowledge and Its Limits* (Oxford: Clarendon Press).

Wilson, Timothy, 2002, *Strangers to Ourselves: Discovering the Adaptive Unconscious* (Cambridge, MA: Harvard University Press).

Winch, Peter, 1972, 'The Universalizability of Moral Judgments', in *Ethics and Action* (London: Routledge and Kegan Paul), pp. 151–70.

Wyvell, Cindy and Kent Berridge, 2000, 'Intra-accumbens Amphetamine Increases the Conditioned Incentive Salience of Sucrose Reward', *Journal of Neuroscience* 20: 8122–30.

—— and ——, 2001, 'Incentive-sensitization by Previous Amphetamine Exposure', *Journal of Neuroscience* 21: 7831–40.

Index

Printed in the United States
By Bookmasters